Poverty Amidst Affluence

Professor Vic George is donating his share of royalties from this book to the Child Poverty Action Group for its work against poverty (CPAG, 4th Floor, 1–5 Bath Street, London EC1V 9PY).

Poverty Amidst Affluence

Britain and the United States

Vic George
Professor of Social Policy and Social Work
The University of Kent at Canterbury

Irving Howards
Professor Emeritus, Department of Political Science
The University of Massachusetts

Edward Elgar

Published by
Edward Elgar Publishing Limited
Gower House
Croft Road
Aldershot
Hants GU11 3HR
England

Edward Elgar Publishing Company
Old Post Road
Brookfield
Vermont 05036
USA

British Library Cataloguing in Publication Data
George, Vic
    Poverty amidst affluence : Britain and the United States.
    1. United States. Great Britain. Poverty
    I. Title II. Howards, Irving
    339.22

Library of Congress Cataloguing in Publication Data
George, Victor.
    Poverty amidst affluence : Britain and the United States/Vic George, Irving Howards.
        p.   cm.
    Includes bibliographical references.
    1. Poor–Great Britain–History–20th century.   2. Poor–United States–History–20th century.   3. Economic assistance, Domestic–Great Britain–History–20th century.   4. Economic assistance, Domestic–United States–History–20th century.   5. Great Britain–Economic policy–1945–   6. United States–Economic policy–1981–
    I. Howards, Irving.   II. Title.
    HC260.P6G46   1991
    362.5'8'0941–dc20   91–9952
                                                                        CIP

ISBN 1 85278 337 0
      1 85278 338 9 (paperback)

Printed in Great Britain by Billing & Sons Ltd, Worcester

Contents

Tables

Introduction

It is now generally accepted that government policies in both Britain and the US led to a widening of income inequalities and to an increase of poverty during the 1980s. Moreover, continuation of the same government policies will lead to even greater inequality and poverty in the 1990s. This book takes the view that poverty in such affluent societies as the US and Britain is morally indefensible. It is also undesirable on economic and social grounds. It leads to massive wastage of ability among the children of the poor; it weakens people's health in a complex web of direct and indirect ways; it renders secure families vulnerable and it breaks up vulnerable families. The justification that poverty is necessary in order to encourage economic growth is not only morally unacceptable but also not sustainable by empirical evidence. It is our view that the abolition of poverty is an issue of the highest priority in both countries and that they both possess enough financial resources to achieve such a modest goal.

The book begins with a review of the various approaches to the meaning of poverty and puts forward the suggestion that poverty is best understood as a continuum of want ranging from starvation to social exclusion from normal life in society (Chapter 1). Most of the empirical evidence on the extent and depth of poverty comes from government data which see poverty as lack of basic necessities. In both countries poverty levels are high though they are slightly higher in the US despite the higher living standards prevailing. It is evidence of the basic principle that economic growth by itself does not abolish poverty (Chapters 2 and 3). Chapter 4 is devoted to a review of the various theoretical explanations of the existence and distribution of poverty. Its main conclusion is that structural factors related to the workings of the labour market, to the education system and to the social security system are the main reasons for poverty. These factors operate through class, gender and ethnicity so that the lower socioeconomic groups, women and black people run the highest risks of being in poverty. The purpose of any long debate on poverty, however, is not so much to document and explain it but to suggest policies which can lead to its reduction and elimination. This is the task of Chapter 5. Its main conclusions are that the social security systems of both countries have contributed to the reduction of poverty but they both need radical reform if they are going to abolish poverty. More of the same will not do. Chapter 6 brings the discussion to a close, positing that the 1990s may well witness a public reaction against the policies of the 1980s which made the rich richer and the poor poorer. It is our hope that this book will make some contribution towards this change in public opinion and government policies.

We are grateful to many people who helped us in one way or another: to Paul Wilding and Peter Taylor-Gooby who read some of the chapters and made helpful comments; to the Directors of the Gordon Public Policy Center at Brandeis University and of the Institute for Research on Poverty at the University of Wisconsin who provided us with office facilities where we could meet to work and exchange ideas. We are also grateful to the Nuffield Foundation which made a grant to one of us to visit the US for a lengthy period. Finally, our thanks to Enid George who typed several drafts of the book before it reached its final version.

We are jointly responsible for the structure, contents and theoretical approach of the book as well as for any mistakes and shortcomings.

Vic George
University of Kent, Canterbury, UK
Irving Howards
University of Massachusetts, Amherst, US

1. Poverty: its Meaning and Measurement

Over the years the poor have been defined and redefined, classified and reclassified in countless ways to estimate how many or how few of them there are and how much or how little is needed to escape poverty. It might, therefore, be seen as unnecessary to spend a whole chapter on the meaning and measurement of poverty. Nevertheless our approach is different and we hope it may be found useful by others, particularly those concerned with historical and comparative studies of poverty. First, we distinguish between the definitions of poverty and the measurements of poverty. Second, we define poverty along a continuum of want that begins with starvation, moves on to subsistence, then to social coping and ends with social participation. Clearly, adjacent points on the continuum of want overlap each other but they are nevertheless different not only in terms of research and debate but for policy purposes as well. Third, we identify three different methods of measuring poverty – the professional, the consumption and the public opinion approach – and we point out that some definitions of poverty are more amenable to some of the methods of measurement than to others. The discussion on definitions precedes the discussion on measurements for logically we need to have some idea of what it is that we want to measure before we can attempt to measure it (Drewnowski 1977).

It is useful to make clear from the outset that all definitions and measurements of poverty involve, to a greater or lesser extent, the values of the definer, the researcher, the policy maker or the author. Poverty may not exactly be, as Orshansky claimed, like beauty that simply 'lies in the eye of the beholder' (Orshansky 1969, p. 37) but it is certainly value-based however simple and precise, complex and broad its definition and measurement may be. As an OECD report aptly put it 'there cannot be any definition of "poverty" which is free from value judgements' (OECD 1976, p. 62). To acknowledge this does not, of course, mean that one should not attempt to collect and analyse data as accurately as possible. It rather makes for more open

1

and frank debates on not only the extent of poverty but also on its causes and its solutions. Poverty is a political issue, not merely a technical problem, and it can only be abolished or reduced by government policies that have implications for other sections of society apart from the poor.

DEFINITIONS OF POVERTY

The simple question of how much or how little money is enough to lift a person out of poverty subsumes three interrelated questions: how many of a person's requirements should be met; the quantity of each of these requirements that is necessary; and the quality of each of these requirements. Thus the most generous definition of poverty contains a very long list of requirements each of which is generously provided for in terms of both quantity and quality. *Vice versa*, the most draconian definition refers to a very short list of requirements, normally food, which is minimally provided for in terms of both quality and quantity. In theory it is possible to argue that, as Table 1.1 shows, a person can

Table 1.1   Definitions of poverty

Number of requirements	Quantity of each requirement	Quality of each requirement
Minimal	Minimal	Minimal
Modest	Modest	Modest
Median	Median	Median

define poverty differently in terms of the number of requirements, the quantity and the quality of each. One can have, theoretically speaking, a minimal definition in terms of number of requirements but a median definition in terms of either quantity or quality or both. In practice, however, this is most unlikely because of the ideological nature of poverty definitions. Thus a person who maintains that only a small number of necessities is required is also likely to maintain that the quantity and quality of each of these should be at minimal or, at best, modest levels. On the other hand, a person who defines poverty in a median way in terms of number of requirements will do likewise in terms of their quantity and quality. Those, however, who define poverty at a modest level in terms of number of requirements may well define these requirements either in modest or minimal levels as far as their quantity and quality are concerned, for it would not be too incongruent with their overall ideological stance on poverty.

Over the years, four distinct definitions to this three-dimensional approach to poverty have emerged, each signifying varying depths of want. The first and most austere definition equates poverty with starvation as the diagram below shows. It lists only one requirement – food –

Figure 1.1   Depths of poverty

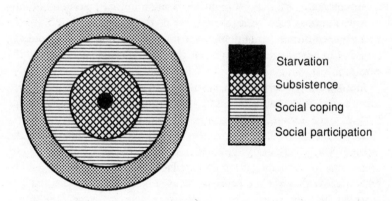

Starvation
Subsistence
Social coping
Social participation

to be met at a minimal level in terms of both quantity and quality. A person, according to this definition, is in poverty if he or she does not have enough money or enough resources to obtain the amount of food that is needed to avoid undernourishment. It then becomes a semi-technical issue as to what quantity and what quality of food is necessary. This is the definition of poverty used in societies with very low levels of economic conditions. It was widely used during the early industrial stages of contemporary advanced industrial societies and it is equally widely used by poverty researchers in third world countries today. Thus Naseem's study of poverty in Pakistan defined as poor 'those with an income less than the amount associated with the purchase of an adequate diet' (Naseem 1977, p. 43) and used local diets, which were cheap, rather than those recommended by the FAO that were expensive for most people in Pakistan even though they made up a balanced diet to avoid undernutrition. Even so, he found that three-quarters of the rural population of Pakistan had incomes below this very austere definition of poverty.

The starvation approach to poverty has no adherents in advanced industrial societies even though it surfaces from time to time. Thus Joseph and Sumption writing of the situation in Britain provided this definition recently: 'A family is poor if it cannot afford to eat. It is not poor if it cannot afford endless smokes and it does not become poor by the mere fact that other people can afford them' (Joseph and Sumption 1979, p. 27). A more careful reading of their discussion, however, shows that they would not define poverty simply in terms of food and that they would include at least clothing and housing in their list of requirements. What they were doing by adopting the starvation defini-tion was simply reacting against some of the less austere definitions. The absence of starvation definitions in affluent societies is an indica-tion that undernutrition, though not totally abolished, is not a signifi-cant problem.

Despite this austerity, there is still a great deal of disagreement as to the kind of diet that is necessary to avoid starvation not only for different age groups, occupations, and different parts of the world (Pacey and Payne 1985) but also between those who maintain that the human body gradually gets accustomed to less food without undernutrition or malnutrition taking place (Sukhatme 1982) and those who dispute that such a process is possible. It is a debate that has featured in third world countries, particularly in India, and it has strong implications for the extent of undernutrition in these countries.

The second main definition of poverty that has emerged over the years is concerned with subsistence. A person is in poverty, according to this definition, if his income or resources are not sufficient to pay for a small number of requirements at the basic level in terms of both quantity and quality. In terms of Table 1.1, it falls into the category of a minimal number of requirements each of which is met at a minimal level in terms of both quantity and quality. Clearly this approach is open to more disagreements than the first approach for very obvious reasons. How long should the list of requirements be and how does one decide how much is needed for, say, clothing in minimal terms as far as quantity and quality are concerned?

Rowntree's study of poverty in York in 1899 best exemplifies this approach. His list of requirements consisted not only of food but of clothing, housing, heating and a few household necessities such as spoons, forks and knives, plates and cooking utensils. All these requirements were to be met at a minimal level in terms of both quantity and quality so that they reflected the low living conditions of working class persons in Britain at that time. The criterion which he used for the quantity and quality of food was precise enough – cheap food that would provide enough calories so that people neither gained nor lost in body weight – but the criteria which he used for the other requirements were, as we shall see later, very imprecise. Nevertheless, the overall effect of his approach was a subsistence definition of poverty within the then prevailing living standards. This is how he described his poverty line:

A family living upon the scale allowed for in this estimate must never spend a penny on railway fares or omnibus. They must never go into the countryside unless they walk. They must never purchase a halfpenny newspaper or spend a penny to buy a ticket for a popular concert. They must write no letters to absent children, for they cannot afford to pay the postage. They must never contribute anything to their Church or Chapel, or give any help to a neighbour which costs them money. They cannot save, nor can they join sick club or Trade Union, because they cannot pay the necessary subscription. The children must have no pocket money for dolls, marbles or sweets. The father must smoke no tobacco, and must drink no beer. The mother must never buy any pretty clothes for herself or for her children, the character of the family wardrobe as for the family diet being governed by the regulation, 'Nothing must be bought but that which is absolutely necessary for the maintenance of physical health, and what is bought must be of the plainest and most economical description'. Should a child fall ill, it must be attended by the parish doctor; should it die, it must be buried by the parish. (Rowntree 1901, pp. 133–4)

An early American study of poverty by Hunter used a definition that was very similar to Rowntree's and indeed acknowledged that fact. People are in poverty, Hunter wrote, when 'they are not able to obtain those necessaries which will permit them to maintain a state of physical efficiency' (Hunter 1904, p. 5). More specifically, he wrote,

A sanitary dwelling, a sufficient supply of food and clothing, all having to do with physical well-being, is the very minimum which the labouring classes can demand.... Such a standard has been established naturally by everyone in his treatment of animals; no one would think of supplying less to any man or beast for whom he was personally responsible. (Hunter 1904, p. 8)

As a radical reformer Hunter was amazed at the extent and depth of poverty and was angry with the indifference of employers and governments.

The subsistence definition of poverty has many supporters in advanced industrial societies even though they would illustrate it in terms of current consumption patterns. They would not be using the same items of diet or clothing nor would they be referring to concerts, church or chapel or to dolls, marbles and sweets but to their counterparts in today's society. It is also the definition which best fits with the current level of assistance benefits paid to the poor in both the US and the UK. People in subsistence poverty for long periods may not necessarily be starving but their life is socially intolerable in advanced industrial societies for their standard of living is so markedly below that of the rest of society. People in subsistence poverty in third world countries, however, constitute such a high proportion of their country's population that their life is the norm in their society. Obviously the subsistence definition of advanced industrial societies provides a much higher standard of living *vis-à-vis* the subsistence definition of third world countries but this is no comfort to those who rely on it for long periods. Indeed the same may apply, though to a far lesser extent, to the subsistence definitions of any two advanced industrial or any two third world countries. It is in this respect that poverty, particularly beyond the starvation level, is relative between countries as well as over time in the same country, to a greater or lesser extent.

The third definition sees poverty not in terms of starvation or subsistence but in a slightly more generous way, in terms of social coping. People are in poverty if their incomes or resources are not sufficient to provide them with those goods and services that will enable them to live a life that is tolerable according to working-class life styles. This definition refers ideally to a modest number of requirements each of which is met at a modest level as regards both quantity and quality. Clearly this approach is open to more disagreements than the second approach because the number of requirements is slightly greater and because the level of satisfaction is slightly less austere. What exactly is a modest number of requirements? It is the minimum number plus a few others which, though not necessary for subsistence, are necessary for a person to cope socially in society. Thus, giving a child a birthday present is not necessary for subsistence but it is socially necessary by the mere fact that it is universally customary in British and US society today. What exactly is a modest level in terms of quality and quantity? In the case of clothing it means not having to rely on second-hand clothing – as distinct from buying such clothing out of choice – and being able to change one's clothing without too much difficulty. Obviously these are imprecise answers and the concept of 'social coping' is open to a great deal of differential interpretation. Nevertheless it is a useful concept for without it one would move from the subsistence to the social participation definition which is much too long a leap on the continuum of poverty. Basically, the social coping definition sees poverty in terms of the living standards of the working class and in this way it arrives at a modest level of requirements in terms of both quantity and quality.

Though there have not been any studies of poverty which explicitly used a social coping definition, there have been some which implicitly apply such a definition. For example, Galbraith's approach to poverty in the US during the late 1950s implies a social coping definition even though he does not use the term. This is how he expressed it:

> People are poverty-stricken when their income, even if adequate for survival, falls markedly behind that of the community. Then they cannot have what the larger community regards as the minimum necessary for decency; and they cannot wholly escape, therefore, the judgment of the larger community that they are indecent. They are degraded for, in a literal sense, they live outside the grades or categories which the community regards as acceptable. (Galbraith 1958, pp. 323–4)

The emphasis in this definition is on the fact that people who are poor do not merely fall behind the rest of society but they do so in a marked way. They are not just unequal; rather they do not have enough income to cope with the basic needs and the basic social expectations of their community and society.

Piachaud's study of child poverty in Britain also seems to imply a social coping definition. He used as requirements food, clothing, footwear, household provisions, heating and lighting, toys and presents, pocket money, costs of schooling, entertainment and holidays; he then allowed a sum of money for each of these items that was higher than that allowed for in the government assistance benefit which represents the second definition. We shall be discussing the methodology he used later but here suffice it to say that he arrived at a weekly amount of money that was 50 per cent higher than that of the assistance benefit amount for children (Piachaud 1979, p. 18).

The US Bureau of Labor Statistics produced for many years estimates of 'what it costs a worker's family to live in the large cities'

(US BLS 1948, p. 3). Its first report in 1948 estimated the expenditure that was necessary not merely for subsistence but for 'a level of adequate living to satisfy prevailing standards of what is necessary for health, efficiency, the nurture of children and for participation in community activities' (US BLS 1948, p. 3). Thus the range of requirements included food, housing, clothing, furniture, personal toiletries, transport and leisure activities. In 1969 the US BLS study constructed three different poverty budgets – the lower, intermediate and higher – reflecting different degrees of generosity *vis-à-vis* the subsistence definition of poverty. This work of the US BLS was discontinued in 1982 but it nevertheless helped to create a definition of poverty that was not as austere as the subsistence definition and not as generous as the fourth definition that we will now discuss.

In several ways it can be argued that the fourth definition is no different from the third because it, too, seeks to define poverty in relation to the prevailing living standards. People are in poverty, Townsend argues, 'when they lack the resources to obtain the types of diet, participate in the activities and have the living conditions and amenities which are customary, or at least widely encouraged or approved in the societies in which they belong' (Townsend 1979, p. 31). There is, of course, some truth in this argument, but the social participation approach is different from the social coping definition in at least two ways. It is more generous and in the context of Table 1.1 it implies a median number of requirements met at the median level both as regards quantity and quality. In other words, both the list of requirements and the level of their quantity and quality is higher than those of the social coping definition. As we shall see below in the work of Townsend the social participation model included not only basic needs and many social requirements but it also covered other aspects of life – work, education, health, leisure and environment. Another way of expressing the difference between the two is to see the social coping definition as a reflection of working-class living standards and the social participation definition as based on the living standards of the whole society. Second, the ideology behind the social participation model is different. It sees poverty programmes as an integral part of the drive to reduce inequalities in society rather than, as in the social coping model, an attempt to provide people with a standard of living slightly higher than that of subsistence. It is accepted that poverty is not the same as inequality but the two are inextricably linked and poverty can only be abolished if inequality is reduced. To abolish poverty, however, one need not abolish inequality. Indeed, as Harrington, one of the supporters of the social participation model, points out, theoretically 'one can at least imagine a society in which there would be no poverty and considerable inequality' (Harrington 1985, p. 72). This is, of course, even more the case with the other three definitions of poverty.

Clearly the social participation definition raises more difficulties than the other three definitions in terms of the range, quantity and quality of requirements. This is why so very few supporters of this definition have attempted to be specific on these issues and why most of them have instead attempted to relate it to the prevailing average income in society. In other words, they have argued that the social participation poverty line should be a certain percentage of either the median family income or the net disposable income per person. Fuchs proposed in 1967 to define as poor 'any family whose income is less than one-half the median family income' on the grounds not only that this definition recognized that poverty lines reflect prevailing living standards and hence change over time but also because such a definition 'represents a tentative groping toward a national policy with respect to the distribution of income' (Fuchs 1967, p. 89). Families, however, vary in size and hence Fuchs's poverty line of 50 per cent of the median family income was bound to be too severe for large families and too generous for the small families. It was therefore understandable that family size should be taken into account and the more recent approach of using the disposable income per person is the result (Walker *et al.* 1984; Beckerman 1979; Callan *et al.* 1988). Some definitions use 40 per cent, others 50 per cent and some others 60 per cent of the median disposable income per person as their poverty line. It is the highest of these figures that can legitimately be placed in the social participation definition. The other two fit the social coping definition just as well.

The social participation definition is usually referred to as the relative definition of poverty in the sense that it is the opposite of subsistence poverty. The term 'relative', however, has been used in three different ways in the poverty literature with the result that it has confused rather than clarified poverty debates: first, relative in historical terms; second, relative in country comparative terms; and third, relative in relation to other groups within any one country at any one time. To some extent all definitions of poverty are relative in historical and country-comparative terms. Even the definition of starvation, let alone the other definitions, has been defined slightly differently over the years as well as between countries to take some account of the differences of prevailing socioeconomic conditions. A 'starving' person in the US today means a slightly different condition from a 'starving' American in the last century and from a 'starving' Ethiopian today. It is the third definition of 'relative' that is in dispute. The social participation view claims that poverty in any one country at any one time can only be defined in relation to the prevailing living standards whilst the other three definitions insist that certain needs are basic to survival and that they have to be included in the definition of poverty irrespective of whether they cannot be afforded by even the majority of the population of a country. It is for this reason that the social participation model of poverty may make sense in affluent societies but it cannot be used by itself to measure poverty in third world countries. It can lead to such unacceptable conclusions that since the vast majority of the population in a country is ill-fed, ill-housed, ill-clothed, ill-educated etc., the majority of the population cannot be in poverty. Only that section of the population whose living standards are at the very bottom of these low national living conditions is in poverty since poverty can only be defined in terms of the prevailing national standard of living. Moreover, it can lead to the equally unacceptable conclusion that the extent of social participation poverty in Britain and India is similar. It is for this reason that in third world countries the more austere definitions of poverty are more useful. As Sen has argued, the notion of relative poverty 'supplements (but cannot supplant) the earlier approach of absolute dispossession' (Sen 1981, p. 22). If the majority of the population of a country lack the basic needs of life then the majority of the population is in poverty.

In conclusion, poverty is best defined in a composite manner, i.e. as a condition that ranges from starvation to subsistence, to social coping and to social participation. Defined in this way, we can meaningfully argue that poverty in Britain and the US has declined in terms of starvation and in terms of subsistence but less so in terms of social coping and it may not have declined at all in terms of social participation. Similarly, when comparing the situation in say Britain and India, we can avoid making such non-convincing statements that poverty is about equally prevalent in the two countries. We can begin to compare like with like, as far as this is possible, in both historical terms and in contemporary comparative terms. It will also enable us to abandon the traditional dichotomy between subsistence and relative poverty for in one sense all definitions of poverty are relative in terms of time and country. What distinguishes the various definitions is their degree of generosity in terms of their list of requirements as well as the quantity and quality of each requirement.

MEASUREMENTS OF POVERTY

Three different methodological approaches have been used over the years to calculate the poverty line: the professional or expert approach, the expenditure or consumption approach and the public opinion or social consensus approach (Piachaud 1987). Each of these three methodological approaches can be used for any one of the four definitions of poverty discussed earlier even though certain historical associations may have been built into the literature of poverty. The importance of discussing these types of measurement lies in the fact that when applied to any one of the four definitions of poverty they may arrive at different poverty lines. For example, if starvation is defined by the professional dieticians and by the opinions of the public it is more than likely that the amounts of money considered necessary to avoid it will be different.

The first approach relies on the opinions of the professional, or the expert, in reaching decisions about the range, as well as the quantity and the quality of requirements for the poor. Rowntree made use of this approach in at least two different ways in his study of poverty in York. First, he used the findings of dieticians to decide how many calories a person needs to maintain health but, second, he used his own judgement as to which diets should be used to provide the necessary number of calories. Thus, the expert can be either an outside professional or the researcher himself. A more recent approach in relation to food is the work of the expert committee of the FAO and WHO which drew up diets that were necessary to provide enough calories for an active working life, as Rowntree did, and diets that were necessary to prevent stunted growth and serious health risks (FAO/WHO 1973). As we saw earlier, researchers in several third world countries modified these diets downwards, again similar to Rowntree, in order to reduce costs and thus to arrive at poverty levels which could not be criticized as being exaggerations of the extent of poverty. Yet this raises the important question of whether a diet considered necessary by expert dieticians to avoid starvation becomes invalid by the mere fact that the majority of the population of an impoverished country cannot afford it.

Even with food, the professional approach has its difficulties: how much account to take of cultural factors or of people's varied nutritional needs that correspond to gender, age, height, type of employment and so on. It runs into even more serious difficulties, however, when it moves beyond food requirements and particularly when it moves beyond the basic necessities. It is very difficult but perhaps possible for an expert in housing to provide useful advice as to how much housing space an individual needs, the quality of the housing and the amount of money thus needed to cover housing costs. It is certainly impossible, however, for experts to provide any valid advice as to how much is needed for such social needs as recreation or presents to children, or even clothing.

It is for this reason that the expert, professional approach cannot be used on its own to measure any other form of poverty, apart from starvation. When it comes to the other three definitions of poverty, the expert approach has to be supplemented with the personal judgement of the researcher and with consumption data. This is exemplified in several studies of poverty in Britain. Piachaud's estimate of the costs involved in bringing up a child was based, to a large extent, on his own judgements as to what to include in the list of requirements and how much to allow for each one of them. But his own views were informed partly by his knowledge of current consumption patterns in Britain. As he repeatedly points out: 'The items included and excluded in estimating this modern minimum cost reflect the author's views of what are minimum requirements' (Piachaud 1979, p. 18). Similarly Bradshaw *et al.* constructed a poverty line that included basic necessities and a few other items and costed these according to the evidence that was available to them from expenditure studies. They acknowledge the complex ways in which personal judgements and empirical evidence combined to produce their budgets for different sized families. 'Drawing up a budget standard inevitably involves judgements – judgements about what *items* should be included, about the *quantity* of items that are required and about the *price* that should be fixed to the items. In each case these judgements can be tempered with survey data' (Bradshaw et al. 1987, p. 169). The inclusion of personal judgements in the professional/expert approach does not make this approach any less useful than the other approaches but it does highlight the point that experts also have values and that facts do not speak for themselves – they have to be interpreted and the values of the researcher are crucial in this.

The second methodological approach to the measurement of poverty is the expenditure or consumption approach. The main claim of this approach is that the best way to estimate the amount of money that people need so that they are not in poverty is by looking at the ways in which the general public spend their incomes. It is not a matter of what the professional or the researcher thinks people should spend their money on but rather attention should concentrate on the way people live, what they purchase, how much they spend on the various items, how expenditure patterns vary according to income, and so on. The crucial question in all this is how to decide where to draw the line below which people's income signifies poverty and above which they are not in poverty. Two main approaches have been used, one in the US and the other in Britain. In 1963, the President's Council of Economic Advisers, using data from the food consumption surveys conducted by the Department of Agriculture in 1948 and 1955 which showed that the average expenditure by all families on food was about one-third of their income, drew up a poverty line for a family of two or more. This was refined by Orshansky in 1965 to take account of the sizes of the family but both measurements were based on the simple proposition that the amount of money a person needs to avoid being in poverty is three times the amount that the average individual spends on food. Orshansky was quite frank that this was not an objective, scientific definition but rather one where value judgements played an important part. The US Department of Agriculture had developed four food plans reflecting varying degrees of generosity. Of these Orshansky chose two – the low-cost budget and the economy budget – which reflected working-class food expenditure patterns and developed two poverty lines one of which was only 80 per cent of the other. It was this lowest poverty line – the economy budget – that was chosen by the Council of Economic Advisers to the President as the official poverty line and has remained so ever since. Orshansky's choice of the two lowest food plans as the bases for the two poverty lines was based on the value judgement that the poverty line should not be too generous or too austere if it is to have any public and political credibility. This is how she reached this conclusion: 'A benchmark should neither select a group so small, in relation to the population, that it hardly seems to deserve a general program, nor so large that a solution to the problem appears impossible' (Orshansky 1969, p. 37).

There are several criticisms of this methodological approach. The first is that the amount of income allowed for in the poverty line is sufficient for emergency periods of need and it is thus an underestimate of the extent of poverty at any one time since many people either on low wages or on benefits are long-term cases. Second, there is evidence which shows that the proportion of income spent on food rises with the size of the family with the result that the multiplier for large families should be more than three in order to arrive at even an 'economy' poverty line (Oster *et al.* 1978, pp. 40–2). Finally, of course, had the low-cost budget rather than the economy budget been used as the basis for the poverty line, then the number and composition of the poor would have been greater and different. We shall examine in another chapter how the US official poverty line has fared over the years. We conclude the discussion here, however, by noting that all the statistical work employed in the construction of the US official poverty line should not hide the fact that it was based on a personal, political decision to use the lowest of food plans – the economy budget – as its basis.

We now turn to a pioneering British study (Townsend 1979) that was designed to measure poverty 'objectively' with the minimum of personal value judgements. Townsend was anxious to construct a poverty line by looking at the ways in which people of different socioeconomic groups live and how they spend their incomes. He acknowledged that a minimal use of value judgements was inevitable but he nevertheless hoped that his methodology would ensure that these value judgements 'will have been pushed one or two stages further back and an attempt made to make measurement both reproducible and more dependent on externally instead of subjectively assessed criteria' (Townsend 1979, p. 60). He therefore began by defining both income and consumption widely. He defined income not simply in terms of earnings and social security benefits but also included income from wealth and from employers' fringe/occupational benefits. He defined consumption widely by the use of 60 indicators of styles of living ranging from diet to housing, education, health, working conditions, environmental conditions, entertainment and so on. Through a complex statistical technique, he correlated income with participation or use of the 60 indicators to establish not simply whether there was a correlation between the two – which is obvious enough – but rather whether there was 'a point in the scale of the distribution of resources below which, as resources diminish, families find it particularly difficult to share in the customs, activities and diets comprising their society's style of living' (Townsend 1979, p. 60). The results substantiated his hypothesis and he therefore concluded that there was a point – which he called the deprivation threshold – below which participation in many of the 60 indicators dropped so sharply that individuals were not simply unequal to others; they were in poverty.

Townsend's methodology has been the centre of a great deal of critical comment – both favourable and unfavourable. The first issue around which debate has centred is the choice of the 60 indicators. How did he come to select these and not others? Obviously through a process that involved personal judgements about existing empirical data on consumption patterns. Inevitably there were indicators which would be generally accepted – amount of food, overcrowding, birthday presents – and others which will be disputed by many – cooked breakfast, children not having friends in the house to play, working mainly or entirely outdoors, etc. Second, Townsend's methodology did not distinguish between those who did not have any one of the indicators out of choice and those who could not afford to. It can, however, be claimed that such a distinction would tend to underestimate poverty since some people would be too proud to admit that they could not afford to buy certain items. Third, some re-analyses of Townsend's data did not substantiate his thesis of a deprivation threshold whilst others did. Piachaud found no such threshold whilst Desai did (Piachaud 1981; Desai 1986). Above all, his methodology and his definition of poverty raise the crucial question of whether it is meaningful or politically useful for a researcher to include in a poverty index conditions that he considers depriving but which the public does not. He wanted to define and measure poverty as a social scientist who was not 'the unwitting servant of contemporary social values' and this led him to a methodology which distinguished between 'actual' needs as he saw them and 'socially perceived' needs or, in other words, 'between *objective* and *conventionally acknowledged* poverty' (Townsend 1969, p. 46). But this raises the important question of the purpose of poverty studies. If poverty is defined and measured in ways in which it is beyond the understanding and support of the public then one runs the risk of being involved in a simply academic study that has no immediate political implications. On the other hand, if a researcher defines and measures poverty strictly in ways in which there is public support for his approach then he runs the opposite risk – of defining and measuring poverty according to conventional wisdom which is dominated in varying degrees by the dominant values of society which support the existing pattern of income distribution. It is a difficult issue and it surfaces again below.

The third main methodological approach to the measurement of poverty is the public opinion or social consensus approach. Basically this approach tries to define and to measure the extent of poverty according to the views of the general public. It can, therefore, lead to both austere and generous definitions depending on the prevailing state of public opinion as well as on the range and phrasing of the questions put to the public. Its fundamental premise is that conditions only become necessities worthy of being included in a poverty index if they are socially perceived as such. It is a theoretical position opposite to Townsend's and it raises the question of how social perceptions about needs develop and particularly of how the public comes to distinguish between the 'needs' of the poor and the 'needs' of the rest of the population.

The justification for public opinion approaches to poverty is twofold. In the first place, it is argued that despite all the problems involved the public is a better judge of what poverty means than either the expert or the researcher. Obviously the public is not a unified whole but so long as one uses a large and representative sample then one will be able to represent the various group interests in the findings. Second, a definition based on public opinion will carry more political weight than studies based on other methodologies. It is acknowledged that governments are influenced by a variety of complex factors but this does not negate the political superiority of public opinion poverty studies over others. On the other hand governments cannot and perhaps should not raise or lower poverty lines according to changing public moods. All that governments can reasonably be expected to do is to bear public views on poverty in mind in formulating their policy programmes.

Public opinion studies on poverty fall into two overlapping types. The first involves simply a small number of questions included in public opinion surveys covering several issues; the second is a specifically designed study covering definition, extent, composition and other issues of poverty. So far, there have been several of the first type but very few of the second. For many years Gallup Poll in the US asked respondents: 'What is the smallest amount of money a family of four (husband, wife and two children) needs each week to get along in the community?' Not surprisingly, the average amount that emerged from these replies has been higher than the government's poverty line. Clearly, the phrase 'get along in the community' signified a level of coping that was more generous than the economy food budget on which the official poverty line is based.

The study of poverty in nine European countries in 1976 is one of the first main attempts to elicit the public's views on what constitutes poverty and how much poverty thus existed. The questionnaire included two questions probing how much income was necessary for a person living in the respondent's neighbourhood first 'to live satisfactorily' and second 'to make ends meet'. As expected, the amount of income needed 'to make ends meet' was considered to be lower than the amount needed 'to live satisfactorily' (Commission of the European Communities 1977, table 9, p. 19).

A more complex and better designed study of public opinion on poverty was that of Mack and Lansley in Britain in 1983. The study asked a national sample to state which of 35 items they considered necessary 'and which all adults should be able to afford and which they should not have to do without' (Mack and Lansley 1985, p. 294). When two-thirds of the respondents considered an item as necessary – as per question – then that item was considered a necessity. Respondents were then asked whether they possessed that item and if they did not whether it was by choice or because they could not afford it. Those who could not afford three or more of the socially perceived necessities were considered by the researchers as poor. The surprising finding was not that the extent of poverty so defined was substantial but rather the high degree of consensus on what the 'necessities' of life were. As Mack and Lansley put it:

> People from all walks of life, from across the generations, from widely varying family circumstances, and with fundamentally opposed political beliefs, share the same view of the kind of society Britain should be in terms of the minimum standards of living to which all citizens should be entitled. (Mack and Lansley 1985, p. 86)

Despite the high involvement of respondents in the definition of necessities, the influence of the researchers was inevitable not only in the phrasing of the questions but also on two strategic decisions – the proportion of respondents' replies needed to designate an item as a necessity and the lack of three items as the poverty benchmark. Both of these decisions could have been left to the respondents. A number of other improvements could also have been made to the study: the size and composition of the sample could have been larger and more representative of the diverse interest groups in society; the poverty line could have been expressed not simply in terms of number of necessities but also in income terms; and so on. The fundamental question yet remains whether public opinion studies, however well designed and conducted, reflect the true extent of poverty or whether they reflect that kind and that degree of poverty which the dominant ideology enables respondents to express. This is fundamentally Townsend's criticism of the Mack and Lansley study and it raises important questions of the nature and distribution of power and ideology in society (Townsend 1985), issues which are beyond the scope of this chapter but are discussed at some length in Chapter 4. Suffice it to say here that both the public and the researcher have views which are in varying degrees within the orbit of the dominant ideology of society. Only radical researchers and radical members of the public go beyond and against the dominant values of society. They both form part of what Parkin calls the 'radical value system', 'which promotes an *oppositional* interpretation of class inequalities' (Parkin 1971, p. 82).

Viewed from a social reform perspective, a case can be made for both radical approaches to poverty which raise challenging questions of how poverty is defined and measured and consensual approaches which involve the public in an issue such as poverty which is or ought to be a public concern. As stated earlier, consensual approaches provide evidence on the nature and extent of poverty which governments will find more difficult to ignore than evidence arrived at through either the expert or the expenditure approach (Veit-Wilson 1987). They may not necessarily represent the 'true' nature of poverty but what they do represent has more public support behind it and perhaps more influence on government policies. Though all the poverty studies based on the consensual approach have so far arrived at poverty lines that are higher than the prevailing 'official' lines, there is no guarantee that they will always arrive at this conclusion. Bearing in mind the austerity of government definitions, however, it is more than likely that this will continue to be a conclusion of future public opinion studies.

There have been several variants of the public opinion or social consensus method of measuring poverty. Some surveys have relied on the views of low-income groups only on the ground that they will have a more realistic idea of what is needed to avoid poverty. Deleeck's study of poverty in Belgium is such a study in the sense that it utilized the replies of only those who regarded themselves as making ends meet with some difficulty (Callan and Nollan 1987, p. 30). Other surveys have used a more complex approach to defining the amount of income needed to avoid poverty. The Leyden poverty line constructed by Hagenaars and Van Praag depended on public responses to a question that asked for six income figures ranging from a very low income to a very high income (Hagenaars and Van Praag 1985). Several US studies also used the subjective approach. Rainwater's study in Boston asked respondents to state how much they thought families of different sizes needed in order not to be 'poor', to 'get along', to be 'comfortable', to be 'prosperous', etc. (Rainwater 1974). Danziger and his colleagues analysed the replies of a large sample to the following question included in the 1979 Income Survey Development Program of the Social Security Administration: 'Living where you do now and meeting the expenses you consider necessary, what would be the very smallest income you (and your family) would need to make ends meet?' They found that the extent of poverty arrived at through this subjective approach was the same as that from the official poverty line though there were substantial variations for some of the subgroups. Thus 40.5 per cent of white aged females were in official poverty but only 18.4 per cent in subjective poverty (Danziger 1984, table 3, p. 504). Another US study which interviewed respondents in Wisconsin several times arrived at a similar conclusion, i.e. that the official and the subjective approaches resulted in the same poverty line (MacDonald 1988). Despite their variations, however, all these studies rely on the public's views on the definition of poverty and they exhibit similar strengths and weaknesses.

Though the three methodological approaches to the calculation of the poverty line have been presented separately, they in fact overlap. In the first approach, the professional's or the expert's views dominate but, as we saw, the expert's views exert some influence on the other two approaches too. In the second approach, consumption patterns dominate the calculations but these same patterns must exert some influence on the views of both the public and the experts. In the third approach, the views of the public are the dominant factor but, again, these views reflect and reinforce expenditure patterns and they must reflect the views of the professionals in varying degrees.

Our discussion of poverty has concentrated on income as a proxy for the possession and consumption of goods and services. This approach has recently been criticized on two grounds: first, that income is not an accurate measure of poverty in terms of consumption and that poverty should be not only defined in terms of consumption of goods and services but it should also be measured as such (Ringen 1988; Mayer and Jencks 1989). There may well be an element of truth in this but, on the whole, people with low incomes and heavy family responsibilities are most likely to have low living standards as we shall show in the next chapter. Second, it has been argued that income poverty does not excite public passion in the same way that malnutrition or homelessness or high infant mortality rates do and it therefore creates little public pressure for government action. In Heclo's words: 'The concept of income poverty is a statistical construction capable of interesting economists and public policy analysts, but lacking a political reality that could animate national action' (Heclo 1984, p. 337). It is thus all the more important to show that income poverty is closely connected with other forms of deprivation and that it has visible and undesirable effects on the lives of people as well as on the prosperity and social cohesion of the whole society.

CONCLUSION

The discussion in the first section of the chapter showed that poverty can best be defined along a continuum ranging from starvation to lack of social participation in order to be meaningfully used not only for national studies but also for historical and comparative studies. The discussion in the second section showed that each of the three methodological approaches to the measurement of poverty has its strengths as well as its weaknesses when adopted for the four definitions of poverty. This suggests that some methodologies are better suited to some definitions of poverty than to others. Thus starvation can best be defined by the expert approach; it would not be useful to define it either through public opinion or through consumption patterns. At the other end of the poverty continuum, it would not be useful to define lack of social participation through expert opinion only; one would have to bring in the views of the public as well as the current consumption patterns of society.

Poverty in advanced industrial affluent societies cannot possibly be defined in terms simply of starvation or basic needs for physical survival. In the midst of unprecedented affluence, it must be defined at least in terms of social coping so that it includes the basic necessities plus a number of social needs all met at a modest level. It would be tempting to suggest that all these needs could be measured by one method – the professional, the expenditure, the public consensus. The reality, however, is that poverty is a complex issue and all three approaches have to play a part in measuring the range, the quantity and the quality of needs to make up a social coping level of poverty. Taking food as an example, we need to know the kinds of diet that are conducive to people's health, which conform to the prevailing diets of society and which will be reasonably priced. It is even more difficult to decide how much to allow for clothing, housing, heating, household sundries and for a small number of social needs. Yet we have to know all this before we can realistically decide how much persons of different ages need to avoid social coping poverty. The real issue, therefore, is not which method of measuring needs is the best but rather which combination of the three methods can provide the evidence for the most accurate poverty line.

For public policy purposes in Britain and the US, there is a strong case for defining poverty in terms of social coping. It is morally unacceptable for governments to define poverty in such affluent societies in terms of either starvation or subsistence. On the other hand, defining poverty in terms of social participation reflecting the living standards of *all* income groups in society would make it politically impossible for any government in the foreseeable future to commit itself to the abolition of poverty. The social coping definition which sees poverty in relation to only working-class living standards offers both a more realistic approach in terms of public policy and a more justifiable approach in terms of conceptual understanding since the poor are, on the whole, part of the working class.

2. Poverty in Britain

The lack of agreement on what constitutes poverty cannot be used to write off its existence any more than the lack of consensus on the definition of wealth can be used to argue that there are no wealthy persons in Britain or the US or other affluent countries. The sad fact is that irrespective of how poverty is defined it exists in both countries even though its extent will be influenced by the definition adopted.

The study of poverty in Britain goes back a long time but in this chapter only the postwar period is covered. Most of the data on the extent of poverty come from government studies and these begin with 1972 and end in 1985. Inevitably the documentation of poverty will be both patchy and sketchy and will leave much to be desired.

EXTENT OF POVERTY, 1950–87

The 1950s were a period when little interest or concern about poverty was shown. There was a general belief that the full employment situation, the rise in economic growth, the improvement in wage levels and the reorganization of the social services during the late 1940s had ensured that few, if any, remained in poverty. Comparisons were understandably made with the prewar situation when unemployment was high, wages low and the social services were most inadequate. Clearly the country had achieved a great deal in economic and social terms. Thus as early as 1950, the Labour Party which formed the government boldly declared that it had 'ensured full employment and fair shares of the necessities of life' and thus 'destitution has been banished' (Labour Party Election Manifesto in Craig 1970, pp. 127 and 132). The first big poverty study conducted by Rowntree in York in 1950 confirmed this general belief in the abolition of poverty. Its main conclusion was that only 1.5 per cent of the population of York was in poverty compared with 18 per cent in Rowntree's previous survey of 1936 (Rowntree and Lavers 1951). A recent re-analysis of Rowntree's data shows that at least 4.9 per cent of all family units in York and perhaps as many as 9.5 per cent had incomes which were below the prevailing national assistance level (Atkinson 1989, p. 74). Nevertheless, very little attention was paid to contemporary criticisms of the study – its methodological weaknesses and the unrepresentativeness of York for the rest of the country (Townsend 1952; Kaim-Caudle 1953). The fact that the study was conducted by Rowntree, who had conducted two previous studies in York in 1899 and 1936, had influenced the reorganization of the social security benefit schemes in the 1940s and had dominated poverty research debates so much, was proof enough of the accuracy of its findings. Not surprisingly, a *Times* leader marvelled at this 'remarkable improvement – no less than the virtual abolition of the sheerest want' (quoted in Coates and Silburn 1970, p. 26).

These feelings of political satisfaction and general consensus were strongly reflected in the social science literature of the period. Bell's end of ideology thesis proclaimed that welfare capitalism had solved the main social problems and that any differences which remained between political parties were confined to means rather than to ends (Bell 1960). Writing from the Left, Marcuse drew attention to the sad fact that consumerism had gained such a stranglehold on societies irrespective of political system that no real ideological differences remained. The one-dimensional man ruled and welfare capitalism was the end of all social evolution (Marcuse 1964).

By the late 1950s, however, disquieting evidence from several local studies was beginning to emerge which showed that poverty was still a significant problem in Britain. Particularly important for the general public was the evidence that the extent of poverty and of general deprivation among the elderly was quite substantial (Townsend 1957; Cole and Utting 1962). It was poverty among a 'deserving' population group that could not easily be explained away through some individual fault. In the US, concern about poverty surfaced slightly earlier than in Britain. Galbraith's lively strictures of US society where private affluence and public squalor existed unnoticed side by side and his condemnation of poverty as being not simply annoying but 'a disgrace' in the late 1950s were part of this early and rising public concern (Galbraith 1958, p. 259). It was not, however, until Harrington's work in 1962 that poverty became a national live issue in the US (Harrington 1962) and not until Abel-Smith and Townsend's work in 1965 that the same thing happened in Britain (Abel-Smith and Townsend 1965). Not for the first time in the history of these two countries poverty was 'rediscovered' and was being seen in 'structural' rather than in 'individual-istic' terms. The US government was more forthright in its condemna-tion of poverty than the British and President Kennedy's forthright stand, followed by President Johnson's declaration of war on poverty fired people's imagination far more than Prime Minister Wilson's tech-nocratic approach. If intentions, declarations, reports and the like were sufficient then the 1960s provided more than its share to abolish poverty! The documentation of trends in the extent of poverty, however, shows that the 'rediscovery' of poverty had only a minor permanent impact on the numbers and proportions of the poor in the two countries over the past three decades.

Abel-Smith and Townsend's study was the first attempt to estimate the extent of poverty in Britain from data that represented the whole country. Until then, poverty studies examined the situation in specific towns or communities and then generalized their findings to the rest of the country. Two features of the Abel-Smith and Townsend study have been incorporated in subsequent studies – the use of the national assistance benefit as the poverty line and the use of the government's family expenditure survey as the source of their data – and they merit serious discussion because they have implications for the extent and the trends in poverty.

The family expenditure survey uses a large national sample but it excludes the homeless, those living in boarding houses, hotels and residential institutions – groups which, on the whole, run a much higher risk of being in poverty than the general population. Moreover, the response rate over the years has averaged to 70 per cent, a fact which again tends to underestimate poverty since those with low in-comes are more likely not to respond to government surveys than other groups. In brief the findings of surveys based on the sample of the family expenditure survey underestimate the extent of poverty, though it is difficult to know by how much.

The use of national assistance benefit plus an amount for rent as the poverty line was justified on the grounds that when it was introduced by the government in 1948 it was designed to ensure that those receiv-ing it would have an income that was sufficient for basic necessities at basic level in terms of both quality and quantity. The amount was based largely on the studies of poverty by Rowntree and it came to be seen both by the public and the government as the 'official' poverty line. Over the years, however, it has been generally accepted that the level of the assistance benefits is too stringent. In the words of the government's own watchdog on social security, these benefit rates 'are too near the subsistence level to provide an adequate standard of living for the poorest people in our society' (Social Security Advisory Committee 1983, p. 94). Most studies of people who rely on assistance benefits conclude that the benefit rates are inadequate. A study of fathers looking after their children on their own with reliance on assistance benefits concluded that 72 per cent of the fathers found them inadequate and even those who found them adequate qualified their statement by saying that the level of benefit 'was adequate for day to day needs but not for the replacement of things which had worn out. It was adequate some weeks but not others. It was adequate for meagre necessities but not for extras' (George and Wilding 1972, p. 84). In a survey of 700 assistance benefit recipients, over half said the benefits were not sufficient to manage on and a further 15 per cent said they could just about manage but could not afford to meet one-off payments for gas or electricity bills or for clothing (Briggs and Rees 1980). Another study of assistance recipients in 1982 showed that indebtedness was very common as a survival mechanism with the result that 'half of all claimants got behind with payments, or had borrowed money during the past year. The most important single form of problem was having to borrow to make ends meet' (Berthoud 1989, p. 28). Bradshaw *et al.* showed that families on assistance benefit could not afford an adequate diet or sufficient clothing, let alone any social needs. The mother, for example, 'can afford one coat lasting 15 years, one nightdress lasting 10 years, one bra every five years, one dress every five years, three pairs of knickers every year, one pair of shoes every one and a half years and a handbag every 10 years' (Bradshaw *et al.* 1987, p. 179).

Despite the stringency of the assistance benefit, Table 2.1 shows that the proportion of the population in poverty has been quite high. The first four columns of Table 2.1 show the proportion of the population in Britain who do *not* receive assistance benefit and whose income is below the assistance benefit level, 10 per cent, 20 per cent and 40 per cent above it. The fifth column of the table shows the proportion of the population in Britain in receipt of assistance benefit over the years. The figures of the fifth column are *not* included in any of the previous four columns. Some of those on assistance benefit will have incomes below the assistance benefit level itself. For example those of the unemployed who are deemed to be 'voluntarily' unemployed or who were dismissed because of 'industrial misconduct' or failure to make

Table 2.1   Extent of poverty in Britain, 1960–87

	Cumulative proportions of persons NOT receiving assistance benefit with net incomes below and above the assistance level				Proportion of persons in receipt of assistance benefit
Year	Below assistance level	Below 110% of assistance level	Below 120% of assistance level	Below 140% of assistance level	
	%	%	%	%	%
1960	3.8*	6.6*	9.0*	14.2*	
1967	3.5*				
1972	3.4	5.5			7.7
1973	3.0	5.9			7.1
1975	3.0	4.8			6.1
1977	4.0	6.0	7.0		8.2
1979	4.0	6.2	9.0	14.4	7.6
1981	4.9	7.8	11.2	16.9	9.1
1983	5.2	8.5	11.7	19.1	11.4
1985	4.5	7.0	9.3	15.6	12.9
1985(a)	5.1	7.8	10.6	16.0	12.9
1987	5.3	7.7	10.2	14.9	13.5

*Based on household unit and hence underestimates extent of poverty.
Sources: 1960   Abel-Smith and Townsend 1965, p. 40
1967   Atkinson 1969, p. 36
1972   Central Statistical Office 1974, p. 123
1973   Central Statistical Office 1975, p. 116
1975   Central Statistical Office 1977, p. 116
1977   Central Statistical Office 1980, p. 141
1979   DHSS 1986, p. 8
1981   DHSS 1986, p. 8
1983   DHSS 1986, p. 8
1985   DHSS 1986, p. 9
1985(a) Johnson and Webb 1990, p. 11
1987   Johnson and Webb 1990, p. 11

genuine efforts to seek 'suitable' employment will be paid only 60 per cent of their assistance benefit entitlement. Others of those on assistance benefit will have incomes above the assistance benefit level because of 'disregarded' income in calculating their benefit entitlement. Still others on assistance benefit will have simply their full assistance benefit and nothing more or less. In other words an unknown proportion of those on assistance benefit – perhaps a minority – will be in poverty as defined in the first four columns of the table. Thus the first main comment on the table is that the proportion of the entire population in

Britain in 1987 with incomes below the assistance benefit level – the most stringent definition of poverty – must be at least 7 per cent and not 5.3 per cent shown in the table.

The second main comment on Table 2.1 concerns the trend on the incidence of poverty. The extent of poverty declined during the 1960s and the early 1970s but it started to rise again during the late 1970s and far more sharply during the early 1980s so that by 1987 it was higher than it was at the beginning of the 1970s. In brief, any progress made in the 1960s has all but been wiped out during the 1980s. Thus despite the rise in economic affluence in the country, the proportion of the population in the most stringent poverty as well as in other degrees of severe poverty has fluctuated but it has not declined. In fact it has risen sharply during the 1980s.

The third comment concerns the enumeration unit used to estimate the number of persons in poverty. Apart from the years 1960 and 1967 when it was the household, the enumeration unit used was the family, i.e. the parent(s) and any dependent children. This is important because it is generally agreed that poverty estimates based on the household rather than the family underestimate the extent of poverty though there is no agreement as to by how much. The reason is the obvious fact that household is a larger unit than family and as such it is more likely to raise the incomes of any one person within it who happens to have a low income on the assumption that there is a sharing of resources within it – an assumption which may not always be true. Piachaud, for example, estimated that for 1960 'the estimates of household poverty should be approximately doubled to indicate the extent of family poverty' (Piachaud 1988, p. 342). Similarly, Atkinson, reflecting on the figure for 1967, concluded that 'the proportion of the population with incomes below the National Assistance scale rates lies towards the upper end of the range 4%–9%' (Atkinson 1969, p. 38). The study by Beckerman and Clark, however, which looked at poverty in terms of households and families concluded that 'the numbers of individuals in poor households is about 30 per cent less than the numbers of individuals in poor "family" units' (Beckerman and Clark 1982, p. 17). Thus the figures for 1960 and 1967 in Table 2.1 underestimate the extent of poverty by at least 30 per cent.

It has been argued that since the level of assistance benefits is being raised annually, the figures of Table 2.1 simply show the proportion of people that falls through the assistance net rather than those in poverty. Such an argument, however, assumes that the assistance benefit level is too generous. We have already referred to several studies which point to the contrary conclusion. Moreover, it is generally accepted that the assistance benefits introduced in the late 1940s were based on the poverty thresholds devised by Rowntree which are generally acknowledged to have been pretty spartan. Since then, benefits have been increased at twice the rate of the rise in prices but at a lower rate than the rise in average earnings. More precisely the level of assistance benefit for a single adult householder, excluding payment for housing, as a proportion of the *gross* average earnings of adult male manual workers in full-time employment amounted to 17.6 per cent in 1948 and 16.0 per cent in 1989. In terms of *net* earnings, government data go back to 1970 only and they relate to all adult full-time male workers rather than merely male manual workers. They show, however, a similar downward trend. The assistance benefit for a single adult householder, excluding housing additions, amounted to 23.7 per cent in 1970 and 18.1 per cent in 1989 (DSS 1989, tables 46.11, p. 432 and 46.14, p. 438).

In other words, people on benefits today are better off than people on benefits in 1948, in much the same way that the rest of the population today is better off than the rest of the population in 1948. But people on benefits today *vis-à-vis* the rest of the population are not better off than people on benefits were *vis-à-vis* the rest of the population in 1948. It does not make much sense in policy terms comparing the living standards of the poor today with those of previous generations in a vacuum that is divorced from the living standards of their contemporaries. To indulge in such absolute comparisons is to expect people on low incomes today to eat the meals, to wear the shoes and clothes, to live in the housing conditions and so on, that were used in past generations. It is for this reason that the Royal Commission on the Distribution of Income and Wealth concluded that 'the fixing of minimum needs cannot be absolute or immutable' (Royal Commission on the Distribution of Income and Wealth 1978, p. 3).

As pointed out in Chapter 1, the definition of poverty influences the extent of measured poverty. The data we have produced so far relate to subsistence definitions of poverty. Clearly more generous definitions will lead to higher rates of poverty. Thus Townsend's study, which used a social participation definition, found that 22.9 per cent of the population of the UK in 1968–69 were in relative poverty as against 6.1 per cent who were in subsistence poverty, i.e. below assistance level (Townsend 1979, table 7.1, p. 273). Similarly, the recent poverty study conducted by the European Economic Community which defined the poor as those whose incomes were less than half the average equivalent disposable income of their country found that poverty in Britain rose from 6.7 per cent of the population in 1973–77 to 12.0 per cent in 1984–85 – a figure that was two-and-a-half times higher than that shown in Table 2.1 (Wintour 1989).

If, however, one adopts a starvation definition of poverty, the problem is far less serious. Evidence on hunger or undernutrition is very sketchy indeed and it is often used interchangeably with evidence on malnutrition. Clearly undernutrition and malnutrition are two separate concepts: undernutrition leads to malnutrition but the latter is not the result of the former only. A person may be malnourished because he or she eats the wrong food even if the amount consumed is plentiful. Bearing all this in mind, there is, first, evidence which shows that the diet of low-income groups is not only inferior to that of other groups but that it is below the professional diet standards in terms of vitamins. Low-income groups consume insufficient fruit and fresh meat and they rely excessively on starchy, fatty diets (MAFF 1985, table 20). Second, evidence from various local studies shows that a proportion of children in low-income families are undernourished. Nelson and Naismith's survey of the diets of 231 children in poor areas in London suggested that at least 11 per cent of the children were undernourished to a moderate degree (Nelson and Naismith 1983). There is evidence that some mothers, particularly in one-parent families, cut down excessively their own food consumption for the sake of their children. Government estimates show that 7 per cent of the elderly were malnourished in 1979 and the proportion was higher among the very elderly (DHSS 1979). All these and many other studies are reviewed by Cole-Hamilton and Lang who show quite clearly that, though it is not possible to document precisely the size of the problem on a national scale, malnutrition is a serious problem among low-income groups and the recent changes in government policy on social security and on school meals have accentuated the seriousness of the problem (Cole-Hamilton and Lang 1986).

Having presented the data on the proportions of people in poverty in Britain, we end this section with some brief discussion on the gap of poverty, i.e. the degrees to which people's incomes fall below the assistance level. Unfortunately, the official data take no account of this nor do most of the non-official poverty studies. Abel-Smith and Townsend's pioneering study, however, showed that of the 3.8 per cent of persons whose incomes were below the assistance level, 0.9 per cent had incomes below 80 per cent of the poverty line, another 0.9 per cent 80–89 per cent and the remaining 2 per cent were closer to the line, 90–99 per cent of it. Another way of measuring the poverty gap is to express it as a percentage of Gross Domestic Product of the country. This figure shows what proportion of the GDP is needed to bring everyone's income up to the poverty line. Clearly the higher the figure the more difficult, in economic terms, it is for the country to abolish poverty and, *vice versa*, the lower the figure the easier it is to do so, again in economic terms. Beckerman and Clark's study found that the poverty gap in Britain for 1961–3 was 0.33 per cent of GDP and for 1974–76 it declined to 0.22 per cent. In terms of absolute numbers it was £82 million and £214 million respectively for the two years – well within the economic capacity of the country though obviously not within the political will of the government (Beckerman and Clark 1982, table 4.4, p. 29).

THE COMPOSITION AND RISK OF POVERTY

Obviously poverty afflicts some population groups more than others and we shall be discussing the explanations for this in Chapter 4. Here we are simply concerned with analysing the composition and the risk of poverty. It is an important distinction because a group may constitute a large proportion of those in poverty because of its large size but it may not necessarily run a high risk of being in poverty. Table 2.2

Table 2.2   Composition of the poor: groups in poverty in Britain, 1960–87

Groups in poverty	1960	1975	1985	1987
The elderly	33%	40%	40%	31%
The low-paid	40%	34%	23%	32%
The unemployed	7%	7%	21%	21%
The sick and disabled	10%	2%	3%	3%
The one-parent families	10%	8%	3%	3%
Other	–	9%	10%	10%
All groups	100%	100%	100%	100%

looks at the composition and Table 2.3 looks at the risk of poverty. It will be seen, for example, that in 1985 the unemployed were the third largest group in poverty but they ran the second highest risk of being in poverty.

Because of their large numbers in the general population, the elderly have been either the largest or the second largest group among the poor in Britain during the period covered by this study. As Table 2.2 shows, the elderly were the second largest group among the poor in 1960 but became the largest group in 1975. By far the main reason for this is the introduction in the early 1970s of a social security benefit for the low-paid family heads which reduced their numbers in poverty. The unemployed were a relatively small group among the poor in 1960 but they became a much larger group in the 1980s because of the rise in the number of people out of work. Thus the composition of the poverty population is a reflection of the size of different population groups and of the degree of coverage afforded to them by the social security system. The fact, for example, that the one-parent families were a smaller proportion of the total number of the poor in 1985 than in 1965 does not mean that either their numbers declined or the ben-

Table 2.3   The risk of poverty for the various population groups, Britain.

Population group		1981	1985	1987
		%	%	%
I	All persons over pension age	12.7	10.6	10.0
	(a) Married couples	10.3	8.2	5.6
	(b) Single persons	15.3	13.1	15.0
II	All persons under pension age by family type	3.8	3.2	4.4
	(a) Married couples with children	3.6	2.8	4.1
	(b) Single persons with children	6.6	3.4	3.4
	(c) Married couples without children	1.6	2.1	2.7
	(d) Single persons without children	6.4	5.3	6.9
III	All persons under pension age by employment status	3.8	3.2	4.4
	(a) Full-time work or self-employed	1.9	1.8	2.9
	(b) Sick or disabled for more than 3 months	6.3	4.2	6.4
	(c) Unemployed for more than 3 months	13.8	12.1	8.7*
	(d) Other	11.9	5.8	
IV	All persons	4.9	4.5	5.3

*Includes other

efits for them improved. Rather it was due to the unprecedented rise in the numbers of the unemployed who swelled the ranks of the poor.

It is, however, the risk of poverty rather than the composition of poverty which has more bearing on the lives of people susceptible to poverty. Table 2.3 shows that in 1985, the population group that ran the highest risk of being in poverty in Britain was the elderly single persons followed by the unemployed and then by the elderly married couples. On the other hand, the group with the lowest risk of being in poverty was the full-time workers and their families followed by the married couples without children or with children – both groups overlap with the group of full-time employees. The existing data do not permit us to make any reliable comments on long-term trends but the years between 1981 and 1985 showed an improvement in the proportion of the elderly and, due to government social security policies, a deterioration in the position of young single persons. The surprising trend is the improvement in the position of one-parent families which seems to have taken place despite their growth in numbers and the absence of any improved social security provisions for them. We shall return to look at all these trends in more detail in subsequent sections of this chapter because average figures can conceal significant variations within any one group.

All the data presented so far refer to persons who are 'poor' at specific times. They provide snapshots of poverty on specific dates. Ideally we should have data that show the flow of people in and out of poverty, the duration of poverty spells as well as the duration profile of poverty at any one time, i.e. the extent to which it is made up of long-term or short-term impoverished people. Unfortunately there are no such data for the whole poverty group though they do exist for some groups as we shall point out later in this chapter. A study by Atkinson and his associates, however, on intergenerational patterns of deprivation is relevant (Atkinson *et al.* 1983). They interviewed the children of most of the fathers who had themselves been interviewed by Rowntree in his study of poverty in York in 1950, some 25 years later, i.e. during the period 1975–78. It needs to be stressed that all the fathers in Rowntree's study were working-class and hence the Atkinson study refers to intergenerational deprivation in relation to the working class and not to the whole population. Their first finding seems to suggest that, as far as the working class is concerned, the risk of poverty does not vary all that much across the generations according to parental income. Thus the proportion of children below 140 per cent of assistance levels in 1975–78 was '24.8 per cent for those where the parents were below 140 per cent of assistance levels, compared with 21.5 per cent for those whose parents were above' – a very small and statistically insignificant difference (Atkinson 1989, p. 82). Their second finding was that intergenerational deprivation was very significant in terms of low pay, i.e. those whose earnings fell in the bottom 20 per cent of the earnings distribution: 'The proportion of children who are low-paid is 50 per cent for those whose fathers are low-paid, compared with 27 per cent for those not low-paid' (Atkinson 1989, p. 82). Moreover, they found that various forms of deprivation overlap across the generations, particularly low income and inadequate housing conditions. We shall return to the issue of multiple deprivation in a later section of this chapter.

GROUPS IN POVERTY

Tables 2.2 and 2.3 have shown the size and risk of the various groups in poverty. In this section, we discuss each one of them separately in order to bring out the facts of their poverty in a little more detail. We begin with the elderly.

Like all other advanced industrial societies, Britain is experiencing a growth in the proportion of the elderly partly as a result of declining birth rates and partly rising longevity. The proportion of the population aged 65 and over in Britain rose from 4.7 per cent in 1901, to 10.9 per cent in 1951, to 15.0 per cent in 1981 and it is estimated that by 2001 it will be 15.1 per cent (Central Statistical Office 1986, table 1.1, p. 19). Moreover, the proportion of the elderly who are over 75 years old has grown faster with the result that today one in three of the elderly are above that age. Since women live longer than men it follows that they will be the majority among the elderly, particularly among the very elderly. Thus while in 1911 there were 3 women for every 2 men aged 75 and over today there are 2 women for every 1 man in that age group. Because of this rise in the proportions of the elderly, fears have been expressed that governments will not be able to meet the costs of providing adequate pensions, health care, community care and other services.

What is important, however, for economic growth is not so much the size of the dependent groups – mainly children and the retired – but the size of the active labour force and the type of technology used in industries, enterprises and elsewhere. There are still millions of people of working age who are unemployed and many more millions of married women who could enter the labour force. In other words there is abundant scope for increasing the size of the active labour force and equally abundant scope for increasing labour productivity.

old

Another aspect of this debate that needs rethinking is the assumption that past experience in the use of services by the elderly is a good guide for future demands. The heavy use of health services by the elderly need not, however, continue at the same rate in the future if more emphasis were placed on preventive care – healthier work habits, more exercise and better diets. In fact some of this is already happening and it may affect significantly the costs of future services for the elderly. It may also well be that future medical discoveries can influence the course of some of the main disorders – such as dementia – of the very elderly and thus reduce the cost of services. In brief, as Thane has argued, we should 'be wary of extrapolating from present patterns to an unknown future' (Thane 1981, p. 379) because living patterns are changing, medical science is always advancing and these factors can affect the demand for services by the elderly.

Table 2.4   Main sources of gross income for the elderly, Britain 1951–85

	1951	1961	1971	1981	1985
	%	%	%	%	%
Social security benefits	43	47	48	59	59
Occupational pensions	15	16	21	21	21
Earnings from employment	27	22	18	10	14
Investment income	15	15	13	10	6
Total	100	100	100	100	100

Source: Adapted from Fiegehen 1986, table A.3, p. 15; Dawson and Evans 1987, table 4, p. 246.

Table 2.4 gives the main sources of income for the elderly for the period covered by this study. It shows that social security benefits have always been the main source of income for the elderly and that this significance has increased over the years. Occupational pension income has also increased in significance over the years while income from employment earnings has declined so much that, unless changes are made in employment policies, it is in danger of disappearing altogether. The essence of Table 2.4, however, is that social security benefits will remain the main source of income and hence the most effective way of abolishing poverty among the elderly.

Class and gender, however, affect substantially the sources as well as the amounts of incomes for the elderly. Occupational pension provision is class- and gender-biased (Government Actuary 1983). Men are not only more likely to qualify for such pensions than women but they are also more likely to receive higher amounts. Similarly managerial and professional employees are more likely than other employees to receive such pensions as well as to receive higher pension amounts. The same comments apply even more so to investment income. In addition to class and gender, age itself influences the sources of income. The very elderly are less likely to receive occupational pensions than the younger elderly, and they are also less likely to be in employment or to have any savings or investment income. In brief, the lower the socioeconomic group and the higher the age the greater the reliance on social security benefits. Since women live longer than men, they are even more likely to rely on social security benefits as their main source of income and they are therefore more likely to be in poverty.

It is true that during the period covered by this study the incomes of the elderly have risen at a faster rate than the incomes of the rest of the population. Thus the pensioners' disposable income per head amounted to 41 per cent of that of non-pensioners in 1951 and to 69 per cent in 1985 (Fiegehen 1986, table A.1, p. 14). This is the result of improved occupational pension provision and of the rise in the real value of the state retirement pension. This overall improvement, however, conceals wide variations and, as Table 2.3 showed, one-tenth of all pensioners were in official poverty in 1985. Moreover, this improvement will not continue in the future now that retirement pensions are raised according to prices rather than wages. The Government Actuary has recently estimated that by the year 2050 the combined value of the state flat-rate and earnings-related pension will amount to only 19 per cent of average male earnings compared with 28 per cent now. Moreover, this decline will not be made good by a corresponding rise in the combined value of occupational and private pensions (Government Actuary 1990).

This type of poverty would be abolished if only pensioners applied for the assistance benefit because there is no legal reason to disqualify them so long as they meet the income test. The fact is, however, that many pensioners do not apply either because they object to means tests, or because of sheer pride or ignorance. These facts have been known for decades now and yet no government has attempted to find ways of overcoming these obstacles. In the present age of computer technology, it would not be beyond the administrative ability of governments to identify those pensioners who are entitled to assistance benefit and to pay it to them automatically. Official poverty among the elderly would then disappear.

Table 2.5   Cumulative rate of disability per thousand adult population, Britain 1985

Severity category	Men	Women	Total
10	3	6	5
9–10	9	17	13
8–10	16	28	22
7–10	24	42	33
6–10	32	58	46
5–10	45	78	62
4–10	58	97	78
3–10	73	115	95
2–10	92	135	114
1–10	121	161	142

Source: Martin et al. 1988, table 3.7, p. 22.

We now turn to look at the financial circumstances of disabled persons. Table 2.5, based on a recent government study, shows the extent and severity of disability in Britain by gender among adults. It does not cover disability among children. Much disability is light in severity – categories 1 to 5 – and has few, if any, public expenditure implications or perhaps even financial implications for the individuals concerned. It is clearly severe disability and particularly categories 9 and 10 that have strong implications for both the individual and the state – not only financial but social as well. As expected, the severity of disability increases with age so that about 55 per cent of all those in categories 9 and 10 are aged 75 and over. The severity of disability is also higher among women than men and bearing in mind that women live longer it is no surprise that about two-thirds of all disabled in categories 9 and 10 are women.

The disabled derive their incomes from three main sources: social security benefits, earnings and other. Each source is of different significance to the different subgroups of the disabled though for the majority of the disabled social security benefits – mainly retirement pensions – are by far the most significant source of income. Only among the married disabled were benefits of lower significance than either earnings or other sources. Bearing in mind, however, that many of the married disabled will have dependent children, they have the lowest income per person while the unmarried non-pensioners with no children have the highest incomes. Thus age, severity of disability and the presence of children have the strongest depressing effects on income.

It is important to compare the incomes of the disabled with those of the general population in order to get some idea of the degree of comparative deprivation that disability incurs. This comparison can be made in at least three different ways, each of which brings out differ-

Table 2.6   Sources of earnings of the disabled, Britain 1985

Sources of income	Non-pensioner				Pensioner		All disabled adults
	1	2	3	4	5	6	
	%	%	%	%	%	%	%
Earnings	33	21	49	60	1	3	24
Benefits	54	70	36	36	76	72	58
Other sources	13	9	15	4	23	25	18
Total	100	100	100	100	100	100	100

Source: Martin and White 1988, table 3.15, p. 26.

1 Unmarried, no children
2 Unmarried with children
3 Married, no children
4 Married with children
5 Unmarried
6 Married

ent aspects of the disparity of living standards between the two groups. First, a comparison of mean equivalent incomes shows that the figure for the disabled amounts to about 75 per cent of that of the general population (Martin and White 1988, table 3.22, p. 31). Second, the same conclusion emerges if one compares the disabled with the non-disabled in terms of income deciles. Thus while 30 per cent of the non-disabled belong to the top three income deciles, the corresponding proportion for the disabled is only 10 per cent. Conversely, while 40 per cent of the non-disabled fall into the lowest four deciles, the corresponding proportion for the disabled rises to 58 per cent (Martin and White 1988, table 3.24, p. 33). Third, the disparity between disabled and non-disabled increases even more if the extra expenses necessarily incurred by the disabled are taken into account. Clearly, there are difficulties in calculating such expenses and they also vary according to the degree of disability. Nevertheless, on average the proportion of the disabled that fall within the three top deciles is only 9 per cent compared with 30 per cent of the non-disabled; whereas the proportion in the lowest four deciles is 65 per cent compared with 40 per cent of the non-disabled. The worst-off group is the unmarried disabled with children where 83 per cent belong to the lowest four deciles (Martin and White 1988, table 5.6, p. 64).

The government study used several methods to measure the living standards of the disabled. The first was whether they possessed such consumer durables at TV, refrigerator, washing machine, telephone, dishwasher, central heating, etc. The general conclusion was, as expected, that they did not do as well as the non-disabled. Second, the study examined the extent to which disabled persons experienced financial difficulties and, as expected, a very high proportion of non-pensioners found themselves in such difficulties. Further analysis of the data showed that this was related to both income and subjective feelings of dissatisfaction. Third, the study used the findings of the Mack and Lansley poverty study on what the general public considered were basic necessities, as we discussed in Chapter 1, and tried to find out the extent to which these were lacking in the households of disabled persons. Table 2.7 shows yet again the greater incidence of poverty among the disabled. Further analysis of the data showed that the unmarried disabled with children were again the most deprived group with 53 per cent of them not being able to afford new clothes and having to rely on second-hand clothing, 50 per cent not being able to afford two pairs of shoes, and so on. Thus whichever method one

Table 2.7   Proportion of households lacking basic items. Britain, 1985

Basic items lacking	All disabled households		General population households	
	1	2	3	4
	%	%	%	%
Meat or fish every other day	13	7	17	8
Roast joint once a week	25	12	13	7
Warm winter coat	12	8	10	7
Two pairs all-weather shoes	22	15	13	9
New clothes	20	17	12	6
Presents once a year	16	13	8	5
Celebrations, e.g. Christmas	24	13	7	4

Source: Martin and White 1988, table 6.14, p. 77.

1 Lacking them
2 Lacking them because can't afford them
3 Lacking them
4 Lacking them because can't afford them

uses, the living standards of the disabled, and particularly some groups of the disabled, are too low both in comparison with those of the non-disabled and, indeed, by the generally accepted standards of the country.

Since the majority of the disabled rely solely or mainly on social security benefits, their standard of living can only be realistically raised through improvements in these benefits. The current system of benefits is far too complex; it treats some forms of disability more ungenerously than others and it provides benefits which are too low. Pressure groups for the disabled and the government's own watchdog on social security – the Social Security Advisory Committee – have been advocating an integrated scheme that provides one benefit made up of various parts that cater for the varying severities of disability. As the Social Security

Advisory Committee rightly pointed out, any benefits scheme for the disabled must measure up to four guiding principles: it must 'provide an adequate basic income', 'help towards the extra costs' of disability, 'provide incentives for disabled people to achieve independence through employment' and be 'readily understandable' (Social Security Advisory Committee 1988, p. 60). Certainly such a reform, coupled with improvements in housing and environmental services and better employment opportunities, would go a long way to reducing poverty and deprivation among the disabled.

Table 2.8   Composition of one-parent families, Britain

Type of family	1971	1986
Single mothers	15.8	22.8
Separated mothers	29.8	18.8
Divorced mothers	21.1	40.6
Widowed mothers	21.1	7.9
All mothers	87.8	90.1
All fathers	12.2	9.9
All one-parent families	100.0	100.0
Proportion of all families	8.0	14.0
Number of one-parent families	570 000	1 010 000

Source: Adapted from Haskey 1989, table 4, p. 30.

One-parent families are currently attracting government attention largely because of their rising social security costs. As Table 2.8 shows, both their incidence and their composition has changed with the result that they are not only a larger group but they are also a 'less deserving group' in the eyes of right-wing commentators and politicians. While they formed 8 per cent of all families in 1971 they rose to 14 per cent in 1986. Moreover, while widows were one of the largest groups in 1971, they are now the smallest group; and while single mothers were the smallest group in 1971, they are now the second largest. Governments have always found it easier to pay benefits to widows than to single mothers or to the separated and divorced. One important feature of one-parent families in Britain, as compared with the US, is that the vast majority of them – 91 per cent – are white and the remaining 9 per cent are made up of all other nationality groups – 5 per cent West Indian, 1 per cent Asian and 1.9 per cent other (Slipman and Hadjipateras 1988, table 4a, p. 9). It is therefore not possible to inject racial undertones in the relevant debates and thus create openly stigmatizing policy packages for the whole group of one-parent families.

As we shall be discussing in Chapter 4, the reasons for the rise in the proportion of one-parent families are rooted in long-term changes of the national economy that brought, among other things, economic independence to women and thus enabled them to live on their own when their marriage or partnership was unhappy. These economic changes have been accompanied by changes in sexual mores as well as easier divorce laws. All these interrelated changes are largely *irreversible* and governments have no option but to live with higher rates of one-parent families and to make adequate provision for them because, if for no other reason, 12.4 per cent of all children in 1986 were living in one-parent families.

Data on the incomes of one-parent families are far from adequate but the general picture appears to be as follows: assistance benefit accounts for 45 per cent of the total income of all one-parent families; employment earnings for 22 per cent; maintenance payments 10 per cent; the remaining 23 per cent from pensions, investments and so on. Expressed in a different way 74 per cent of all one-parent families draw assistance benefits, some of whom combine it with earnings from part-time employment and/or with income from maintenance payments. Another 23 per cent of one-parent families rely on earnings from full-time employment, some of whom again combine it with income from maintenance payments. The remaining 3 per cent may either have independent incomes or rely exclusively on maintenance payments (DSS 1990, vol. one, p. 3). Let us now look in more detail at employment earnings, assistance benefits and maintenance payments.

Beginning with employment, the facts are that lone mothers do not perform all that differently from married mothers with dependent children. Government data show that during 1985–87, 42 per cent of lone mothers and 54 per cent of married mothers with dependent children were in employment. Of the lone mothers, 18 per cent worked full-time and 24 per cent part-time. The corresponding proportions for married mothers were 17 per cent and 37 per cent respectively. (Office of Population Censuses and Statistics "General Household Survey 1987" table 2.37, p. 105, HMSO, 1989). Bearing in mind all the problems – lack of child care facilities, low wages and having to combine work with mothering single-handed – it is surprising that such a high proportion of lone mothers go out to work. It is a reflection of their adherence to dominant work values as well as the result of the low level of benefits. This is confirmed by several studies. Weale *et al*., for example, found that 93.5 per cent of working lone mothers gave money reasons as their first reason for working and almost half gave social reasons as their second reason (Weale *et al*. 1984, table 9.7, p. 138). However, the decision to go out to work was not an easy one and, as the authors point out, it 'depends on a complex interaction of preferences, child care constraints, job opportunities and financial returns' (Weale *et al*. 1984, p. 190).

Since for most lone mothers going out to work makes no good economic sense due to low wages and high child care costs, it is worth looking further at employment rates in more detail. The first point that emerges is that the proportion of lone mothers with a child under five years – thus needing child care facilities – in full-time or part-time employment is only a third of those with no children under five in employment. Indeed, a similar picture emerges in relation to married women. The second point is that of all lone mothers, it is the single mothers who are least likely to work because of young children, lack of work experience and hence low wages. If there is one conclusion that can be drawn from all this, it is that lack of affordable child care facilities appears at first to be the main impediment to employment for lone mothers and, indeed, for married women with children under five. This conclusion, however, may not be valid if one takes into account the fact that the majority of the public feel that when there are children under five, the preferred arrangement is for the father to work full-time and the mother to stay at home (Ashford 1987). Thus both lone mothers and married mothers with children under five may well be taking a positive decision that it is in the best interests of their children that they should not go out to work but stay at home and look after them.

The present social security arrangements for one-parent families have been in existence with only very minor changes since the reorganization of the social security system in the 1940s. Basically there is an insurance benefit for widows with the result that all others have to apply for means-tested assistance benefit. It is therefore not surprising that a very high proportion of lone mothers receive assistance benefit or that they receive it for very long periods. While only one-sixth of one-parent families received assistance benefit in 1961 the proportion shot up to two-thirds in 1987 (Bradshaw 1989, p. 10). Moreover, almost one-third were on benefit for more than five years. Brown provides official statistics which show that in 1986 27.2 per cent of single mothers, 12.4 per cent of separated mothers, 36.0 per cent of divorced mothers and 30.0 per cent of widowed were on assistance benefit for more than five years (Brown 1989, table 1.11, p. 13). Because of their long stay on benefit, it has become fashionable to refer to this as the culture of dependency, implying that lone mothers have acquired values that inhibit them from work. It is more to the point, as we shall be explaining at length in Chapter 4, to refer to this as the structure of dependency, i.e. lack of affordable child care facilities coupled with low wages that make it very difficult for many lone mothers to escape enforced dependence on assistance benefits.

Maintenance payments from fathers amount not only to a negligible proportion of the income of lone-mother families but they also constitute an unreliable and bothersome source of income for the caring mother. Only 30 per cent of lone mothers received regular payments of maintenance while the remaining 70 per cent received such payments irregularly or not at all. In some cases the mother herself pursues the father in the courts to recover the arrears while in other cases this task is taken over by the DSS. Where the DSS intervenes, the success rate is extremely low – in only 23 per cent of cases is the full amount of arrears recovered and this amounts to only 5 per cent of the total value of the arrears (DSS 1990, vol. one, p. 3). This unsatisfactory state of affairs has led to the recent government proposals to pursue a more active policy which ensures that absent fathers make more adequate as well as more regular contributions towards the maintenance of their children. Whilst the principle is widely supported, there is justifiable criticism on two issues: first, the amount of maintenance payments proposed by the government may be so heavy for some fathers that it will force them and their second family, if any, to live in poverty. Second, lone mothers on assistance benefit do not benefit financially from this new government drive since the amount of the maintenance payment is taken fully into account when calculating the amount of assistance benefit paid to them. It is for this reason that the government proposals can be seen more as an attempt to reduce public expenditure than to improve the financial position of lone mothers and their children. Similarly the government's anxiety to encourage more lone mothers to work full-time is impeded by its refusal to provide more child care facilities in an effort to keep public expenditure down.

The overall result of the structure of dependency is that living standards for most one-parent families are low and compare unfavourably with those of two-parent families. Whether they go out to work or stay at home, most one-parent families will have incomes hovering around the official poverty line and, as Table 2.3 showed, they will run a higher risk of being in poverty than two-parent families. In terms of housing, they are less likely to own or to be buying their house, they are more likely to be living in second-rate rented housing and to be homeless than two-parent families. Their children too, are more likely to suffer from ill-health, to be received into the care of local authorities and to experience school difficulties than the children of two-parent families. All these and other disadvantages are to be expected in societies where the two-parent family is considered the norm and where public and private provision are geared to this. The social security system is still based primarily on the norm of a patriarchal two-parent family.

The lack of consensus on what is to be done about the poverty of one-parent families is far wider than in the case of the elderly or the disabled because it raises fundamental questions in such crucial areas as the family, parental responsibility, child welfare, work incentives and the role of women in society. We shall be dealing with policy issues in Chapter 5 but now we move on to look at the unemployed who also raise difficult and controversial policy debates.

Issues of unemployment have dominated public debates during the past ten years and they will continue to be at the forefront so long as unemployment remains high. During the 1950s and 1960s unemployment in Britain was below 1.5 per cent per annum; it rose during the 1970s so that by the end of the decade it reached 6 per cent and then, due largely to government monetarist policies, it shot up to 13 per cent in 1983 and it has since declined to 7.3 per cent in December 1988, according to official figures. Part of the recent reduction, however, is due to several downward government redefinitions of unemployment. Thus the unemployment rate claimed by the government for December 1988 was estimated by an independent research unit – the London Unemployment Unit – to be 10.1 per cent.

Clearly unemployment strikes some groups more severely than others. The lower socioeconomic groups are about six times as likely to be unemployed as the top socioeconomic groups, as Table 2.9 shows. They are even more likely to be long-term unemployed, i.e. unemployed for more than 12 months simply because there are fewer job vacancies for them.

Age is another factor influencing the risk of unemployment in the sense that those aged 55 or over are more likely to be made redundant

Table 2.9   Unemployment rates by occupational group, Britain, Spring 1986

Occupational group		Men %	Women %	All %
I	All non-manual	4.01	4.98	4.50
	Managerial and professional	3.2	3.9	3.5
	Clerical and related	5.8	5.0	5.2
	Other non-manual	6.7	7.3	7.1
II	All manual	9.87	7.98	9.27
	Craft and similar	7.8	9.2	7.9
	General labourers	21.3	17.8	21.0
	Other manual	10.9	7.7	9.5
III	All occupations	11.1	9.9	10.6

Source: Department of Employment 1988, table 8, p. 34.

and less likely to be re-employed than younger workers. In addition the younger age groups, 16–25, suffer from high rates of unemployment but their spells of unemployment are of short duration. Ethnic minority groups are also more vulnerable than white persons irrespective of educational qualifications. Government data show that in the Spring of 1985 and 1987 the unemployment rates for white males of working age according to qualifications were as follows: for those with higher qualifications the unemployment rate was 3 per cent; for those with other qualifications the unemployment rate was 9 per cent; and for those with no qualifications, it rose to 18 per cent. The corresponding rates for all ethnic minority groups were 9, 19 and 25 per cent. A similar, but not as extreme, picture emerges in relation to women's unemployment by qualifications and race (Department of Employment 1988, table 9, p. 642). Clearly either discrimination or inappropriateness of qualifications or both account for the higher rates of unemployment among qualified ethnic groups. It is another aspect of the structural explanation of poverty that we develop in Chapter 4.

There are three main benefits for the unemployed: redundancy payments, unemployment insurance benefit and assistance benefit. Redundancy payments are lump sums paid to employees who are made redundant, the amount of which depends on years of full-time service with the same employer, gross weekly pay and age. Those who lose out on this scheme are part-time workers, those who move from job to job and the low-paid. But even the largest redundancy payments are not sufficient replacements of earnings – they serve 'more as a consolation prize for the loss of the job than as a resource for ongoing income' (Root 1986, p. 40).

The initial intention of the Beveridge Report, the basis for the reorganization of social security benefits in the 1940s, was that the majority of the unemployed would qualify for the insurance benefit and only the few who failed to do so would have to apply for the means-tested assistance benefit. So long as unemployment was low and few people worked part-time this expectation worked well enough though not perfectly. With the rise of unemployment and particularly long-term unemployment, however, the whole idea collapsed in practice, as shown by Table 2.10. In 1988 only a minority relied on unemployment benefit and about two-thirds relied on assistance benefit. It was the inevitable result of the rule that the unemployment insurance benefit can be paid for a maximum of 12 months. The figure referring to those receiving no benefit in 1988 is an underestimate and it is the result of

Table 2.10   Social security benefits for the unemployed, Britain

		1961	1988
		%	%
I	Unemployed male claimants receiving:		
	unemployment benefit only	40.2	16.3
	unemployment benefit and assistance benefit	9.4	7.2
	assistance benefit only	21.9	61.2
	no benefit	27.6	15.2
II	Unemployed female claimants receiving:		
	unemployment benefit only	39.7	29.7
	unemployment benefit and assistance benefit	2.5	3.1
	assistance benefit only	12.2	43.4
	no benefit	45.5	23.7

Source: Central Statistical Office 1990, table 5.8, p. 90.

recent redefinitions of who counts as an unemployed person to be included in the official statistics.

The social security system treats the unemployed more harshly than other groups of claimants in at least four ways. First, unemployment benefit is paid for a maximum period of 12 months while insurance benefits for other contingencies – sickness, disability, widowhood and retirement – are paid for as long as the contingency lasts. Second, the amount of unemployment benefit as well as assistance benefit is lower than the corresponding benefits for other groups. Third, there is far more social security policing of the unemployed than other comparable groups. Fourth, unemployment benefit can be withheld for short periods if it is felt that a person made himself 'voluntarily' unemployed; if he was dismissed for 'industrial misconduct' and if he refuses 'suitable offers' of employment or training. In such cases assistance benefit can be paid but at a reduced rate. These four harsh attitudes and practices against the unemployed are found in the social security systems of all industrial countries. They reflect the dominant values of society, they reinforce industrial discipline and they benefit the higher socioeconomic groups in society.

Bearing all these in mind, together with the fact that part-time employment does not qualify a person for unemployment benefit, it is no surprise that the risk of poverty among the unemployed is the second highest of all groups, as Table 2.3 showed. There is also a great deal of evidence which confirms the obvious point that unemployment depresses living standards (Moylan *et al*. 1984) and thus renders the living standards of the unemployed inferior to those of people in employment. Bradshaw *et al*., for example, summarize their findings on the financial impact of unemployment by concluding 'that the living standards of the long-term unemployed are lower than those in short-term unemployment and that the living standards of both are below those of the poorest families at work' (Bradshaw *et al*. 1983, p. 450). It needs to be remembered, however, that though the likelihood of unemployed persons being in poverty is certainly high this may well be confined to the middle and lower socioeconomic groups. In other words, it would be wrong to give the impression that unemployed persons from the higher socioeconomic groups find their standard of living dropping below that of the poorest families at work. Even unemployment is not such a strong economic leveller.

The extent of low pay depends to some extent on how it is defined. The three main definitions are in order of generosity: the Council of

Europe definition which is equivalent to 68 per cent of full-time mean earnings; the London Low Pay Unit definition which amounts to two-thirds of median male earnings; and the definition put forward by the Trade Union Congress which is two-thirds of mean male manual earnings. Using the Low Pay Unit definition, which was £157.00 p.w. in April 1989 as compared to £163.00 for the first definition and £145.20 for the third, Table 2.11 shows that 16.7 per cent of all male workers and 47.9 per cent of all female workers in full-time employment were low-paid, making up a total of 27.3 per cent of all adult workers as low-paid. Clearly the extent of low pay is higher among manual than non-manual workers and it is also higher among women than among men. Young workers under the age of 20, not included in Table 2.11, are more likely to be low-paid since their earnings are only about half those of older workers. Finally, Table 2.11 shows the very high amount of overtime work performed by male manual workers clearly because it is the only way that they can earn enough wages for their family needs.

Table 2.11   Proportion of low-paid employees, Britain 1989

	Category of workers	Including overtime pay	Excluding overtime pay
		%	%
I	Male, full-time workers on adult rates		
	Manual	22.8	36.7
	Non-manual	10.3	11.9
	All	16.7	24.6
II	Female, full-time workers on adult rates		
	Manual	75.3	81.7
	Non-manual	40.5	42.7
	All	47.9	51.0
III	All men and women	27.3	33.6

Source: Bryson, 1989, table 2, p. 12.

Low wages have always been a main reason for poverty in Britain. Rowntree's study of poverty in York in 1899 found that low wages were the single most important reason for poverty – they accounted for 74 per cent of the poor in York. The study by Abel-Smith and Townsend found that low wages were still the single most important reason for poverty in the whole country, accounting for 40 per cent of the poor in 1960. Several factors contributed to the relative decline in the significance of low pay to family poverty – the introduction of child benefits in 1945, the rise in the two-wage families, the growth in the numbers of retirement pensioners and so on. It is doubtful whether one of the reasons was the relative improvement of low wages since the lowest decile of the earnings of full-time manual male workers as a proportion of the median earnings has changed very little over the years. It was 68.6 per cent in 1886, 67.7 per cent in 1938, 70.6 per cent in 1960, 67.3 per cent in 1970, 68.3 per cent in 1979 and declined to 63.9 per cent in 1989. Table 2.2 showed that low wages accounted for 23 per cent of the poor in 1985, making the low-paid the second largest group of the poor after the elderly poor. The main reason behind this relative decline in the significance of low pay to poverty was the introduction of the government scheme in 1971 that supplemented the low earnings of workers with children. To avoid any misunderstanding, it is worth repeating that these figures do not refer to the risk of being in poverty for this risk is very low as far as those in full-time employment are concerned. Thus Table 2.3 showed that only 1.8 per cent of those in full-time employment were in poverty in 1985 – the lowest degree of risk of all groups. The fact that low pay accounts for such a high proportion of the poor is due to the numerical size of the employed population *vis-à-vis* other groups and not to the degree of risk involved.

Low pay, however, accounts for poverty not only in the direct way just discussed but also in several indirect but significant ways. As mentioned in the discussion on the unemployed, the lower socioeconomic groups are far more likely to find themselves out of work and for longer periods than other groups. A similar relationship exists between low pay and unemployment for there is a general relationship between low pay and socioeconomic grouping (Bazen 1988, table 7, p. 16). Low pay is also related to occupational pension provision even though most of the evidence refers to socioeconomic groups. Bazen's analysis of government data for 1980, however, showed that while 42.6 per cent of all male and female employees were covered by an occupational pension, the proportion of the low-paid, defined as two-thirds of median earnings, was only 13.3 per cent (Bazen 1988, table 8, p. 17). Clearly low pay is also related to housing, to investment and to the amount of savings that a family possesses. It is also related to levels of education and degrees of sickness though the relationship in these two areas is often a two-way process. All this lends support to the argument that low pay is significantly related to poverty in direct and indirect ways. It is, however, also true that single low-paid people may not be in poverty, as it is officially defined. Similarly the existence of two low-paid wage earners may avoid poverty in many families. Nevertheless, many families may be in poverty despite the fact that the family wage earner is not low-paid, because of the large size of the family. All these qualifications are correct but they do not demolish the basic argument that low pay is the direct and indirect cause of a large proportion of those in poverty. It is for this reason that it has rightly been claimed that the low-paid worker of today will be the impoverished pensioner of the future. It has also been shown that a large proportion of single mothers in poverty were also poor prior to motherhood; and so on. Low pay is a focal part of the web of disadvantage that we discuss in the next section.

So far we have concentrated on the effects of low pay on poverty. But there is another unacceptable side to it – the degree of economic exploitation involved in very low wages. These two different aspects of low pay have necessitated two different types of government programmes: supplementation of the earnings of low-paid family heads to reduce family poverty; and minimum wage legislation. Clearly minimum wage legislation can only be useful if it is national, set at a respectable level, upgraded regularly and rigorously enforced. All these have been lacking from the British minimum wage legislation. Minimum wage legislation is not national but rather involves certain industries covering only one-sixth of the labour force; it has been irregularly updated and it has been very inadequately enforced. Instead of improving it, the government has now decided to abolish it altogether. Wage supplementation has been a more useful policy although its take-up rate has ranged from 50 per cent to 75 per cent of those entitled to it. A government study in 1972 showed that wage supplementation does not abolish poverty altogether among wage earners and families but reduces it. Of those families whose head had his wage supplemented, 13 per cent were still in official poverty; without wage supplementation, however, the proportion would have been 29 per cent

(DHSS 1976). Government schemes to raise low pay either through minimum wages or through wage supplementation are not only useful in relation to low pay but also in relation to other social security beneficiaries, particularly the unemployed. By raising wages, such schemes allay the fears, real and imaginary, that people on decent benefits would not want to give up their benefits in return for wages. In this way, wage supplementation removes one justification for reducing the level of benefits for such groups as the unemployed and the one-parent families. A society which cannot bring itself to be generous towards the low-paid will hardly be generous towards the unemployed and the one-parent families.

INEQUALITY, POVERTY AND DEPRIVATION

Both in Chapter 1 and in this chapter, it has been pointed out that though poverty and inequality are different, they are closely related. The life chances of a person whose income is just above the poverty line, by a few pence or dollars, cannot be all that different from those of another person whose income is just below or on the poverty line. It is in this sense that poverty is a class issue irrespective of whether class is defined in Marxist or Weberian terms. Poverty in terms of income is also related to other forms of deprivation – in terms of housing, health and education. In this section we shall therefore discuss income and wealth inequalities in Britain and the relationship between low income and material forms of deprivation.

Beginning with wealth, Table 2.12 shows the position in terms of marketable wealth, i.e. wealth which a person can use and trade with as distinct from wealth which includes rights to state and occupational pensions. Despite the fact that the figures for 1960 are not strictly comparable with those for subsequent years, nevertheless the long-term trend has been a reduction in the heavy concentration of wealth among the top 1 per cent towards a wider concentration among the top 50 per cent most wealthy adults. It is difficult to know what proportion of this spread is between related adults – husbands, wives, children – in an effort to reduce tax liability. Moreover, a good part of this spread has been the result of the rise in house ownership which is a different type of wealth in terms of the person's ability to receive an income from it or to trade with it. Thus dwellings (net of mortgage debt) amounted to 22 per cent of net marketable wealth in 1971 and 32 per

Table 2.12   Distribution of marketable wealth, UK

Per cent of wealth owned by:		1960	1971	1981	1985	1987
		%	%	%	%	%
Most wealthy	1% adults	38.2	31	21	20	18
Most wealthy	5% adults	64.3	52	40	40	36
Most wealthy	10% adults	76.7	65	54	54	50
Most wealthy	25% adults		86	77	76	74
Most wealthy	50% adults		97	94	93	93

Source: Central Statistical Office 1990, table 5.19, p. 96
For 1960, Royal Commission 1974, table 45, p. 102.

cent in 1985. Other types of wealth are more concentrated. Despite the
paucity of statistics it is well known that share ownership is heavily
concentrated notwithstanding government efforts to spread it out. In
1986, only 14 per cent of the population owned any shares and, what is
more, most of the shares were owned by a smaller proportion of these.
As one would expect, wealth distribution is heavily class-based. Thus
in 1986, the two higher socioeconomic groups – professional and
managerial – owned 42 per cent of all the country's wealth; 29 per cent
was owned by the junior administrative and professional, the clerical
and supervisory group; 19 per cent by the skilled manual workers; and
the remaining 10 per cent by retirement pensioners, the semi-skilled
and the unskilled workers. If one takes into account the fact that most
of the wealth of the skilled, semi-skilled and unskilled manual workers
consists of their houses, it means that most of the income-generating
wealth belongs to the two top socioeconomic groups. Finally, what
Table 2.12 also shows is that 50 per cent of adults in the country
owned only 7 per cent of the national wealth in 1987. The concentration of wealth, particularly in terms of land, property, stocks and
shares, is important not only because of the income it generates but
also because of the economic and political power that it bestows on its
holders.

The distribution of income is obviously far less concentrated than
wealth because it includes earnings from employment, social security
benefits as well as income from investment and from savings. Table 2.13

Table 2.13   Distribution of income in the UK before and after tax

	Before tax			
Group	1949	1972	1982	1985
	%	%	%	%
Top 1%	11.2	6.4	6.0	6.4
Top 10%	33.2	26.9	28.3	29.4
Top 50%	76.3	75.0	77.3	77.8
Bottom 50%	23.7	25.0	22.7	22.2
All groups	100.0	100.0	100.00	100.00
	After tax			
Group	1949	1972	1982	1985
	%	%	%	%
Top 1%	6.4	4.4	4.6	4.9
Top 10%	27.1	23.6	25.6	26.5
Top 50%	73.5	73.2	74.8	75.1
Bottom 50%	26.5	26.8	25.2	24.9
All groups	100.0	100.0	100.0	100.0

Source: For columns 1949 and 1972, Royal Commission 1975, table 15, p. 45
For columns 1982 and 1985, Central Statistical Office 1988, table 5.14, p. 92.

distinguishes between the distribution of income before and after taxation and it shows that post-tax income has always been slightly less
concentrated. The general trends for both pre-tax and post-tax income
distribution however have been very similar. There was a substantial
reduction in the concentration of income among the top 1 per cent
during 1949–82 and though the trend has since been reversed this
group is still worse off than it was in 1949 in terms of both pre- and
post-tax income. The trend has been different for the next group, i.e.
the next 9 per cent of highest income earners. Their share of the total
income declined slightly during 1949–72 but it picked up after that so
that by 1985 they were slightly better off than they were in 1949 for
both before- and after-tax income. The position of the next group, 10–
50 per cent of income earners, improved between 1949 and 1972,
remained static up to 1982 and declined after that but still left them

better off than they were in 1949. As for the bottom 50 per cent of income earners, their position improved slightly during 1949–72, declined after that and today they are worse off than they were in 1949. In brief, the top 1 per cent and the bottom 50 per cent are worse off today than they were in 1949 which shows that the small amount of income redistribution has been from the very high to the high- and middle-income earners.

The recent government data on households with below average incomes show quite clearly that their position deteriorated significantly during the 1980s. Table 2.14 shows that while the median income of

Table 2.14   Rise in median disposable incomes by decile group, Britain 1981–87

Decile group	Per cent rise before housing costs	Per cent rise after housing costs
Lowest decile	9.3	2.3
2nd decile	7.5	4.4
3rd decile	10.1	6.0
4th decile	12.3	9.5
5th decile	14.6	13.0
Total population	20.6	19.8

Source: Government Statistical Service 1990, tables A.1 and D.1, pp. 10 and 26

the entire population in Britain rose by 20 per cent during 1981–87 the income of the poorest 10 per cent rose by only 9 per cent before housing costs and by a mere 2 per cent after taking into account housing costs. Similar comments apply to the other deciles with below average incomes. Table 2.15 tells the same story but from a different perspective. The number and proportion of both individuals and children with incomes below half the average disposable income increased quite considerably during this period particularly when housing costs are taken into account. Obviously housing costs rose more for the low-income than the high-income groups. Whichever figures one uses the conclusion that Thatcherite policies widened inequalities is inescapable. The message is clear: politics do matter.

Table 2.15 *Proportion of individuals and dependent children with incomes below half the average disposable income, Britain*

		Before housing costs		After housing costs	
		1981	1987	1981	1987
Individuals	– Number (thousands)	4,390	7,720	6,370	10,500
	– Proportion (%)	8.2	14.3	11.9	19.4
Children	– Number (thousands)	1,790	2,420	2,360	3,090
	– Proportion (%)	13.7	20.2	18.0	25.7

Source: Government Statistical Service 1990, tables C1, p. 20; C3, p. 24; F1, p. 36; F3, p. 40

Wealth and income inequalities are associated with privilege and advantage at one end of the distribution scale and with deprivation and disadvantage at the other. The connection between low income and individual forms of deprivation has long been known and has been fairly well documented (Berthoud 1976; Brown and Madge 1982; George and Wilding 1984; Mack and Lansley 1985; Le Grand 1982). What is less adequately documented is the relationship between low income and multiple forms of deprivation. The Black Report in 1980 re-awakened interest in the relationship between low income, bad housing and ill-health (DHSS 1980) and several studies have since shown that this link, which was once thought to have disappeared, is still very much with us (Byrne *et al.* 1986; Blackman *et al.* 1989). The relationship between low pay and unemployment, that was referred to above, extends to physical and mental ill-health as so many studies have shown over the years (Jahoda 1933; Brenner 1973; Fagin and Little 1984). Similarly, the relationship between family background, education, income and unemployment is widely accepted and well-documented in all advanced industrial societies as Chapter 4 will show. All these multiple forms of deprivation as well as of advantage are testament to the validity of the importance of structural factors in people's lives. This is a crucial issue in the debates on the causes of poverty and will be discussed at length in Chapter 4.

CONCLUSION

Six main conclusions stand out from the discussion in this chapter. First, whichever of the four definitions of poverty is adopted, poverty is still prevalent in Britain. In terms of starvation, poverty has declined but pockets of it remain in a much more affluent society. In terms of social participation, the evidence is very sketchy but it suggests that little, if any, progress has been made. Since no studies have used a social coping definition, it is impossible to make any comments. In terms of subsistence, i.e. incomes below assistance benefit level, poverty has not declined at all during the period 1960–90. It has fluctuated but it is as high today as it was in the early 1960s. The government has recently replaced the statistics on poverty in terms of assistance benefit level with a new series that refers to the distribution of disposable income per person in the various deciles.

Second, the distinction between the deserving and the undeserving poor is still with us. It was allowed to decline during most of the postwar years but it has been intensified during the 1980s. The unemployed have always been treated more harshly than other groups and in recent years they have been subjected to relentless pressure by a never-ending list of increasingly harsh social security regulations in an effort to drive them off the registers and into any kind of work. One-parent families, apart from widows, have also been the subject of harsher regulations over the years but in the past couple of years they have been made to feel that they are to blame for their poverty. The elderly are treated more liberally than other groups with higher benefits and fewer regulations governing their benefits. Dominant social values will inevitably influence social security provisions at any time but particularly when administered by extremist right-wing governments.

Third, class, gender and race are the underlying structural factors in the risk of poverty. The lower socioeconomic groups are, on the one hand, more likely to find themselves unprotected by the social security system than other groups and, on the other, to have fewer private or occupational resources that they can rely on in times of financial emergencies. There is no doubt that gender, too, both independently and in conjunction with class, has an effect on the risk of poverty. The inferior position of women within the labour market and the traditional underlying principles of the social security system result in women either receiving lower benefits than men or no benefits at all. The social security system has still not fully accepted the fact that the periods of maternity and of child rearing should be considered as qualifying periods for social security benefit entitlement. Moreover, the exclusion of part-time employment from benefit entitlement discriminates more heavily against women. It is thus no surprise that women run a higher risk of being in poverty than men and that the majority of the poor are women, particularly in view of the greater life expectancy rates of women. Thus the feminization of poverty thesis is valid, if it is defined in terms of either prevailing risk or extent of poverty. Data on race and poverty are very inadequate but from what we know about race in relation to earnings, unemployment, occupational pensions and attitudes within the social security system, the conclusion must be that certain ethnic groups run higher risks of being in poverty than the rest of the population.

Fourth, income poverty is only one part of the web of deprivation that afflicts the lives of so many people in the country. Multiple deprivation exists side by side with multiple advantage in contemporary Britain without so far evoking much government or indeed public concern. People have been prepared to accept the government claim that increased inequality and poverty were necessary to bring about higher rates of economic growth from which all groups in society would benefit. Yet this has not happened – which leads to the fifth conclusion. The 1980s witnessed in Britain an unprecedented degree of government largesse to the rich and the very highly paid. Marginal tax rates were reduced from 83 per cent in 1979 to 40 per cent today and company dividends increased by five times during this period. On the other hand, the range and level of benefits have declined so that the incomes for the low-paid have suffered. Yet, as Keegan points out, rates of economic growth have not improved. The average rate of annual growth in the economy was 3.2 per cent during 1959–69, 2.4 per cent for 1969–79 and only 2.2 per cent for the decade 1979–89. The policy of squeezing the poor and pampering the rich has not brought about the economic miracle that the government envisaged. It has merely deepened economic and social divisions in British society (Keegan 1990, p. 10). Very similar policies in the US have led to very similar results to those in Britain, as the following chapter will show.

Sixth, the Beveridge approach to social security served the country well for several decades and it achieved a great deal in maintaining incomes and in reducing poverty. It is now, however, out of step with the changed demographic, economic and social conditions of the 1990s. As Chapter 5 shows it cannot, as it stands, abolish poverty. There is an urgent need for a more coherent social security approach – one that makes the elimination of poverty its top priority.

Finally, the discussion in this chapter has shown how inadequate data on poverty are. The recent decision by the government to replace the assistance poverty line with a new poverty line that simply shows the proportions of people with incomes below the national average disposable income will make the situation worse and will render historical comparisons impossible. The assistance poverty line had clear policy implications – the achievement of a minimum income for all – whilst the new poverty line has none even though it is useful for comparative purposes. The way forward would have been to produce both sets of poverty data for they serve different purposes. The decision to replace one set of data with another was based on political rather than research considerations. It reflected the government's lack of commitment to a basic minimum income for every citizen in the country – a commitment that was accepted by all other postwar governments.

3. Poverty in the US

As previously indicated, analysis of the extent of poverty in the two countries is complicated by disagreements about how to define and measure poverty. The controversy in the US is suggested by Sawhill's observation that poverty in the US 'reflects off the green eyeshade of the statistician' (Sawhill 1988). Nevertheless, tacit agreement exists in the US that 'official' poverty should be measured in terms of the number of people living below a 'poverty line'. Therefore, official poverty will be used as the basis for analysis in this chapter.

The line, first established by Orshansky in 1963, assumed that a non-farming family of two adults and two children required approximately $3000 each year to stay out of poverty. The $3000 was arrived at by assuming that minimally adequate meals would cost $1000 a year and other essentials of life would cost twice that amount. The line has been adjusted each year to reflect price increases. By 1989 it was $12 675 for a family of four (US House of Representatives, Committee on Ways and Means 1990, table 1, p. 1021).

Although the poverty line provides the basis for analysing the extent of poverty, some adjustments must be made even when using this measure if we wish to get an accurate picture of poverty in the US. First, it must be recognized that the poverty line fails to reflect earnings increases and therefore living standards. The 1989 poverty line merely recognizes that it takes almost $13 000 to buy the same food, goods and services that cost approximately $3000 in 1965. It makes no adjustment for improved living standards since it was first used in 1965. Our analysis will, therefore, examine the extent of poverty when improved living standards are considered. We shall look at the resulting disparities between income levels which result from the practice of ignoring changing living standards.

An additional problem with relying on the official poverty line is that it uses the availability of pre-tax money income as the basis for determining if people are out of poverty. This creates a number of problems in estimating the poverty levels. For example, poverty rates may be quite different if adjusted for in-kind benefits, e.g. food stamps and Medicaid (which provide financial aid to the medically indigent), subsidized housing and school lunch benefits. Furthermore, the term 'pre-tax money' requires elaboration. To illustrate, official rates of poverty in the US are based on post-transfer poverty, i.e. the percentage of people who are below the poverty line after receiving benefits from cash social insurance and public assistance programmes. Cash social insurance programmes include Old Age and Survivors' Insurance (OASI), which provides benefits (pensions) to qualified retirees, disability insurance, which provides benefits for workers too disabled to continue in their jobs, and Unemployment Insurance (UI), which provides unemployment compensation to workers who are unemployed. Public assistance programmes designed for poor non-workers include Aid to Families with Dependent Children (AFDC) and Supplemental Security Income (SSI). AFDC provides cash benefits to single-parent families in need while SSI provides cash benefits to the poor aged, blind and disabled. The $208 billion spent for retirement and disability benefits in 1987 far exceeded the $63 billion for AFDC and SSI in the same year (Munnell 1987).

Poverty rates can also be based on pre-transfer or pre-welfare income. Pre-transfer income indicates the extent of poverty before any government transfers and therefore offers essential information about the target population which needs income supplementation. Pre-welfare income suggests the extent of poverty after income from cash social insurance programmes. In addition, it is generally agreed (Sawhill 1988) that the use of pre-tax income provides an unrealistic view of the resources which should be used in gauging whether people have escaped poverty. The consensus reflects the obvious, i.e. that paying taxes reduces the ability to escape poverty. And some account must be taken of the fact that poverty rates will vary if assets, in addition to pre-tax money income, are counted when determining the extent of poverty which exists in the US.

A further problem with using the official poverty rates relates to the time period chosen to judge the extent of poverty. This is because official poverty presents a snapshot of poverty at a particular time even though people move in and out of poverty at various times in their life cycle. More people are temporarily poor than permanently or chronically poor and poverty varies according to whether one is in childhood, a member of a single-parent family, a labour force participant, or an elder (Palmer, Smeeding and Torrey 1988, p. 16).

Finally, the official poverty rate must be adjusted to take account of whether poverty is defined according to household or family composition. As pointed out in Chapter 2, it is generally agreed that poverty figures based on the household underestimate the extent of poverty, although there is no agreement by about how much. Furthermore, poverty rates vary within families. Thus 'a four-person family consisting of two parents and two children [the standard used in determining official poverty in the US] might require more or less income to achieve the same standard of living as a single parent with three children' (Palmer *et al.* 1988, p. 11). One effort to provide a base for determining poverty for a family of four, focused on an 'income to needs' ratio, and concluded that a family of four adults had a 'poverty threshold (in 1985) of $11,085, compared to $11,268 for three adults and one child, $11,899 for two adults and two children, and $10,937 for a family of four consisting of one adult and three children'. The obvious implication is that the financial needs of an adult family are greater than those of a family with children because children share the income received by the adults in the family.

Because of these considerations this chapter will:

- examine pre-transfer, pre-welfare and in-kind poverty;
- analyse the poverty gap in the US;
- look at relative poverty by noting the disparities between income groups;
- examine the persistence of poverty for various segments of US society;
- note how poverty varies by different income and asset measurements; and
- evaluate how poverty is affected by various demographic characteristics e.g., age and family composition.

Because poverty among the elderly and children is an important issue in the US, the two groups will be analysed in some detail.

POVERTY IN THE US: 1950–89

The passage of the Social Security Act in 1935 initiated a nationwide concern with the issue of poverty since, for the first time, it provided that the national government (rather than individual states) would have the bulk of the responsibility for aiding the needy. Until this Act was passed states and their local governments haphazardly provided such aid. But the depression of the late 1920s and early 1930s made it clear that state aid was insufficient given the vastly increased needs resulting from the massive economic upheaval.

The Act reflected a reluctant concern about the poor. It emphasized national social insurance programmes, i.e. pensions to former workers who had retired, and the unemployed. Retirees and the unemployed were considered entitled to benefits because they had worked and anticipated their needs by making payroll tax contributions to pay for their benefits. This approach contrasted with public assistance programmes for the needy poor, i.e. Old Age Assistance (OAA), Aid for Dependent Children (ADC) and Aid to the Blind (AB). State governments essentially determined who was poor enough to qualify, and benefits varied according to state determination of qualification. In addition, political support for ADC was secondary to the provision of benefits for needy aged because it was anticipated that OAA would 'wither away' as the pension programme became more generous and needy elderly died (Steiner 1966, Chapter 2).

Although the programmes expanded in the next 15 years a policy of 'benign neglect' was pursued toward the poor (Patterson 1981, pp. 78–9) which reflected the view that the poor would disappear, a sentiment which was reinforced by post-World War II prosperity. Employment was high, and average personal income rose. The percentage of families with annual incomes below $3000 dropped from 51 per cent in 1935–36, to 20 per cent by 1960. Using definitions of poverty then current, it was found that the percentage in poverty fell from 48 per cent in 1935–36 to 33 per cent in 1940, 27 per cent in 1950 and 21 per cent in 1960. Even the poor were judged to be 'staggeringly well off' compared to the poor elsewhere (Patterson 1981, pp. 79–80). There was agreement that, eventually, people would be able to work their way out of poverty.

By the late 1950s the policy of benign neglect was replaced by the 'rediscovery of poverty' (Patterson 1981, Chapter 6). Galbraith criticized Americans for allowing private affluence and public squalor to exist unnoticed side by side, and condemned poverty as 'a disgrace' (Galbraith 1958, p. 259). Harrington made a powerful and emotional indictment against a society that allowed 40 to 50 million poor, and warned that such a system was 'designed to be impervious to hope' (Harrington 1962, p. 10). Harrington's warning was well received by

US intellectuals. Macdonald reviewed Harrington's book favourably in the January 1963 issue of the *New Yorker* and an 'avalanche of books and articles on poverty rolled off the presses' (Patterson 1981, p. 99). The publicity had an impact. John Kennedy, the newly elected President, noted in his inaugural speech that a society which fails to help the poor also cannot save the rich. He initiated programmes which, ultimately, became part of the 'War on Poverty' during the administration of President Lyndon Johnson (Patterson 1981, pp. 100–4). An official poverty line was established. Although 'unrealistically low' (Duncan *et al*. 1984, p. 37), and designed for 'temporary or emergency use' (Orshansky, New York Times, 1989), it provided a basis for comparative data on poverty, and served as an inducement for expanding existing government programmes so that poverty could be reduced.

Continued prosperity brought with it a conviction that the newly discovered poverty could be eliminated if government programmes were expanded to help those who were unable to escape poverty. Keyserling, a liberal economist who served in President Truman's administration, wrote in 1964 that more jobs and massive government spending would eliminate poverty in ten years (Keyserling 1964). The president of the American Economic Association spoke of the 'threshold of the golden age' (Stigler 1965). After a study of 5000 US families, the prestigious Survey Research Center of the University of Michigan proclaimed that poverty could be abolished with expansion of government programmes. The views reflected the faith that an affluent society could (and should) dedicate its resources to providing relief for the destitute.

The support for expanded government programmes was successful. Between the mid-1960s and the early 1970s a 'stunning enlargement of social welfare programs' occurred (Patterson 1981, p. 157). Benefits and coverage were increased for traditional programmes established under the Social Security Act of 1935. But even more significant were large programme additions during the 1960s. The War on Poverty resulted in a plethora of new programmes devoted to improving the working skills of the poor, upgrading educational opportunities for pre-school children and labour-force poor, providing additional food assistance and school lunch programmes to the needy, and encouraging the poor to play an increased role in improving their economic position in society. But the most important additions were Medicaid and Medicare in 1965, programmes which became the cornerstone of US health policy for the next 25 years. Medicaid subsidizes medical care for qualified poor; Medicare subsidizes hospital care for the elderly who qualify for retirement benefits under OASI. Doctors' care is also subsidized by Medicare if beneficiaries agree to purchase supplemental medical insurance (SMI) by paying a monthly premium.

As a result of the expansion, federal expenditures grew significantly through the mid-1970s. By 1984, some analysts characterized the US welfare state as 'generous' and 'comprehensive' (Moynihan 1986, p. 120). Almost 42 million non-farm households received government benefits by 1978. By 1984, over half of US households had members who received government benefits (Moynihan 1986, pp. 120–21). The growth in expenditures for particular programmes was especially impressive. Programme costs for OASI (the federal pension programme) increased by 350 per cent. Medicaid was 5 per cent of means-tested programmes in 1966; by 1985 it had risen to 40 per cent. Cash and in-kind expenditures, as a percentage of the gross national product (GNP) increased from 1.2 per cent to almost 3 per cent between 1965 and 1984 (Burtless 1986, pp. 23–4, 30–32). However, by the late 1970s expansion during the Carter administration slowed to less than 4 per cent of the GNP and only one new programme was added to help the low-income people (Low Income Energy Assistance). For all practical purposes, growth came to a complete halt during the first term of the Reagan administration when significant reductions were made, especially in public assistance programmes for the poor. Indeed the growth rate of social programmes declined to 1.5 per cent per year.

Initially, there was much enthusiasm about the impact of the massive infusion of government aid to the needy. Patterson, a respected analyst of the US scene, referred to the decline of poverty from 1965 to 1973 as the 'revolution in social welfare'. From his perspective, there had been a 'fantastic drop in the number of poor' in post-transfer (official) poverty (Patterson 1981, p. 157). And as Table 3.1 suggests his assessment seems accurate.

Thus the post-transfer poverty rate, which was 20 per cent in 1960, declined dramatically from 1965 to 1973. In 1965 there were 32 million Americans (17.3 per cent) in post-transfer poverty, 7 million less than five years earlier. Eight years later there were approximately 11 per cent, or 9 million fewer persons in post-transfer poverty. The decline was attributed to the consequences of the War on Poverty, expansion of government benefits, and the expansion of the economy because of the Vietnam War.

Unfortunately the sharp decline in poverty was a short-term phenomenon. Indeed, as Table 3.1 indicates, assessment of poverty in the

Table 3.1   Percentage of persons in poverty, US, 1965–88

Year	Pre-transfer	Pre-welfare	Post-transfer (official)	Adjusted
1965	21.3	16.3	17.3	16.8
1966			14.7	
1967	19.4	15.0	14.2	
1968	18.2	13.6	12.8	
1969	17.7	13.3	12.1	
1970	18.8	13.9	12.6	
1971	19.6	13.8	12.5	
1972	19.2	13.1	11.9	
1973	19.0	12.4	11.1	
1974	20.3	13.1	11.2	
1975	22.0	13.7	12.3	
1976	21.0	13.1	11.8	
1977	21.0	13.0	11.6	
1978	20.2	12.6	11.4	
1979	20.5	12.9	11.7	7.0
1980	21.9	14.2	13.0	8.1
1981	23.1	15.1	14.0	9.3
1982	24.0	15.9	15.0	10.3
1983	24.2	16.1	15.3	10.6
1984			14.4	9.8
1985			14.0	9.3
1986			13.6	
1987			13.4	
1988			13.1	

Source: Danziger and Weinberg 1986, table 3.1, p. 54; US House of Representatives 1990, table 2, p. 1024.

US depends on the year that is chosen. By 1975, official poverty began to climb sharply, reaching a high of 15.3 per cent by 1983 before declining again to 13.1 per cent in 1988, a rate which represents almost 32 million people. Thus, official poverty in 1988 was essentially the same as it was 20 years earlier. And projections suggest that the poverty rate is unlikely to return to the 11 per cent level of the mid-1970s (Danziger and Gottschalk 1985). Thus 'poverty [i.e. official post-transfer poverty] has never faded to insignificance in the years since the War [on Poverty] was declared'. In 1985, one in seven Americans were still poor using the official definition of poverty as the index (Danziger, Haveman, Plotnick, 1986, p. 55).

We shall analyse the suggested causes of the continued high rate of post-transfer poverty in some detail later. For now, it is appropriate to note that there are differences of opinion about the causes for this situation. Some maintain that the condition began with the recession which started in 1980; others argue that high rates of poverty are the result of benefit reductions during the Reagan administration; and others maintain that high rates of poverty reflect a population unwilling to work because of dependence on unnecessarily generous government benefits. Whatever the cause, it is obvious that despite large-scale expenditures, cash social insurance and public assistance programmes have been unable to eliminate, or even reduce significantly, the overall rate of poverty in the US.

Ignoring whether the poverty rates are strictly comparable, we can see that the trend in US poverty rates is similar to that in Britain (see Table 2.1). In both countries there was a decline between 1960 and the late 1970s followed by a rise during the 1980s; by the mid-1980s the poverty rate was similar to that of the mid-1960s. However, official poverty in the US has always been higher than in Britain, although the disparity between the two has narrowed over the years. Thus, the US rate was at least five times greater than the rate in Britain in 1960, but by 1985 it was only three times as large.

The trend in the pre-transfer poverty rate in the US is especially discouraging. As Table 3.1 indicates, pre-transfer poverty has been consistently higher than official (post-transfer) poverty. Pre-transfer poverty declined from 21.3 per cent in 1965 to 19 per cent by 1973, and then started to increase; by 1983 it was actually higher than it was in 1965. The increase has been profoundly disturbing because it suggests the inadequacy of the 'trickle down effects of economic growth, especially as it affects the number of people in the labor-market, and the antipoverty impact of welfare programs' (Danziger, Haveman, Plotnick, 1986, p. 57).

The level of pre-transfer poverty is a crucial measurement for another reason: it suggests the proportion of people who are moved out of poverty as a result of benefits from cash social insurance pro-

Table 3.2   *Anti-poverty effectiveness of cash and in-kind income transfers, US, 1967–86*

Year	Cash social insurance	Cash means-tested	All cash transfers	In-kind transfers	All transfers
	Percentage of all poor persons removed from poverty				
1967	22.7	4.7	27.3	*	*
1979	33.2	6.3	39.6	10.2	49.8
1985	30.3	4.2	34.5	7.1	41.6

* Comparable data not available.
Source: Sawhill 1986, table 5.

grammes, means-tested public assistance programmes and in-kind programmes (e.g. Medicaid and Medicare). Therefore the extent of pre-transfer poverty is used as a barometer to gauge the effectiveness of 'anti-poverty income transfers' (Sawhill 1988). Two points are especially noteworthy in this regard. First, as Table 3.2 indicates, cash social insurance programmes (particularly the pension programme) have accounted for approximately 83 per cent of the percentage of persons removed from poverty in 1985, and the remaining 17 per cent by in-kind transfers. Therefore, cash means-tested programmes (e.g. AFDC) have had an inconsequential impact as anti-poverty tools, despite the fact that 1983 expenditures for means-tested programmes totalled $31 billion (Sawhill 1988). Second, the effectiveness of the programmes, as anti-poverty tools, peaked in 1979 (39.6 per cent) and then declined to approximately 35 per cent in 1985. The continuing high level of pre-transfer poverty has provided 'damning' evidence to some that government programmes discourage work incentive and initiative. President Reagan, for example, suggested that the continued high levels of post-transfer and pre-welfare poverty was proof that in the War on Poverty 'poverty won' (Moynihan 1986, pp. 78–9).

The trend in pre-welfare poverty is also troubling since it suggests that poverty continues at high levels despite large social insurance expenditures. As Table 3.1 indicated, pre-welfare poverty declined from over 16 per cent in 1965 to 12.4 per cent in 1973 but then began a steady ascent so that by 1983 it was essentially the same as it was in

1965. It is only when in-kind benefits are considered that the rate of poverty shows an overall downward trend. Thus adjusted poverty, when in-kind benefits are added, was reduced by almost half between 1965 and 1985. The reduction reflects the fact that food stamps, Medicaid, subsidized housing and school lunch benefits constitute the main expenditures for poverty relief – almost two-thirds of total assistance in 1987.

THE POVERTY GAP

The poverty gap is another important indicator of the extent of poverty since it shows the difference between household income and the poverty line. The gap can be measured in terms of the dollar amount necessary to bring all poor households up to the poverty line (Danziger, Haveman, Plotnick, 1986, p. 58) or as the proportion of the gross national product (GNP) needed to bring everyone's income up to that level. Clearly, the higher the dollar amount, or percentage of the GNP, the more difficult it is to abolish poverty.

Table 3.3 shows that there is a similarity in the trend in the poverty gap as indicated by the official measure and the poverty gap as measured in dollars. The official poverty gap began to increase in 1980; the

Table 3.3   Total poverty gap, US, 1979–88 (millions of 1987 dollars)

Year	Official measure	Pre-transfer measure
1979	35.9	100.3
1980	41.4	111.6
1981	46.8	118.2
1982	51.3	123.6
1983	53.2	126.7
1984	50.7	122.5
1985	50.5	122.3
1986	51.0	122.9
1987	51.7	124.3
1988	50.1	122.0

Source: US House of Representatives, Committee on Ways and Means 1990, table 15, p. 1041.

gap in 1988 was over $14 billion more than it was in 1979. As noted, pre-transfer data are particularly revealing since they provide dramatic information about the differences between income and the poverty line before any government transfers. Using this measurement one can only come to pessimistic conclusions about the nature of the problem in the US. The pre-transfer gap has risen significantly since 1979. By 1988 it had reached $122 billion, almost $22 billion more than in 1979.

The poverty gap expressed as a percentage of the GNP suggests a similar trend and problem. The gap of 1.29 per cent declined gradually to 1.02 per cent by 1979 and then rose to 1.47 per cent by 1982 (Uhr and Evanson 1984, table 3, p. 7). It is important to remember, however, that the poverty gap is expressed in terms of the amount of money necessary to bring an individual, a family or a household up to the relevant 'poverty line'. As we have argued several times so far, the poverty line is austere and at best a crude index of income necessary to stay out of poverty. A more generous poverty line will obviously mean a greater poverty gap than that indicated by current government poverty statistics, as Chapter 2 pointed out when discussing the situation in Britain.

RELATIVE POVERTY

The trend in US poverty is even more disturbing because official poverty fails to take account of changing standards of living. As a result there is 'a growing disparity between the status of the poor and that of the rest of the population' (Schiller 1980, p. 19). The disparity is dramatic. The official poverty line for a family of four was 49 per cent of the median US income of four-person families in 1959, 42.3 per cent in 1964, 35.2 per cent in 1969, 34.9 per cent in 1983 and 32 per cent in 1986 (Kahn 1986; Sawhill 1988). The average family income of the poorest fifth of the population declined by 5.1 per cent from 1979 to 1988, while income for the richest fifth of the population rose by 11.8 per cent. The average family income of the poorest fifth of the population dropped from $5782 to $5424 between 1973 and 1988 (after adjusting for inflation); the family income of the top fifth increased over $9000 to $72 759 (US House of Representatives, Committee on Ways and Means 1990, p. 1070). In short, the poor have been getting poorer and the rich richer even though official poverty is adjusted to take account of price changes.

Haveman provides further confirmation about the seriousness of the problem in the US when he found that the share of income received by working-age families in the bottom 20 per cent declined from 5.3 per cent in 1967 to 3.9 per cent in 1983; during the same period the share of income of the top 20 per cent increased from 41.4 to 43 per cent. The recent government analysis notes that 'the poverty rate of married-couple families with children and female-headed families with children who have significant work, increased between 1979 and 1987'. Poverty of married-couple families increased from 4.1 to 4.8 per cent; poverty in female-headed families with children increased from 11.1 to 14.8 per cent (US House of Representatives, Committee on Ways and Means 1990, p. 1029). In addition, the Gini concentration index, a standard measure of inequality, increased by 4.2 per cent for the total population and well over 10 per cent for non-aged families (Haveman 1988, p. 54).

The growing gap in income inequality is heightened by inequalities of assets and wealth. Almost 70 per cent of wealth in the US is concentrated in the hands of the richest 10 per cent. Furthermore, the problem is getting worse because 'the share held by the very rich increased by nearly 19% from 1962 to 1983 while the share held by the bottom 90% fell by about 5%' (Haveman 1988, p. 55).

The work of the Luxembourg Income Study Group provides an opportunity to compare relative poverty in the US with that in Britain. The study indicates that relative poverty in the US is higher than that in Britain. Thus, for 1979–81, the proportion of the population with an income below 50 per cent of the median income was 16.9 per cent in the US and 8.8 per cent in the UK (Kahn 1986). Therefore, whether one uses the official definition of poverty, or a relative definition, the level of poverty is substantially higher in the US than in Britain.

As we know, pre-tax money is used as the measure for determining whether families remain in post-transfer poverty. However, official poverty rates would be different if money income were adjusted to take account of tax payment and if assets were counted since money income is less after tax payments. Adjusting to take account of tax payments increases the poverty rate while adding assets lowers the percentage in poverty.

At first observation, it seems logical to ignore taxes when determining levels of poverty because the income of the poor is usually too low to be taxed. This is especially true since the passage of the Tax Reform Act of 1988 in the US which eased the tax obligations of the very poor.

However, it must be noted that the tax liability for the poor still 'begins at income levels substantially below the poverty line' (Sawhill 1988). Furthermore, poor working families pay payroll taxes. As a result 'by 1984 a four-person family with poverty-level earnings was paying 10.1% of its earnings in income and payroll taxes'. If this is taken into account the 1985 poverty rate would have been one percentage point higher, i.e. 15 per cent instead of 14 per cent (Sawhill 1988).

Using pre-tax money income as a basis for determining whether poverty exists means that assets such as homes, automobiles and other consumer durables are excluded. Yet a 1983 study indicated that 31 per cent of the poor own their own home and 48 per cent own a car (Sawhill 1988). The addition makes a difference. With assets the 'mean net worth' of poor is 28 per cent of the non-poor, compared to 17 per cent if only money income is counted. What this means is that there may be 'fewer poor people both absolutely and relatively than one might assume on the basis of reported income figures' (Sawhill 1988; Weisbrod and Hansen 1968, p. 58; Moon 1977).

The next section will look at the composition of the poverty population and the risk of poverty for various population groups.

COMPOSITION AND RISK OF POVERTY

As noted in Chapter 2, the distinction between poverty composition and risk is important. Composition of poverty reflects the proportion of a group in poverty compared to the total poverty population; risk reflects the risk which that group has of being in poverty. The two measurements can be different for the same population group. For example, Table 3.4 indicates that over two-thirds (68 per cent) of the poor in the US are white in 1986 compared to under 30 per cent for blacks. The difference reflects the obvious fact that there are more whites than blacks in the US. However, Table 3.5, which provides figures on the risk of poverty, indicates that the risk of being in poverty for blacks in 1988 was three times greater than for whites (31.6 per cent for blacks compared to 10.1 per cent for whites). Thus the risk of poverty for blacks is greater than for whites even though they constitute a smaller proportion of the total poverty population. The situation is similar for people of Hispanic origin. Their risk of being in poverty was well over twice as great as that for whites even though they made up less than 25 per cent of the white population in poverty in 1988.

Table 3.4   Composition of the poverty population, US

Group	Percentage distribution			
	1959	1969	1979	1988
Total (percentage)	100.0	100.0	100.0	100.0
Age				
Elderly	13.9	19.8	14.1	11.0
Adult	41.7	40.0	46.1	50.3
Children	44.4	40.1	39.8	38.7
Household status				
Female-headed family	17.8	28.5	36.6	52.9
All other families	69.8	50.9	41.1	47.1
Unrelated individuals	12.5	20.6	22.3	NA
Race/ethnicity				
White	72.1	69.0	66.0	65.3
Black	25.1	29.4	30.9	29.5
Other	2.7	1.6	3.1	5.3
Hispanic origin	NA	NA	11.2	16.9

NA   Data not available

Sources: Sawhill 1988, table 2; US House of Representatives, Committee on Ways and Means 1990, table 10, p. 1032.

Further anomalies are obvious when comparing the composition of poverty with its risk. Table 3.4 divides up the poor according to age, household status and ethnicity and shows the significance of various sub-groups to the total number of people in poverty. The differences compared to Britain are noteworthy (see Table 2.2). The elderly constituted 11 per cent of the poor in the US in 1988; the corresponding figure in Britain in 1985 was 40 per cent. On the other hand, children account for 38 per cent of the poor in 1988, compared to 14 per cent in Britain. The proportion of persons in poverty in female-headed households is also significantly different: in the US 37.8 per cent were in poverty compared to only 3 per cent in Britain. Figures on ethnicity are not comparable because of the lack of data in Britain. Nevertheless, it is clear that blacks would not account for 29.5 per cent of the

Table 3.5   *The risk of poverty for various population groups, US*

Group	Percentage distribution			
	1969	1979	1986	1988
Total (percentage)	12.1	11.7	13.6	13.1
Age				
Elderly	25.3	15.2	12.4	12.0
Adult	8.7	8.9	10.8	NA
Children	14.0	16.4	20.5	19.7
Household status				
Female-headed family	38.2	34.9	38.3	37.4
All other families	7.4	6.3	7.3	NA
Unrelated individuals	34.0	21.9	21.6	20.4
Race/ethnicity				
White	9.5	9.0	11.0	10.1
Black	32.2	31.0	31.3	31.6
Hispanic origin	NA	21.8	27.3	26.8

NA   Data not available
Source: Sawhill 1988, table 2; US House of Representatives, Committee on Ways and Means 1990, table 11, pp. 1024–25.

poor in 1988, as they do in the US, because of their smaller proportion among the general population.

Table 3.4 suggests three main trends in the composition of US poverty of particular importance to this study. First, and most noticeable, is the significant rise in the growth of poverty among female-headed families. They accounted for 17.8 per cent of all the poor in 1959 and almost 53 per cent by 1988. The growth has given rise to the term 'feminization of poverty'. Second, even though the percentage of elderly among the population has increased, their share of the total number of poor dropped from 13.9 per cent in 1959 to 11 per cent in 1988. Third, there has been a relatively small increase in the proportion of black persons among the poor from 1959 to 1988, despite their rise in the general population.

One must look at the trends in the risk of being in poverty to understand why the composition of poverty for such groups has declined or remained essentially the same. The elderly, for example, feature prominently among the poor because of the size of the elderly population, but their risk of being in poverty is less than for other groups. This is because of the success of large-scale government programmes aimed at supplementing the income of the elderly. At first observation, the risk of poverty for blacks seems to have improved markedly, especially compared to 1959. But black poverty has been over 30 per cent since 1969, a rate which is exceeded only by female-headed families. And poverty among those of Hispanic origin has risen since 1979 so that it is third highest among the groups listed in Table 3.5. The group, however, with the highest risk for the whole period of 1959 to 1986 was female-headed families. The trend has been described as proof that feminization of poverty and welfare dependency exists among female-headed families. Table 3.5 does not provide data about the poverty risk of the unemployed. Other data, however, address this issue. In 1984, of all those age 22 to 64 who did not work, 50 per cent were in poverty; the corresponding proportion for men was 36 per cent while the rate for women was 64 per cent (Department of Health and Human Services 1987, table 11, p. 77). It is, however, true that debates on poverty in the US have not concentrated on unemployment as much as debates in the UK have done over the years because of the popular belief that there are jobs for all who really want to work.

PERSISTENCE OF POVERTY

Official poverty figures, such as those quoted so far, provide snapshots of poverty, i.e. data about who are 'poor' at the time of measurement. It is important, however, for both the poor themselves and for government policy makers to have data on how long poverty lasts for the various poverty groups.

Estimates on the persistence of poverty differ according to whether they are based on data relating to people in poverty at any one time, or whether they are based on data referring to people who ever enter poverty. Bane and Ellwood use the analogy of hospital patients to explain the difference between the two approaches:

> Most of the persons admitted in any year will require only a very short spell of hospitalization. But a few of the newly admitted patients are chronically ill and will have extended stays in the hospital. If we ask what proportion of all admissions are people who are chronically ill, the answer

is relatively few. On the other hand, if we ask what fraction of the number of the hospital's beds at any one time are occupied by the chronically ill, the answer is much larger. The reason is simple. Although the chronically ill account for only a small fraction of all admissions, because they stay so long they end up being a sizeable part of the hospital population. (Bane and Ellwood 1986, p. 11)

Data from the Panel Study of Income Dynamics (PSID) for the years 1970 to 1982, excluding those over the age of 64 years, and using the official poverty line, show that, as in hospitalization, the majority of all spells of poverty are of short-term duration. The minority of spells, however, which last a long time account for most of the poor at any one time. Column 1 of Table 3.6 shows that 44.5 per cent of all periods in poverty last for 1 year only; 15.8 per cent last for 1–2 years, 9.8 per cent for 2–3 years and so on. In other words, 70.1 per cent of all spells terminate by the end of the third year; a further 17.9 per cent by the end of the ninth year; and only 12 per cent of spells last beyond that.

Table 3.6   *Duration of completed and uncompleted spells of poverty for persons aged below 64 years (%), US*

Spell	Persons beginning a spell	Persons poor at a given time	
	Completed spell duration	Completed spell duration	Uncompleted spell duration
1 year	44.5	10.6	23.0
2 years	15.8	7.6	13.3
3 years	9.8	7.0	9.5
4 years	6.2	5.9	7.1
5 years	4.7	5.6	5.7
6 years	2.8	4.0	4.5
7 years	2.1	3.5	3.9
8 years	1.0	2.0	3.4
9 years	1.1	2.3	3.1
Over 9 years	12.0	51.5	25.6
Total	100.0	100.0	100.0
Average	4.2	12.3	6.2

Source: Bane and Ellwood 1986, table 2, p. 12.

Looking at column 2, however, the 12 per cent of all spells lasting for more than 9 years account for 51.5 per cent of those in poverty at any one time. Thus the overall conclusion is that: 'Most people who are ever poor have short spells. Most people who are just beginning a spell of poverty will have a short spell. But the bulk of those poor at a given time and the bulk of the person-years of poverty are accounted for by the long-term poor' (Bane and Ellwood 1986, p. 13).

There is abundant evidence that persistent poverty is heavily concentrated among the black population and particularly among black female-headed families in the US. Low wages and unemployment are the primary reason for persistent poverty among black male-headed families to a greater extent than among white male-headed families. Particularly worrying is the finding that persistent poverty is a serious problem among children, especially black children: 'The average poor black child today appears to be in the midst of a poverty spell which will last for almost two decades' (Bane and Ellwood 1986, p. 21).

Persistence of poverty for such groups is even greater when the percentage who have been in pre-transfer poverty from 1965 to 1983 is considered. Studies have found that the pre-transfer poverty rate for white females with children actually increased from 48.5 per cent in 1965 to over 50 per cent in 1983. The rate of pre-transfer poverty among non-white females with children did decline from the high of 80 per cent in 1965. However, it is impossible to take comfort in the downward trend because almost 70 per cent remained in pre-transfer poverty in 1983 (Danziger and Weinberg 1986, table 3.5, p. 63).

The persistence of poverty raises a number of questions, but none more important than whether poverty is transmitted from one generation to another in the same families. Corcoran and her associates refer to the evidence from the PSID which showed that though there was a correlation between parental poverty and children's later income, there was also substantial upward mobility:

> Only one in five individuals who were at or near the poverty line as children was at or near the poverty line after leaving home. Further the majority of those who escaped poverty were not clustered just above the poverty line and there was substantial economic mobility even among young adults from the very poorest of the poor families. (Corcoran *et al.* 1985, p. 530)

Evidence also showed that it was not attitudes and values that accounted for the limited extent of intergenerational poverty but structural factors relating primarily to employment.

ELDERS AND CHILDREN IN POVERTY

Elders and children constitute 'the nation's two largest dependent groups' (Palmer, Smeeding and Torrey 1988, p. 1). This has resulted in an intergenerational controversy because poverty rates for the elderly have declined while they have increased sharply for children. Table 3.5 indicates poverty for children has risen from 14 per cent in 1969 to almost 20 per cent in 1988 while during the same period the poverty rate for the elderly declined from 25.3 per cent to 12.0 per cent. As a result some have called for 'intergenerational equity' aimed at redistributing existing resources, away from relieving poverty among the elders, to reducing the high poverty rate among children (Palmer, Smeeding and Torrey 1988, p. 413).

Because of the importance of these two groups, this section will focus on the elderly and children by examining how their poverty varies by age, sex, race and ethnic composition. In addition, we shall look at family composition to see what impact the growing trend toward single-parent families has on poverty among children in the US.

We have already noted that conclusions about poverty in the US depend on the time chosen for comparison. This is particularly true for poverty of the aged and children. We can appreciate this point by looking at Table 3.7 which provides information about poverty rates for children and elderly men and women from 1969 to 1988. In 1969, the 14.5 per cent poverty rate for children was almost 8 per cent less than that for men and about 18 per cent less than the rate for women. However, the trend was reversed in the next 18 years. By 1988 poverty increased to 20.9 per cent for all children while declining to 10 per cent for elderly men and 16.7 per cent for elderly women.

The trends in poverty are essentially similar when age is taken into consideration. Thus in 1969 poverty was more for elderly men and women of all age groups than for children in various age categories. But again by 1988 the trend was reversed. For example in 1988 children 6–17 years of age were well over twice as likely to be poor as elderly aged 65–74 even though they were less likely to be poor in 1969. However, it is important to note the high poverty rates for elderly women of all age groups. Indeed, the rates were almost equivalent to those for children. By 1988, poverty rates for elderly women were higher than those for men in every age group. Because of different methods of assessing pre-tax income poverty, rates in Table 3.7 are different from those cited in Table 3.5.

*Table 3.7	Poverty rates for children and elderly, US, 1969–88*

	Percentage of poor persons		
Age group	1969	1979	1988
Children			
Under 6	15.5	18.3	22.6
6 – 17	13.4	15.5	18.2
All	14.5	16.9	20.9
Elderly men			
65 – 74	18.9	9.3	6.9
75 – 84	27.2	13.5	9.1
85 and over	36.7	14.5	14.0
All	22.2	10.6	10.0
Elderly women			
65 – 74	28.8	16.7	12.4
75 – 84	36.5	29.5	18.0
85 and over	35.4	27.0	19.7
All	32.1	18.0	16.7
All persons	12.1	11.7	13.1

Source:	Palmer, Smeeding and Torrey 1988, table 3.1, p. 33.

Demographic changes, income sources and the economy have been offered as reasons for the trends in poverty among children and the elderly. Table 3.8, which provides data about the composition of the population and poor children, clearly demonstrates the importance of demographic changes upon poverty rates for children.

It is apparent that the increase in the number of children in the population affected the number of children who are poor. Thus, when the proportion of children in the population increased from 25.1 per cent in 1939 to 31.6 per cent in 1959, their share of the poor rose from 29.3 per cent to almost 37 per cent; when the percentage of children in the population declined in 1969 and 1979, the percentage of children who were poor also declined. But it is obvious that the increase in

Table 3.8   *Composition of the population and poor children under
15, selected years (%), US*

	1939		1959		1969		1979	
	Persons		Persons		Persons		Persons	
	All	Poor	All	Poor	All	Poor	All	Poor
Children under 15	25.1	29.3	31.6	36.8	28.8	31.4	23.2	30.4
living with 2								
parents	22.6	26.0	29.2	29.6	25.3	18.9	18.9	14.8
living with 1								
parent	2.5	3.3	2.5	7.2	3.6	12.5	4.3	15.6

Source: Palmer, Smeeding and Torrey 1988, table 3.2, p. 37.

single-parent families is the key for understanding why poverty rates
for children have risen so sharply. Table 3.8 indicates that in 1959 poor
children living in single-parent families were approximately three times
their proportion of the total population – 7.2 as against 2.5 per cent. In
1979, when children living with two parents had dropped to less than
19 per cent of the population and 14.8 per cent of the poor, poor
children living with single parents were almost four times their proportion of the total population, 15.6 as against 4.3 per cent.

Table 3.9   *Composition of child poverty population by family type
and race, selected years, 1966–88 (%), US*

Year	Total poor (in thousands)	Female head			Male present		
		Non-white	White	% of total	Non-white	White	% of total
1966	12 146	18	17	35	23	42	65
1971	10 344	23	24	47	16	38	54
1976	10 080	28	27	55	12	33	45
1981	12 069	26	26	52	12	36	48
1988	12 295	30	30	60	11	30	41

Source: US House of Representatives, Committee on Ways and Means 1990, table
48, p. 946.

Table 3.9 provides a more recent view of the impact of family composition upon the poverty of children. From 1966 to 1988 the percentage of poor children in female-headed families increased from 35 to 60 per cent while the percentage of poor children in families with a male present declined from 65 to 41 per cent.

The growth of children living with single parents was reflected by a growth in their poverty rate. The 1979 poverty rate for children was almost 17 per cent; by 1988 it was over 20 per cent. What these data suggest, then, is that the poverty rate of children is high because the rate for children living in single-parent families is also high. And it is likely that high poverty rates for children will continue; by 1985 49.9 per cent of children lived with single-parent families (Palmer, Smeeding and Torrey 1988, p. 41).

Income sources are an important factor affecting the poverty of children and elders. For the elderly, poverty rates are affected significantly by social security (pension) benefits. Thus elderly poverty has declined as cash benefits from pensions have increased. Social security benefits increased about 40 per cent between 1950 and 1960, and grew rapidly between 1970 and 1980 – another 35 per cent. The recent government study notes that: 'The percentage of elderly individuals removed from poverty due to social insurance programs (including benefits from social security) increased from 69.3 per cent to 73.6 per cent from 1979 to 1988' (US House of Representatives, Committee on Ways and Means 1990, pp. 1039–40). The reduction is reflected in the declining poverty rates for elders. The plight of women has been attributed, in part, to their longevity compared to elderly men, and the consequent increase in widowed women. This in turn has resulted in increased poverty because 'social security benefits for a widow fall by one-third when a husband dies' (Palmer, Smeeding and Torrey 1988, p. 36).

The rise in the percentage of children in single-parent families is accompanied by an increase in children's poverty. The implication is obvious: limited income is 'an important contributor to child poverty, especially since 1969' (Palmer, Smeeding and Torrey 1988, p. 41). The logic seems inescapable. Income for female-headed families declines because of limited cash income available compared to a two-parent family and because of low wages for working women. In addition benefits under Aid to Families with Dependent Children (AFDC), the programme in the US which provides aid to single-parent families, have remained essentially stagnant since 1970. For example, by 1980 'the typical retired couple received almost twice the benefits of a three person family with a prime-age head' (Palmer, Smeeding and Torrey 1988, p. 45). This has given rise to the demand for intergenerational equity referred to above. In addition income for single-parent families during the 1970s and 1980s declined because of the slowdown in the economy. As a result about two-thirds of the poverty rate for children in 1985 (20.1 per cent) 'was due to the failure of poverty rates to decline as fast as they had in the period before 1969' when the economy was booming (Palmer, Smeeding and Torrey 1988, p. 41).

Colour of skin, ethnicity and sex are factors which affect poverty rates of children and elderly. Table 3.10 indicates that, overall, white children and white elders are far less likely to be in poverty than their non-white counterparts. Thus in 1988, the 14.6 per cent poverty rate for white children was far less than the rates for non-white children. Similarly, the rate for white elders was far less than the rate for all

Table 3.10   Poverty rates for children and the elderly, by race, ethnicity and sex, selected years (%) US

Age group	1975	1980	1985	1988
Children under 18				
Black	41.7	42.3	43.6	44.2
White	12.7	13.9	16.2	14.6
Hispanic	NA	33.2	40.3	37.9
All	17.1	18.3	20.7	19.7
Elderly men, 65 & over				
Black	31.0	31.5	26.5	23.7
White	9.5	9.0	6.9	6.2
Hispanic	NA	NA	NA	NA
All	11.4	10.9	8.5	8.0
Elderly women, 65 & over				
Black	40.2	42.6	34.8	38.0
White	16.1	16.8	13.8	12.6
Hispanic	NA	NA	NA	NA
All	18.1	19.0	15.6	14.9

NA   Data not available

Source: US House of Representatives, Committee on Ways and Means 1990, tables 47, 6, pp. 945, 1000.

other non-whites of whatever age and category. Poverty rates among black and Hispanic children were more than twice the poverty rates of white children in 1988. As Table 3.10 indicates, the rate for black children was 44.2 per cent; the poverty rate for Hispanics was almost 38 per cent. Finally, it is clear that black women over age 65 are particularly susceptible to poverty in the US. In 1988 the poverty rate for black elderly women was 38 per cent, over three times the rate for white women, and more than six times the rate for white elderly men.

CONCLUSION

In Chapter 1 we defined poverty along a continuum that ranges from undernutrition, to subsistence, to social coping and finally to social participation. This chapter has been predominantly concerned with poverty as it is officially defined – a definition that corresponds to subsistence poverty.

One of the main achievements of economic growth and of the various social security benefits has been the very substantial reduction of undernutrition. As in Britain, however, so in the US too, undernutrition still exists even though there are conflicting opinions of its extent and severity (J.L. Brown 1989; Cohen 1989). Cohen's analysis draws attention to two main reasons for the persistence of undernutrition: the level of benefits and of food stamp allowances are too low and, second, many people do not apply for various food assistance programmes to which they are entitled.

Our analysis of the US experience confirms the British conclusion that economic growth by itself does not abolish poverty even when this is defined in official subsistence terms. Indeed, the extent of poverty before the receipt of benefits rose from 21.3 per cent in 1965 to 24.2 per cent in 1983. The receipt of benefits obviously reduces the extent of poverty but even then it has remained at fairly high levels in the US. It declined from 17.3 per cent in 1965 to 11.4 per cent in 1978; it then crept up gradually so that by 1983 it reached 15.3 per cent but declined again to 13.1 per cent in 1988. It is only when benefits in kind are taken into account – food stamps, health care, etc. – that poverty rates declined: from 16.8 per cent in 1965, to 7.0 per cent in 1979 and to 9.3 per cent in 1985. However this measure of poverty is of uncertain validity because of the difficulty involved in determining the cash value of some of the in-kind benefits. As Sawhill aptly points out the inclusion of medical benefits to the poor as an in-kind benefit 'would imply that people who have poorer health are better off, other things being equal' (Sawhill 1988, p. 1078). Finally, if one looks at poverty in terms of the proportion of people with incomes below 50 per cent of the median income, the picture is equally discouraging: 16.9 per cent of the population in the US compared with 8.8 per cent in the UK were in this position during 1979–81. Another measure of the seriousness of poverty is the size of the poverty gap. Again the picture is not at all encouraging. Over the years it has followed the same trend as the extent of poverty with the result that it declined from 1.29 per cent of GNP in 1967 to 1.02 per cent in 1979 only to rise to 1.47 per cent in 1982 – figures which seem to be consistently higher than those for Britain. In terms of absolute amounts of dollars the rise is, of course, even greater over the years.

We were able to get some insights into the immediate reasons why poverty remains high by looking at the composition of poverty and the risk that certain groups have of being in poverty. Two main trends are especially important about the composition of poverty in the US since 1959. First, the percentage of poor female-headed families in the US almost tripled from 1959 to 1988. Second, the proportion of poor elderly declined during the same period even though they constitute a growing percentage of the total population. These trends contrast with Britain where the percentage of poor elderly is a significant problem and the percentage of female-headed families is negligible compared to the US.

There have been suggestions that some people stay in poverty over the years because of a 'culture of poverty' and because some are willing to await general benefits from government programmes. We have found these allegations to be grossly overstated. Over 60 per cent of the poor under 64 years of age are out of poverty after two years. Poverty is persistent, however, among female-headed families, especially if black. Poverty for black children can last almost twenty years. But reliable studies attribute poverty longevity to inadequate wages and unemployment rather than a disposition to stay in poverty because of cultural attitudes and values. This is a crucial issue which we discuss in some detail in Chapter 4.

Further insight into poverty was gained by examining poverty among the nation's two largest groups. The analysis was particularly pertinent because of the clues it provides about poverty in the US, and because of a developing conflict between advocates for children and advocates for the elderly over the fact that poverty has been increasing for children while declining for the elderly. Children's advocates argue that programmes should be redirected so that benefits for children can be increased, even if this means that they will be lowered for elders. Naturally elder advocates disagree.

Three developments bear on poverty of these two groups (and by implication poverty in the US) and the argument for intergenerational equity. First, poverty among children is a function of the growing trend toward single-parent female-headed families since the income of single-parent families is less than that of two-parent families. Second, the distinction between poverty of the elderly and poverty of children largely disappears when colour of skin is taken into account. Thus in 1988, the poverty rate of the elderly male blacks (23.7 per cent) was almost four times that of white male elders, while poverty of black elderly women 65 and over (38.0 per cent) was three times that of elderly white women. The situation was essentially the same for non-white children; the poverty rate for black children (44.2 per cent) was over three times that for white children. Third, the increase in children's poverty was affected by the stagnant economy during the 1970s and 1980s since fewer and lower-paying jobs resulted in lower incomes for single-parent families headed by females. The inevitable result has been an increase in poverty among children. Thus the state of the economy, colour, gender and socioeconomic grouping account for the distribution and persistence of poverty in the US as in Britain.

4. Explanations of Poverty in Advanced Industrial Societies

In the previous chapters we discussed the various definitions and measurements of poverty, and we documented the extent of poverty in Britain and the US. We showed that poverty is still very prevalent in both these countries and so is inequality of income and wealth. Though poverty and inequality are two separate concepts, they are related in the sense that in both countries today poverty is the tail end of income inequality. Our preferred definition of poverty in terms of social coping implies that it is possible, theoretically, for a society to abolish poverty but to retain inequality albeit of a reduced kind. It is a moot question, however, whether once poverty is abolished it will not set in motion new demands for a more generous definition of poverty whose abolition will make more inroads into the pattern of existing inequalities.

In this chapter we attempt to review the various explanations of poverty and to put forward our own approach. Bearing in mind the relationship between inequality and poverty, it is to be expected that some of the discussion is relevant to both. Even if poverty is defined in pathological terms and as a condition afflicting a very small minority of the population it is still not possible to have distinctive theories of poverty that have no implications for the explanation of inequality. We shall review all these theories and hence the discussion in the chapter touches on the explanations of both inequality and poverty.

The various theories of inequality and poverty are discussed at two related levels. First, the explanations of why there is inequality and poverty in advanced industrial societies and, second, the explanations of why some population groups rather than others are likely to be in poverty. It is an important distinction which has not always been observed, with the result that the *incidence* or the existence of poverty has often been confused with its *distribution* (George 1980). The first explains why there is poverty in society while the second explains which individuals or groups of individuals are likely to be poor. It is a mistake to assume that what decides the distribution of poverty at an individual level also explains the causation of poverty at an aggregate level. This becomes clearer when applied to low wages which directly and indirectly underlie poverty. It is generally accepted that education and training have some influence on the level of wages. But if all citizens in Britain or the US were equally well educated, would they also be equally paid? Surely not. What decides unequal pay is the nature of jobs in society. We need to explain why there are low-paid, medium-paid and high-paid jobs if we are to understand why there are low- and high-paid workers. So long as there are low-paid jobs, individuals will be found to fill them even though the personal characteristics of these individuals may change over time. We need to explain the incidence of low pay and poverty before we explain their distribution in society.

Thus the chapter is divided into three sections. The first examines the three main explanations for the existence or the incidence of inequality and poverty in society – the functionalist, the Marxist and the structuralist. The second section looks at the main explanations for the distribution of poverty, i.e. which groups of individuals are most likely to be in poverty. The third section considers the reasons why the social security/income maintenance systems of the two countries have had varying degrees of success in ensuring that people receive benefits which lift them up to the poverty line. Social security systems have several aims but one of them is the abolition of poverty and the section explores the various reasons for this failure despite the mounting costs of these systems in both countries.

EXPLANATIONS OF THE INCIDENCE OF POVERTY AND INEQUALITY

The three theories discussed in this section are part of a very long tradition in the debates on social stratification. They each have different intellectual origins among classical theorists: the functionalist theory can be traced to the work of Durkheim with his organic and holistic perspective on society. Durkheim saw society as similar to a biological organism with various interrelated parts each of which served specific functions. The emphasis, therefore, is on the whole of society rather than on its parts and on order and stability rather than on conflict and change. Society functions for the benefit of all its members and the state epitomizes the values of the whole society and tries to serve the interests of all. The Marxist tradition clearly has its roots in the work of Marx for whom society is divided into classes with unreconcilable interests under capitalism. Power is unequally distributed along class lines and the state serves the interests of the capitalist class in varying degrees depending on the specific balance of class power in society at any one time. The structuralist school has its intellectual origins in the work of Weber who, like Marx, saw society in conflict terms but, unlike Marx, saw divisions in society not only along class lines but, equally important, along group lines. For Weber the origins of inequality are multidimensional and though they emphasize material factors they do not discount social values. Thus though the Marxist and Weberian perspectives are similar in many ways they are also different in several important respects as will be shown in the discussion later in this section.

The Functionalist Explanation of Inequality and Poverty

Of modern functionalist writers on inequality, Davis and Moore stand out as the most prominent because their work on inequality and stratification is concise and clear. The work of Parsons is far more comprehensive and conceptual but at the same time too complex for the purposes of this discussion.

Every society, according to Davis and Moore, has to find ways and means of placing its members in the various jobs and, once in those positions, to encourage them to fulfil their duties satisfactorily, if that society is to grow and prosper. If all jobs had the same functional utility to society, it would not matter which individuals occupied which jobs. But since different jobs have different functional utility it matters a great deal how the allocation of individuals to jobs takes place. It is, therefore, in the interests of all members of society that the most able persons occupy the most functionally important jobs and the best way of achieving this is through unequal pay. Other factors such as the pleasantness of a job or esteem may carry some weight but it is financial rewards that are the primary motivations. Hence inequality is 'an unconsciously evolved device by which societies insure that the most important positions are conscientiously filled by the most qualified persons' (Davis and Moore, 1945, p. 243). The degree of income inequality necessary to achieve this will vary from one society to another according to its technological, educational and other such characteristics but income inequality is necessary, inevitable and beneficial to all in all societies. Society is considered as integrated with high levels of consensus among its members, with few important conflicts of interest, so that it can somehow reach decisions on such a weighty issue as the distribution of income in an unconscious and amicable way.

The criticisms of the functionalist thesis have been many and varied but the most noteworthy focus on the functional importance of jobs and the distribution of power in society. What kind of characteristics determine the varying functional importance of jobs? Davis and Moore claim that, in general 'those positions convey the best reward, and hence have the highest rank, which (a) have the greatest importance for the society and (b) require the greatest training or talent'. Of these two characteristics, it is the first that has been subjected to intensive criticism. How can the 'importance' of jobs to society be defined and measured? Davis and Moore provide two guidelines both of which are difficult to apply convincingly. These are '(a) the degree to which a position is functionally unique, there being no other position that can perform the same function satisfactorily; (b) the degree to which other positions are dependent on the one in question' (Davis and Moore, 1945, p. 243). One can find as many examples of jobs which do not fit in with these two criteria as those which do. It can be argued that the position of the President of the US or of the Prime Minister of the UK is 'more important' than that of a minister of religion and hence it commands higher pay. But why does it command less pay than the position of the general manager of a large company? Surely it cannot be because it is less 'important'. Coming down to more ordinary jobs, why are the wages of a skilled worker higher than those of a nurse; or the earnings of an accountant higher than those of a teacher in terms of job 'importance'? Similarly, how can the criterion of other jobs being dependent on a position be usefully applied? It may help explain why the salary of a headmaster is higher than that of a teacher but it does not explain why the salary of a headmaster can be less than that of a bank manager. Moreover the functionalist theory does not show how or why the prevailing relativities of jobs in terms of earnings change over time. When all these criticisms are put together they render the 'greatest importance for society' explanation worthless (Tumin 1953). All that then remains of the functionalist explanation is the 'training or talent' explanation. Its claim that 'talent' is limited and hence it must be unequally rewarded is clearly not so. Many more people have the ability to train as accountants or doctors but they do not do so either because there are not enough university places or because they cannot afford long university education or some other such reason. As far as the value of training to earnings is concerned, this is generally recognized but one does not have to accept the entire functionalist explanation because of this particularly in view of the fact that for the functionalist the importance of training is secondary to the 'functionality' of the job. Finally, the assumption of the thesis that the distribution of power in society is not unequal and that it, therefore, permits such an important decision on the distribution of income to be reached in an unconscious and trouble-free way has been questioned by many. It flies in the face of reality in contemporary societies irrespective of whether one adopts a Weberian or a Marxist view of the nature and distribution of power.

Apart from the theoretical criticisms, there is also the ideological criticism, i.e. that the functionalist explanation of inequality is a conservative justification of the status quo. It justifies all types and degrees of income inequalities on some spurious abstract justification without ever raising any questions concerning the role of power in earnings distribution or the possible 'dysfunctional' effects of excessive inequality to society, let alone issues of workers' exploitation through low pay. For all these reasons, the functionalist explanation of inequality, of high and of low pay, is not only unconvincing and misleading but unhelpful to any efforts to eradicate poverty among wage earners' families since this is presented as a natural and inevitable state of affairs.

The clear implication of the functionalist thesis is that low pay and hence poverty among the wage-earning section of the population is the result of individual inadequacies – low intelligence, lack of motivation, low educational and technical levels and so on. What is more, these individual inadequacies are attributed mainly to either genetic or familial causes, as we shall see later.

The Marxist Explanation of Inequality and Poverty

Marx's views on class divisions, class conflict and class exploitation in capitalist societies are known well enough to warrant not repeating them here. In brief, Marx saw inequality in capitalist societies as the inevitable result of the exploitation of the working class by the capitalist class. This state of affairs is perpetuated because of the superior economic and political power of the capitalist class and because of the development of a dominant ideology that justifies and legitimizes inequality. Moreover, workers' exploitation is the very basis of profit making and hence of the capitalist system and it cannot be attributed to the personalities of the individual industrialists. The clear implication is that workers' exploitation and hence poverty can only be abolished after the abolition of the capitalist system. Marx did not claim that the abolition of the capitalist system would in itself lead to the abolition of poverty or inequality; rather that it was a necessary precondition.

The classical Marxist analysis of society concentrated on class conflict and class inequality and neglected conflicts and inequalities within the working class. With the growth of capitalism, however, the working class has ceased to be a monolithic entity and contemporary Marxist theorists have tried to accommodate this change. They recognize that there are divisions within the working class with the result that different sub-groups possess differential bargaining power *vis-à-vis* their employers and *vis-à-vis* one another in the pursuit of higher wages. In their study of contemporary Britain, Westergaard and Resler present the following picture of working class fragmentation: 'The labour market is in effect a patchwork of markets where skilled and unskilled blue-collar and white-collar employees, men and women, workers in this industry and that, one region and another, sell their labour on different terms' (Westergaard and Reisler 1975, p. 347). This is a generally accepted view among Marxists today and it differs very little from that of structuralist writers of the Left.

Inequality within the working class is thus the result of this fragmentation and stratification of the labour market. Poverty is similarly explained because it is seen as part of inequality. There have been very few attempts to develop an explicit Marxist explanation of the incidence of poverty as distinct from the incidence of inequality. The few attempts made so far show the divergence of opinion within contemporary Marxism as well as the substantial degree of overlap with left-wing structural explanations on poverty. We examine two such attempts here that bring out the essence as well as the differences within Marxism. Wachtel identifies the three basic institutions of capitalism that result in poverty as class relationships, markets in labour and the state. The division of society into classes inevitably means that poverty is a working-class problem. The type of job that people do influences not only whether they will be in poverty whilst at work but also when they are not at work as a result of unemployment, disability or retirement. Unskilled or semi-skilled workers are likely to receive low wages, to suffer more from unemployment or industrial injuries and to have few, if any, assets so that when they are not at work they are likely to be in poverty unless they qualify for social security benefits, which is not always the case.

The labour market is seen in similar terms to those of structuralist writers discussed in the following section – along segmented and stratified lines. The division of the labour market into high-, low- and medium-paid jobs is the result of many economic processes but also of the educational system which trains young people for different positions in the labour market. Since the education that young people receive is related to their class and family background which in turn is affected by the labour market, a vicious circle is created between class, the family, the school, the labour market and poverty. Thus the forces 'that determine an individual's status in the labor force lie outside his or her control' (Wachtel 1972, p. 191) and solutions to that problem also lie in changes in societal structures rather than in individuals. It might be argued that despite these disadvantages, working-class people can rely on protection from the government. But this is most unlikely because the government or rather the state is seen by Marxists not as an impartial arbiter but rather as the defender of the existing socioeconomic system and hence of the interests of the higher socioeconomic groups. The result is that government policies on wages, taxation, social security and elsewhere either reinforce or do not change in any big way the existing patterns of inequality. Thus inequality and poverty are 'a logical consequence of the proper functioning of the capitalist institutions of class, labor markets, and the state' (Wachtel 1972, p. 193).

Indeed inequality and poverty perform several positive functions for capitalism – a view that echoes Gans's approach from the structural school. They are necessary to encourage workers to do 'alienating work'; they control militancy by reminding workers what might happen to them if they misbehaved; they depress wages in general; and they also allow more income to accrue to the better-paid as well as to employers. It is these functions that explain 'the tenacity of poverty in the face of wars against it' (Wachtel 1972, p. 188). In brief, poverty is the result of the capitalist system; it can be reduced somewhat by government policies but it cannot be abolished within capitalism.

A rather different and more historical attempt to explain the incidence of poverty in capitalist societies has been made by Novak in his work on the British situation. He looks at the creation and continuation of poverty in a historical way beginning with the collapse of feudalism and the rise of early capitalist forms of industrialization. The explanation of poverty centres around Marx's thesis that 'Poverty as such begins with the tiller's freedom' (Marx *Grundrisse*, p. 735 quoted in Novak 1988, p. 3). Though starvation, deprivation and inequality have always existed, poverty is the direct result of capitalist forms of production. Poverty is not just insufficient income to buy the necessities for life but it is also the lack of economic security – something which by definition no employee possesses in a capitalist society. Thus poverty in capitalist societies is not a minority group condition but rather it is 'a condition that ultimately threatens a majority of the population' (Novak 1988, p. 26). Even the prosperous middle-class sections of society are not safe from the threat: 'they too are no more than a few weeks removed from the threat of poverty that can arise with sudden illness or redundancy' (Novak 1988, p. 27). In brief, poverty is tantamount to economic insecurity and its causes are to be found in the very essence of capitalist forms of production. The abolition of poverty is thus only possible when the capitalist forms of production have themselves been abolished.

The strength of Novak's approach is that it sees poverty in structural, political terms both in relation to causation and solution. Its weakness, however, is to equate poverty with economic insecurity, so that it leads to some unconvincing claims. Thus the argument that, despite the prevalence of starvation and deprivation, poverty did not exist under feudalism because individuals had a secure position in the production process or in society is a self-defeating proposition. Similarly, the claim that a starving person under feudalism was not in poverty whilst a well-fed worker under capitalism is either in poverty or in constant fear of poverty is a caricature of the notion of poverty. Finally, to maintain that the situation of a well-paid professional employee is different only in degree from that of an unskilled low-paid worker is a gross oversimplification which misrepresents social reality. It is more than likely that Novak's views on the nature of poverty may not find wide support even amongst Marxist writers on these issues. It blunts the central Marxist thesis that poverty is inevitable among working-class families – not middle-class families – and particularly unskilled working-class families because of the inevitable exploitative relationship that is inherent in capitalist forms of production.

The Structuralist Explanation of Inequality and Poverty

This perspective has its theoretical roots in the work of Weber and Wright Mills and other writers of the Left with the result that it is similar to but also different from the Marxist perspective in several ways which, I hope, will become clear in this discussion.

Like the Marxist perspective, it sees industrial societies not in consensus terms but in conflict terms. Advanced industrial societies are stratified along class, gender and race lines so that economic and political power is unequally distributed. A person's economic position and hence the risk of poverty is decided largely by his family background, education, gender, race and occupation. There is a complex web that runs through these factors so that they are interrelated to a large extent and most people's careers and living standards are influenced by them. There are always exceptions to any generalization so that upward and downward social mobility, particularly between adjacent rungs on the ladder, takes place. The risks, however, of a child born in a rich family ending in poverty as an adult are limited; conversely, the opportunities of a child born in persistent poverty rising to a wealthy position as an adult are also limited.

Family background affects a child's educational achievement and also influences his outlook towards the kind of jobs open to him. Societal values towards the role of women in society have implications for their education and the job careers which are usually beyond the control of the individual. Discrimination against racial groups also has adverse effects on both their education and their job careers. Thus the educational achievement of workers is seen as the result of primarily structural factors rather than of individual traits. Moreover, educational standards are not seen as such an important factor in determining the unequal earnings derived from different occupations as the functionalist thesis claims.

What largely decides the unequal earnings attached to different jobs is their position within the totality of the labour market. For this reason the labour market is seen as 'balkanized' or 'stratified' or simply 'dual', consisting of different strata which provide unequal pay, security, fringe benefits and scope for promotion. There is no agreement on the degree of labour market stratification but three main approaches stand out. First, there are those who see the labour market in dual terms, i.e. consisting of a primary sector that is well-paid, secure and full of promotion opportunities and a secondary sector which is the exact opposite

(Doeringer and Piore 1971; Gordon 1972). Second, there are those who divide the labour market into three sectors. An example of this is Bluestone's 'tripartite economy', consisting of the 'core economy' of industries 'which comprise the muscle of American economic and political power'; the 'peripheral economy' with such areas of work as retail trade, agriculture and subsidiary manufacturing; and the 'irregular economy' made up of irregular, episodic work such as the informal economy of the city ghettoes (Bluestone 1970, pp. 24–6). Third, there are those who view the labour market as a 'differentiated structure of mini-systems' (Townsend 1979, p. 918), each of which provides different levels of pay, working conditions, fringe benefits and so on.

Crucial to all types of labour market stratification is the question concerning the criteria that determine the allocation of jobs to one or other of the various labour market strata. There is no agreed list but on the whole it will include many or all of the following: 'capital-labor ratios, political power of the industry and locality, degree of market concentration, power of the trade union, profit rates, the industry's association with the state, industrial base of the local labor market, rate of growth of the local labor market, etc.' (Wachtel 1972, p. 191). All these structural factors together decide the position of a job within the labour market and hence the rewards and injuries attached to it. It is not so much the characteristics of the individual as the features of a job that decide the amount of earnings that a person employed in a certain job will have. What the individual characteristics decide is which individuals will enter which jobs and the scope of upward mobility.

The operation of the labour market affects the incidence of poverty in another way, through high rates of unemployment. Though structuralists will agree with Marxists that unemployment is due largely to such structural factors as new technology, declining industries and competition, they will reject the Marxist claim that this is inevitable in capitalist societies only and that there is a historical tendency towards increasingly deeper troughs of economic recessions. The end result, however, is the same as far as poverty is concerned. High rates of unemployment increase the incidence of poverty in society and, as we shall see in the next section, certain groups suffer the ill effects more than others.

The structural explanation of earnings inequality shares with the Marxist perspective the essential claim that both high and low income from work are part and parcel of the stratification of the labour market. Thus poverty is endemic to advanced industrial societies and it can only be abolished through structural changes. In Townsend's view , poverty to be abolished 'there must be less differentiation hierarchi cally of the employed population *and* a smaller proportionate share of total national resources of higher groups' (Townsend 1979, p. 919). It follows that the abolition of poverty is very difficult but most writers in this group are cautiously optimistic that this is possible within capitalist societies if governments of the Left are determined enough.

Another important corollary to the structural perspective is that improvements in the relative educational standards of working-class groups, anti-discrimination legislation and positive discrimination practices are all important steps to a fairer allocation of workers to jobs and may also contribute somewhat to the reduction of the earnings inequalities attached to different jobs. However, without a fundamental restructuring of job inequalities within the labour market, inequality and poverty will remain. Since such a restructuring not only appears remote at present but may well be impossible, the inequalities of the labour market and hence poverty have to be reduced through a combination of measures which include some form of government social security and labour programmes – minimum wage, wage supplementation, child benefits and the like.

Finally, a structuralist perspective sees poverty in affluent societies not as a paradox, i.e. as an illogical state of affairs, but rather as an inevitable result of the ways in which the social, economic and political systems of advanced industrial societies operate. For this reason some writers have argued that poverty plays a very important part in maintaining the existing socioeconomic system. Gans has identified 13 different ways in which other groups in society benefit from the existence of poverty: the poor perform all the menial jobs in society, they buy shoddy and damaged goods, they help to legitimize the dominant ideology by providing examples of deviance, they absorb most of the costs of economic change and so on (Gans 1973). Gans is not in any way arguing for the continuation of poverty but rather, because of its place within the country's economic, political and social system, highlighting the problems involved in any attempts to abolish it. Poverty is not simply dysfunctional to society as some reformers have claimed, but it also performs a number of positive functions for the higher socioeconomic groups and indeed for the better-paid working-class groups.

Concluding this section four main conclusions can be drawn. First, all three theories view poverty as part of inequality; second, all three consider that inequality and poverty are the inevitable results of the operation of the labour market. Third, they will agree that poverty and inequality perform crucial functions for society as a whole – the functionalist view; for the upper class – the Marxist view; or for the higher socioeconomic groups, including some working-class groups, according to the structuralist view. The implication is that inequality and poverty are endemic to industrial societies and hence very difficult to eradicate. Fourth, each has different implications for the explanations concerning the distribution of poverty. The functionalist view concentrates on individual characteristics which are individually or familially determined whilst the other two attribute the distribution of poverty to structural factors or to individual factors that are largely structurally determined.

EXPLANATIONS FOR THE DISTRIBUTION OF POVERTY

Having discussed the three main explanations for the *existence* of poverty, we now move on to discuss the various explanations for the *distribution* of poverty. Since poverty is part and parcel of the economic and social structures of advanced industrial societies at present, we need to know which individuals or groups of individuals are most likely to become poor. We place the various explanations under the two headings of individualistic and structural, the first of which is related to the functionalist and the second to the structuralist explanation of the existence of poverty and, to a lesser extent, to the Marxist explanation.

Individualistic Explanation of the Distribution of Poverty

The implication of the functionalist explanation is that in the same way that high income is the result of high ability, high motivation and high qualifications, poverty, too, is the result of low ability, low motivation and low qualifications. What is more these individual deficiencies are not the result of broad structural factors but rather of individual, familial factors. It is for this reason that many have referred to this group of individual factors as character deficiency, personal fault or flawed character explanations (Townsend 1983, p. 70; Schiller 1980, p. 39). In brief, the three main issues we shall discuss here from this individualistic perspective are the influence of intelligence, education and values on poverty.

Over a very long period now, there have been those in both Britain and the US who have argued that intelligence, as measured by IQ scores, is largely inherited (Eysenck 1971; Hernstein 1971 and 1973), that it influences educational achievement, which in turn influences occupation and income. Beginning with intelligence, there is evidence which shows that the IQ scores of working-class children are lower than those of middle-class children and that the IQ scores of black children are lower than those of white children. This, however, is not the issue. Rather, what is at issue is whether these differences are due to largely hereditary factors that are immune to the influences of the environment. All the massive evidence that has been accumulated on the topic argues against the hereditary proposition. To begin with, IQ tests, despite improvements over the years, are still not totally culture-free. They reflect to some extent the dominant culture of society which is more in tune with the experience of middle-class than working-class children as well as of white than black children. Second, evidence shows that teaching and practice can improve the IQ performance of children, even those children who are mentally retarded. Third, the IQ scores of all children have been rising over the years, an indication that the improvement in living conditions is a relevant factor, unless it were argued that this is due to selective breeding! Fourth, the IQ scores of black children moving from rural to urban areas rise, again an indication of the role of environment. Fifth, when black and white children from similar backgrounds are compared, their IQ scores are much more similar than general differences between black and white children. These and other types of evidence show the overwhelming role of environmental factors on intelligence as measured by IQ scores.

The influence of educational achievement on income can best be examined either in relation to earnings from work or in relation to income in general. If it is the latter, the topic can easily be dispensed with since individuals who are born in wealthy families and who inherit substantial amounts of wealth will have high incomes irrespective of their educational achievement or IQ scores or any other personal characteristic, let alone any earnings from work. All the evidence shows that there is a crude correlation between years of schooling and levels of earnings (Blaug 1972, chapter 2). This applies to both advanced industrial as well as industrializing countries. The important question, however, is how strong the correlation is after family background is taken into account. Becker's evidence from the US showed that, even after ability and family background were taken into account, further education correlated with high earnings (Becker 1964). Even though Bowles's study showed that social class background was more important than years of schooling for a person's earnings (Bowles 1972), the general consensus today is that years of schooling in themselves do have an influence on earnings. Accepting this general conclusion, can working-class children compete with their middle-class peers in this? In other words, is it possible in Britain and the US for children of working-class families to go to the same schools and universities and to stay as long as their middle-class peers? The answer surely is that on the whole this is not possible though many working-class children can achieve this. In costly and competitive educational systems, family backgrounds are bound to play a big part and, hence, middle-class children are bound to be the winners in the educational race. This is crucially important in societies, such as those of Britain and the US where educational requirements for jobs are constantly raised, sometimes because of the genuine requirements of jobs but sometimes as a means of rationing jobs among a large pool of more than sufficiently educated applicants. In this competitive situation, those with lower educational achievements will be the losers and these are predominantly working-class or black children. It is not their intelligence or even the lack of familial interest in education that is at fault. Rather it is the unequal family background that, for most, will be the telling factor in a competitive race for educational qualifications. The more competitive the race, the lower the chances of working-class children in receiving higher education; and conversely, if higher education places were substantially expanded to reduce the intensity of competition, then more working-class children will benefit. More detailed discussion of this will be found in the section on the structural explanation of the distribution of poverty.

Herein lies the difference between an individualistic, flawed character explanation and a structural explanation of the importance of intelligence and education on earnings and on poverty. The flawed character explanation will see intelligence as due primarily to heredity; educational achievement as the result of this largely inherited intelligence; and the two as the primary determinants of earnings from work. Inequality and poverty under this scenario are individually caused and are independent of structural factors. A structural explanation will see the determination of earnings from work as the result of several other structural factors apart from educational achievement and intelligence which are themselves influenced in a big way by structural factors.

A more widely known thesis within this tradition is the claim that poverty is distributed according to people's values and attitudes, i.e. that individuals with 'dysfunctional' values will find themselves in poverty. It is important to put this thesis within the wider debate on the nature and significance of value systems to individual and collective behaviour. It is true that social theorists of different political persuasions have stressed the importance of values on people's behaviour. Marxists have argued that the dominant values of a society serve the interests of the dominant groups because they encourage the dominated groups to behave in certain ways and because they ostracize forms of behaviour that are threatening to the status quo. Weber saw the influence of the 'protestant ethic' as a paramount factor in the economic development of European societies. Without this 'ethic' – the emphasis on hard work and savings with divine undertones – economic growth and development would not have taken place at the same pace. Durkheim attributed political stability to public passive acceptance of the status quo engendered through the culture of the country. 'What is needed if social order is to reign', he wrote, 'is that the mass of men be content with their lot. But what is needed for them to be content, is not that they have more or less but that they be convinced that they have no right to more' (Gouldner 1962, p. 200). Writers may disagree on the origins of social values and on who benefits through value consensus but they do agree on the basic premise that values influence behaviour at the individual and the collective level in varying degrees.

Divisions of opinion between the various schools of thought, as well as contradictions within them emerge on the nature of the value system of a society. These differences of opinion are of two types: first, who benefits most out of the general observance of society's value system and second, is there a unitary or a fragmented societal value system? The functionalist school sees the social value system of a society as the result of an unconscious gradual process that benefits all members of society more or less alike. Hence, the value of inequality benefits all in society, as we saw earlier. The Marxist and structuralist schools tend to see the dominant value system as benefiting the upper groups in society, even though structuralists will be less certain than Marxists that this applies to all aspects of life. They will agree with Marxists that the values of inequality and private property benefit most the higher income groups but they will part company with Marxists on the claim that individual freedom and the right to vote under capitalism are concealed forms of upper-class domination. What concerns us most, however, for the current debate is the unitary versus the fragmentary nature of societal value systems.

Though both functionalism and Marxism begin with a unitary value system they end with a fragmented value system. Thus Marx and Engels claimed that the dominant values of any society are the values of the dominant class and that these are legitimized to become generally accepted to the obvious benefit of that class. Engels's discussion of the working class in Britain, however, led him to the conclusion that working-class culture was very different indeed from the culture of the bourgeoisie. Because of its harsh living conditions,

> the working class has gradually become a race wholly apart from the English bourgeoisie. The bourgeoisie has more in common with every other nation of the earth than with the workers in whose midst it lives. The workers speak other dialects, have other thoughts and ideals, other customs and moral principles, a different religion and other politics than those of the bourgeoisie. Thus they are two radically dissimilar nations, as unlike as difference of race can make them. (Engels 1892, reprinted 1969, p. 154)

He was in many ways reiterating Disraeli's famous phrase of the two nations in nineteenth century Britain – the rich and the poor –

> between whom there is no intercourse and no sympathy; who are as ignorant of each other's habits, thoughts and feelings, as if they were dwellers in different zones, or inhabitants of different planets; who are formed by a different breeding, are fed by a different food, are ordered by different manners, and are not governed by the same law. (Disraeli 1845, p. 76)

Interestingly, however, Engels saw the working-class culture as superior in some ways and inferior in others to upper-class culture. It was, on one hand, more humane but more brutal on the other, both being the result of depriving living conditions which had to be changed if the culture were to change too. Engels was, of course, writing at a period of massive rural migration to the towns, of rapid industrialization and before the mass media dominated people's ways of thinking. It is most unlikely that he would have described the working-class culture in the same terms today. Most contemporary Marxists view the dominant ideology as having permeated and shaped the individual value systems of most people in society.

The functionalist thesis of social consensus is based on the notion that the social values of society are perpetuated from one generation to the next through child socialization, schools, mass media, etc., as well as through social control mechanisms for those who break society's values and norms. Thus it is accepted that a minority of society's members – the deviants – behave in ways that are contrary to established norms because they have not been socialized well enough into the values of their society. Here there is a claim for a causal relationship with values being the cause of deviant behaviour which needs to be changed through resocialization and social control mechanisms. This is in marked contrast to Engels's view that it was the harsh realities of everyday life that accounted for working-class behaviour – humane as well as brutal. This is an important distinction which will emerge again in our discussion – it is the distinction between the structure and the culture of poverty.

The claim that poverty is the result of the values, attitudes and beliefs of the individual and that it is transmitted through socialization from one generation to another has a very long history in both Britain and the US (Patterson 1981; de Schweinitz 1943; MacNicol 1987). Here we are simply concerned with debates during the postwar period covered by our study. Though social work literature from the 1940s onwards tended to see 'problem families' as possessing different values and behaving differently from the rest of society, it was not until the early 1960s that the 'culture of poverty' thesis was developed and popularized first in the US and later in Britain. The irony was that the best known exponents of the thesis in the US were Marxists/structuralists – Lewis and Harrington – whilst in Britain it was a Conservative government minister – Sir Keith Joseph. There have, of course, been plenty of right-wing supporters of the thesis in the US but there have been no left-wing supporters of it in Britain.

Lewis's work on the culture of poverty has been so controversial that it merits detailed examination. For him the culture of poverty consists of three interrelated parts: a range of values, attitudes and beliefs which are different from those of the rest of society: fatalism, helplessness, dependency, inability to defer gratification of pleasure and so on. Second, a range of forms of behaviour which are either antisocial or which simply ignore established norms: promiscuity, illegitimacy, family violence, non-participation in the political, social or community institutions and so on. Third, a set of undesirable living conditions: overcrowding, unemployment, ill-health, illiteracy and general deprivation. Of these three parts, it is the first – the values – that are the dynamic force that shapes the other two and it is this part of his thesis that is the most controversial.

Lewis's anthropological studies of urban large poor families (Lewis 1961 and 1965) led him to the conclusion that in capitalist societies, but not in socialist countries such as Cuba, particularly during periods of mass migration from rural to urban areas, as was the case in Latin America, a culture of poverty develops as a mechanism of coping with the harsh realities that poor people have to face. This then is the first feature of the culture of poverty thesis: an adaptation of the values and attitudes of the poor to their harsh socioeconomic environment with the result that their values and attitudes become different from those of the rest of society. Indeed the nature of these values is such that they are not only different but less worthy than the dominant values of society. People immersed in the culture of poverty 'are aware of middle class values, talk about them and even claim some of them as their own, but on the whole they do not live by them' (Lewis 1968, p. 51). Grand movements in which the poor get involved may change this culture and Lewis referred to the civil rights movement in the US, the Algerian war of independence and the Cuban revolution as instances of this process.

Though Harrington's description of the culture of poverty was not based on any research evidence as such and it was less methodical than Lewis's (Harrington 1962), it was nevertheless most important because of its influence on American debates and policies on poverty. Both Lewis and Harrington were reformers who somehow believed that the culture of poverty would be tackled not just on its own but as part of a series of structural changes to improve the lot of the poor. In the hands of more conservative thinkers, however, the culture of poverty thesis became a far more reactionary and stigmatizing stereotype. Thus Banfield is not only more categorical in his description but far more ready to draw conclusions: 'The lower-class forms of all problems are at bottom a single problem: the existence of an outlook and style of life which is radically present-oriented and which therefore attaches no value to work, sacrifice, self-improvement, or service to family, friends, or community' (Banfield 1968, p. 211). The implication, of course, is that poverty cannot be eradicated through social action programmes involving work and benefits but rather through the cultural resocialization of the poor and particularly the ghetto poor. Even more worrying was Joseph's response in Britain; he was afraid that because of the higher birth rates among mothers in the lowest socioeconomic group 'the balance of our population, our human stock is threatened' and therefore birth control should be made available to those mothers (Sir Keith Joseph, Speech in Birmingham, 19 October 1974, quoted MacNicol 1987).

The second main feature of the thesis is its intergenerational perpetuation through family socialization. Lewis's description of child socialization as a cause of poverty amounts to almost biological determinism:

> The culture of poverty, however, is not only an adaptation to a set of objective conditions of the larger society. Once it comes into existence it tends to perpetuate itself from generation to generation because of its effects on children. By the time slum children are aged six or seven they have usually absorbed the basic values and attitudes of their sub-culture and are not psychologically geared to take full advantage of changing conditions, or increased opportunities which may occur in their lifetime. (Lewis 1968, p. 50)

The result of this process is that over the generations, the poor become cut off from mainstream society, they become, in Harrington's phrase, 'internal aliens' (Harrington 1962, p. 24). One is reminded not only of Disraeli's two nations but of some of the harshest critics of the 'undeserving poor' in the nineteenth century. What is so odd is that both Lewis and Harrington were reformers of the structuralist ilk but somehow failed to see the implications of their emphasis on a culture of poverty. Indeed, Lewis in his later writings reacted strongly against the criticism that the culture of poverty thesis was reactionary in its implications by claiming that his thesis

> is an indictment not of the poor, but of the social system that produces the way of life... with its pathos and suffering. It is also an indictment of some members of the middle class, government officials, and others who try to cover up the unpleasant and ugly facts of the culture of poverty. (Lewis 1967, p. 492).

The third main feature of the thesis is its policy implications. Lewis's claim that poor children may not be 'psychologically geared to take full advantage of changing conditions or increased opportunities which may occur in their lifetime' (Lewis 1968, p. 50) logically suggests that the way forward is for public policy to concentrate on resocialization measures particularly for children. Lewis, however, never specifically suggested such an approach and, indeed, under criticism he came to almost refute the policy implications of his thesis. This is how he expressed his position in his debates with one of his severest critics, Valentine:

> The crucial question from both the scientific and the political point of view is: How much weight is to be given to the eternal, self-perpetuating factors in the subculture of poverty as compared to the external, societal factors? My position is that in the long run the self-perpetuating factors are relatively minor and unimportant as compared to the basic structure of the larger society. (Lewis 1969, p. 192)

Harrington's approach to the policy implications of the culture of poverty was explicit from the start. He proposed a comprehensive series of government programmes that would deal with all aspects of the culture of poverty – its psychological, social, physical and economic aspects (Harrington 1962, p. 164). In contrast, Sir Keith Joseph's solution to the 'cycle of deprivation' was primarily to change the values and practices of poor families through education, social work and nursery programmes for parents and children (Holman 1978, p. 120). What actually happened in both Britain and the US was an expansion and improvement of social policy provisions through the 1960s and early 1970s. In the US more than in Britain, a common platform for many of the programmes was the idea expressed in the report of the Council of Economic Advisers to the President that 'if children of poor families can be given skills and motivation, they will not become poor adults' (Council of Economic Advisers Report 1964, p. 75). Though the culture of poverty did not understandably initiate any structural changes to employment and wage patterns it did not lead to any reactionary policies either. It was not until 20 years later when the new Right rediscovered some of the same ideas and interpreted them differently that demands for public expenditure cuts were voiced and partly accepted by governments in both the US and Britain.

Criticisms of the culture of poverty have been many and varied and we can only summarize them briefly here. In the first place, many people were unconvinced that such large numbers of people in the US were motivated by values and attitudes that were contrary to those of the rest of society. Initially Lewis implied that his thesis referred to all the poor in all capitalist countries but later he modified, or perhaps clarified, his position by stating that his thesis was far more relevant to developing third world countries than to advanced industrial societies and, as far as the US was concerned, only 20 per cent of the officially classified poor could be said to belong to the culture of poverty. This is how he expressed this:

> Because of the advanced technology, high level of literacy, the develop-ment of mass media and the relatively high aspiration level of all sectors of the population, especially when compared with underdeveloped nations, I believe that although there is still a great deal of poverty in the United States... there is relatively little of what I would call the culture of poverty. (Lewis 1968, p. 57)

Second, several studies in the US, Britain and Latin America failed to corroborate the culture of poverty thesis though some studies con-firmed it. In the US Hylan Lewis's study of mother-headed Negro families in Washington in the mid-1960s found no support and con-cluded as follows:

> The evidence suggests that Negro mothers from the low-income category, as much as any mother in any category of our population, want and prefer their men to be strong and supportive in marriage, family, and community relationships. There is no need to invoke the mystique of matriarchy to explain low-income, female-headed child-rearing units when we take into consideration the economic pressures of late twentieth-century urban living upon the young adult Negro male, and especially the ways in which these alter the choices open to low-income women and men. (H. Lewis 1967, p. 158)

Goodwin's long-term study of work orientations with a sample of 4000 persons concluded that there was 'no difference between poor and nonpoor when it comes to life goals and wanting to work'. The study attributed the condition of the poor not to their having 'deviant goals or a deviant psychology' but to their 'different experiences of success and failure in the world' (Goodwin 1972).

A large-scale study of 1400 adult Americans by Rokeach and Parker in 1968 found some support for the culture of poverty thesis. They administered a questionnaire which covered 18 'terminal values', i.e. values which are for goals or ends in life, and 18 'instrumental values' which are means to achieving the goal values and found significant differences between rich and poor. They concluded that 'these groups are characterised by profoundly different value systems and may be subculturally distinct' but they also noted that these differences be-tween rich and poor 'are not to be thought of in a dichotomous way, but in terms of a continuum of status (Rokeach and Parker 1970, p. 103). In other words they found substantial differences in the shades of support that these two groups gave to the list of values in the questionnaire.

A British study of poverty in a working-class district in the late 1960s by Coates and Silburn found no support for the culture of poverty thesis. Coates and Silburn were very careful to point out the real difficulties involved in exploring people's values in a survey situation. Nevertheless their main conclusion was as follows:

> Excepting the so-called 'problem families' the poorer households could not be said to be culturally distinct from the richer; they appeared to respond to the same values, to share the same basic assumptions, to accept similar restraints. Far from the lower pitch of their stated aspirations being evidence of a detachment from the accepted value system, it could simply be the expression of a 'realistic' appraisal of their possibilities, given that they had so little power at their disposal to change them. (Coates and Silburn 1970, p. 155)

Most studies in Latin American countries which attempted to test Lewis's thesis failed to find support for it. Thus Bonilla's study of the favelas of Rio in Brazil – a group that would be expected to be characteristic of the culture of poverty thesis – not only found no evidence for different values but also concluded that 'a great many favela families are relatively stable, have fairly regular employment and are even rigidly conventional by middle class standards' (Bonilla 1970, p. 75).

Finally several US studies have introduced the notion of value-stretch, i.e. that the poor accept the dominant values but they modify them slightly to suit their particular situations. Rodman's study, which set the scene for other such studies, concluded that members of the lower class 'share the general values of the society with members of other classes, but in addition they have stretched their values, or developed alternative values, which helped them to adjust to their deprived circumstances' (Rodman 1963, p. 209). This is not unique to the poor because other socioeconomic groups modify their values to suit their particular situation. The dominant values of society are the core of society's values but in large heterogeneous societies it is inevitable that all socioeconomic groups will not live their lives totally according to these values.

Before leaving the question of whether the poor live by all the unsavoury values packed into Lewis's culture of poverty, it is worth making the point that several writers have questioned the implied assumption that the rich live their lives according to the opposite values which are deemed to be the dominant values. Is it true that the rich postpone their pleasures, that they work hard, that they are honest to the full, that they are law-abiding and so on? One critic of the culture of poverty, Leacock, has this to say on the ability of the middle and upper classes to defer gratification:

> Culture-of-poverty theorists all too often talk about the 'orality' of the poor and their inability to delay gratification, forgetting that the more affluent take for granted as necessities a good diet, comfortable surroundings, and the constant enjoyment of many other such gratifications that the poor must defer for their lives long, with at best, perhaps, some forlorn hope for gratification in an after life. (Leacock 1971, p. 27)

Though no anthropologists or other social scientists have spent any time living among the rich observing their practices and analysing their beliefs and values, the various biographies and autobiographies of the rich and the famous show no evidence of either monasticism or austerity or deferred gratification dominating their social or sexual lives.

The general conclusion from all the studies must surely be that one of the central theses of the culture of poverty – that the poor have values which are contrary to those of the rest of society – either remains unproven or has been proved to be false. But even if we suppose that it is true – and this leads to the third criticism of the culture of poverty thesis – the crucial question still is whether the values are the causes of poverty or whether they are its consequences. Many writers in this debate agree that the values of the poor were either influenced or shaped by their environment to begin with but thereafter the disagreements begin. Lewis claims that once established, values become a force in their own right and they determine the continuation of poverty across generations. In the quotation cited earlier, however, he draws back from this position considerably to make societal changes the primary factor and value changes the secondary in government policies to abolish poverty. By doing this he brings himself closer to such structuralist writers as Gans who stresses societal changes but does not ignore programmes directed at the values and practices of the poor (Gans 1962). He is still, however, considerably apart from other structuralist writers and from those who advocate the structure of poverty thesis. Liebow, for instance, in his study of two dozen Negro men on a street corner of Washington concluded that their values were not dissimilar to those of the rest of society. Indeed, it was because they supported the dominant ideology that they considered themselves as failures. Nonetheless they modified and stretched their values in order to make them more relevant and less painful to their particular situation. What is significant for this discussion, however, was Liebow's claim that similarities in living standards and life styles across the generations were not due to child socialization but to the similarity in the situation of poverty confronting each generation.

'Many similarities between the lower-class Negro father and son (or mother and daughter) do not result from "cultural transmission" but from the fact that the son goes out and independently experiences the same failures, in the same areas, as his father (Liebow 1967, p. 223). In other words it is not the culture of poverty but the structure of poverty that is responsible for the existence and continuation of poverty and it is this that has to be changed for poverty to be abolished.

Empirical evidence cited in Chapters 2 and 3 shows that not all the children of the poor remain poor as the culture of poverty claims. There is upward social mobility even though most of it is to adjacent rungs on the social ladder. Corcoran *et al.* refer to evidence from the PSID panel study which showed that though there was a correlation between parental poverty and children's later income, there was also upward social mobility. 'Only one in five individuals who were at or near the poverty line as children was at or near the poverty line after leaving home' (Corcoran *et al.* 1985, p. 530). Moreover, it was not attitudes and values that accounted for the limited extent of intergenerational poverty but structural factors relating primarily to employment – a finding that confirms Duncan's earlier work from PSID data again (Duncan *et al.* 1984, p. 61).

What then can be concluded from all this debate? Most of the evidence shows that the values and the attitudes of the poor are essentially the same as those of the rest of society and their values cannot therefore be held responsible for their poverty. There are inevitably exceptions to this in the same way that not all the middle- and upper-class individuals are motivated by exactly the same dominant values. In large, heterogeneous societies there will inevitably and thankfully be variations of the dominant value system but this is unrelated to the economic status of the individual. What is not possible to maintain is that millions of Americans and Britons are immune to the dominant values of their society despite the all-encompassing mass media and that this explains their poverty. What is even more untenable is the policy implication that to abolish poverty, governments must initiate nationwide resocialization programmes. Neither logic nor research supports such a proposal and, interestingly, Lewis withdrew from such a position while Harrington never advocated it.

Debates on the culture of poverty had hardly died down when they were succeeded by similar debates around a very similar thesis – the underclass (Levy 1977). It was not until the publication of Auletta's book in 1982, however, that debates on the underclass began to dominate in the US though in Britain they are still marginal and the notion is far less well-known than the culture of poverty. Most of the issues raised in this debate are similar to those of the culture of poverty and we shall thus be brief. Perhaps the main difference is that while debates on the culture of poverty were accompanied by an expansion of social programmes, the opposite has happened in the case of the underclass. The political climate has been influenced far more by ideas of the new Right and we will discuss these as they refer to the notion of the underclass.

Auletta acknowledges that there is no agreement on most issues relating to the underclass – its definition, its composition, its size and its explanation. His own definition combined income and behaviour characteristics though most of his discussion focuses on the latter which are threatening to US society. Thus the underclass is a group which 'feels excluded from society, rejects commonly accepted values, suffers from *behavioral* as well as *income* deficiencies. They don't just tend to be poor; to most Americans their behavior seems aberrant' (Auletta 1982, p. xiii). It is a definition that is open to wide variations in interpretation. Auletta's attempt to specify the number of groups belonging to the underclass, useful though it was, did not improve matters. Members of the underclass, he wrote,

can be grouped into four distinct categories: (a) the *passive* poor, usually long-term welfare recipients; (b) the *hostile* street criminals who terrorise most cities, and who are often school dropouts and drug addicts; (c) the *hustlers*, who, like street criminals, may not be poor and who earn their livelihood in an underground economy, but rarely commit violent crimes: (d) the *traumatised* drunks, drifters, homeless shopping-bag ladies and released mental patients who frequently roam or collapse on city streets. (Auletta 1982, p. xvi)

Attempts have been made by others to define the underclass more rigorously so that it can be better measured (Ricketts and Sawhill 1988) but such attempts have inevitably come under criticism because definitions have implications not only for the size and composition of the group but also for policy initiatives (Hughes 1989). At present it is correct to say that there is no agreement on either the definition, the composition or the size of the underclass. Estimates of its size vary considerably: from 0.8 to 5.3 per cent of the US total population; or from 7.1 per cent of the US poor to 37.5 per cent (Sawhill 1988, table 7, p. 1108). In all the debates, however, four features of the underclass usually appear: heavy concentration in urban areas, antisocial behaviour, weak labour attachment, and an obsession with ghetto black single mothers, their children and the fathers of the children. Thus it is not urban concentration of all the persistent poor which is the issue because, as Corcoran *et al.* show, this is not the case (Corcoran *et al.* 1985, p. 526), but rather the concentration of young unmarried and unemployed blacks who in their work, sexual and moral practices present a threat to white middle-class US norms.

There is even less agreement on the causes and the solutions to the underclass. We shall deal with policy proposals in general and in relation to the underclass in the next chapter. Here we concentrate on debates concerning its causes. There are essentially two main schools of thought reflecting the earlier debates on the culture of poverty even though they now appear under new headings. The first sees the underclass as the result of the values of the poor whilst the other sees structural factors as the cause. We shall concentrate on the first here and deal with the structural explanation briefly because it will be discussed more fully in the next section.

The deficient-value explanation has now been taken up by new Right writers and it has been linked to the welfare dependency thesis. In other words, the deficient values of the poor are the result of over-generous government social security benefits. There are three main variations to this basic theme represented by the works of Gilder, Murray and Mead. Gilder sees the welfare state as the source of all social ills in US society:

> Welfare now erodes work and family and thus keeps poor people poor. Accompanying welfare is an ideology... that also operates to destroy their fate. The ideology takes the form of false theories of discrimination and spurious claims of racism and sexism as the dominant forces in the lives of the poor. (Gilder 1982, p. 128)

With such clear views of the causes of the problem, Gilder sees the solution as equally self-evident: do away with benefits for the unemployed, the one-parent families and such other groups, allow the market to operate freely and force those dependent on benefits to look for jobs to support themselves and their children. In this way the work ethic, familial responsibility and other such virtues will flourish and gradually abolish poverty. Murray takes a slightly different position as far as the causes of the underclass are concerned but adopts a very similar position in relation to its solution. It is not so much dysfunctional values, argues Murray, but logical calculated individual strategies that lie behind welfare dependency and the formation of the underclass. It simply pays more to be on welfare benefits than to be at work, particularly for young people and one-parent families. The solution to the problem, therefore, 'consists of scrapping the entire federal welfare and income support structure for working-aged persons, including A.F.D.C., Medicaid, Food Stamps, Unemployment Insurance, Workers' Compensation, subsidised housing, disability insurance, and the rest' (Murray 1984, pp. 228–9). Another response from the new Right takes a more moral, authoritarian line towards both the causes and the solution to the underclass. Mead sees the underclass as the result of weakly held work values so that for members of the underclass 'work is something they would like to do, but not something they must do at any cost. It is an aspiration, but not an obligation' (Mead 1989, p. 162). The solution lies not in scrapping social security benefits but in making their payment conditional to work – compulsory workfare programmes on lines similar to schooling. 'Just as we require children to attend school, so we should require adults to do something to improve themselves if they are employable yet on welfare' (Mead 1989, p. 166). Such a compulsory approach to work is not, argues Mead, a form of state coercion but a state recognition that it has a duty to help its weak citizens. In brief all these three approaches to the underclass and to the poor of working age blame government expenditures for undermining such traditional values as work incentives, marriage, familial responsibility, self-reliance and, as a result, for creating a population group that is impoverished both morally and financially. But do social services undermine economic growth and do they create more dependent individuals?

The argument that public expenditure undermines economic growth has been voiced in Britain too, and it has been very influential in shaping recent government policies. It is a complex issue and it needs detailed discussion. Some services such as education, industrial training, road building and the like clearly encourage economic growth. Other services such as defence, health care and pensions for the very elderly and the very disabled clearly do not encourage economic growth because they do not contribute anything to the national work effort. A group of other services ranging from health care and benefits for those of working age, to prisons, the police and social work can have both positive and negative effects on work depending on costs and results. Interestingly, the demand has been not to reduce expenditure on the second type of services but on some in the third group which contains the most vulnerable groups in society.

But even if we concentrate on social rather than public expenditure, the claim is not substantiated by comparative evidence. Table 4.1 clearly shows that there is no correlation between the annual growth in

Table 4.1   Social expenditure and economic growth

Country	Social expenditure, % of GDP		Growth of expenditure	Annual growth in GDP per capita
	1960	1981	1960–81	1960–81
	%	%	%	%
Germany	18.0	26.5	47.0	3.1
France	13.4	23.8	78.0	3.6
Italy	12.7	22.7	79.0	3.6
UK	10.3	18.9	84.0	1.8
US	7.3	14.9	104.0	2.1
Japan	4.0	13.8	245.0	6.4

Source: Adapted from Burtless 1986, table 2.2, p. 46.

GDP per capita on one hand and either the volume of social expenditure or the growth in social expenditure on the other. If the overall growth of expenditure for the 21-year period is used as the basis for the debate, then Japan ranks first both in the rate of growth of expenditure as well as in the GDP per capita – exactly the opposite of what one would expect from the thesis. The country with the lowest percentage figure of growth in expenditure – Germany – has a lower rate of GDP growth than either France or Italy which had higher rates of expenditure growth. The UK had a lower rate of expenditure growth than the US but it also had a lower rate of GDP per capita. If one uses another basis for the debate, i.e. the level of expenditure in 1981, the conclusion remains the same. It is true that Japan, with the lowest level of social expenditure, had the highest growth in GDP per capita. But the US and the UK had the next two lowest levels of social expenditure in 1981 but they experienced the two lowest rates of growth in GDP per person. The fact is that economic growth in a country depends on a far more complex web of variables than simply the rate or level of public or social expenditure.

The second main criticism that social security benefits have encouraged the creation of single mother-headed families and thus increased poverty is a uniquely US debate. Yet all the evidence suggests that benefits are only a minor factor in the creation of single-parent families in the US. Ellwood provides statistical evidence which shows first that 'the highest percentages of children living in female-headed families in 1980 are often in the states with the *lowest* benefits' and not the highest benefits as one would expect from the welfare dependency thesis (Ellwood 1988, p. 61). Second, during the period 1972–84, the number of children in female-headed families increased by three million despite the fact that the value of benefits declined and the number of children in such families receiving benefits also declined. Thus the rise in the number of children in female-headed families must be attributed largely to factors other than the benefit system. McLanahan and Garfinkel also show that benefits have had a negligible influence on the rise of mother-only families in general, but they show that this influence was noticeable among the poorer sections of the population: 'the threefold increase in A.F.D.C. and welfare-related benefits between 1955 and 1975 may account for as much as between 20 and 30 per cent of the growth in mother-only families among the bottom half of the income distribution' (McLanahan and Garfinkel 1988, p. 15). But even this still leaves the other 70–80 per cent of the rise attributable to other factors. What is at fault is not the payment of benefits but rather the absence of benefits for children in all families and the lack of benefits for unemployed persons and their families other than those covered by the insurance scheme. The absence of these benefits may discourage both marriage and two-parenthood family life. Ultimately, however, it has to be acknowledged that structural factors which have brought about greater economic independence for women have also enabled them to live more happily alone rather than stay in unhappy marriages or get married for economic reasons. Similarly structural factors involving high rates of unemployment or very low wages for young men discourage married life. The influence of benefits on human behaviour, whether that refers to work effort, to child bearing or to family formation remains minimal for, if for no other reason, they are of such low level in all countries. International comparisons show that neither birth rates nor proportions of one-parent families relate to a country's payment of benefits to families or individuals.

This leads us to a brief reference to Wilson's structural explanation of the underclass but with cultural undertones. The trend for the better jobs to be located outside the city centre has meant that blacks with good educational and technical qualifications left the city centres to take up jobs in the suburbs. At the same time, the number of blue-collar jobs in the city centres declined and the qualifications demanded by employers increased. These structural changes in employment have resulted in greater difficulty by blacks in city centres in finding jobs and an absence of successful black role models with whom they can identify. In such circumstances, emphasis on early sexuality, dropping out of school, drink and crime have become more acceptable and more prevalent in city centres. Marriage rates inevitably dropped because young blacks are unable to maintain a family through working. The solution to the problem, argues Wilson, lies primarily through the creation of more jobs for inner city areas, stricter enforcement of anti-discrimination legislation as well as better educational and training programmes (Wilson 1985; Wilson 1987).

What then can be concluded from the discussion on the underclass? First, that its existence is still a matter of dispute. Jencks has recently tried to be more specific by carving up the underclass into three slices – the economic, the moral and the education underclass – but, he admits, that 'even with these adjectival modifiers the term remains full of ambiguities' (Jencks 1989, p. 25). Second, even if it exists, it refers to a very small minority of the poor; third, that structure rather than culture accounts for its existence; fourth, that the benefit system for one-parent families in the US needs to be changed towards a more universal scheme; and fifth, this should be complemented with higher employment opportunities as well as higher wages for young people in city centres and elsewhere if poverty among this group is to be abolished. The current low wages mean that the majority of mother-only families – 61 per cent of the white and 71 per cent of the black – cannot lift themselves above the official poverty line in the US even if they worked full-time (Finnie 1988, table A16, p. 217). The debate on the underclass has not been taken seriously in Britain largely because there are no large urban black ghettoes with rates of mother-only families receiving public assistance on the US scale. The overall conclusion of this section is that individualist explanations relying on intelligence, motivation, values and attitudes are a diversion from the real causes of the distribution of poverty in both Britain and the US.

Structural Explanations for the Distribution of Poverty

It is worth summarizing what has been said so far in this chapter before proceeding. In the first section the three main theories of the existence or incidence of poverty and inequality were discussed – the functionalist, Marxist and structuralist. It was concluded that the structuralist explanation was the most adequate. Its main thesis was that the incidence of poverty and inequality is to be found mainly in the existence of low-paid jobs in the labour market and in the contractions of the labour market that result in job losses for many people. These basic processes influence people's life chances whether they are at work or out of work. This section is concerned with the distribution of poverty, i.e. which individuals or groups of individuals are likely to be in poverty. The distinction between the incidence and the distribution of poverty is a central theme in this chapter for the first explains why there is poverty while the second explains which individuals are likely to be poor. Two main explanations of the distribution of poverty are discussed: individualistic explanations which maintain that those individuals with inadequate or faulty characteristics – low intelligence, insufficient schooling, faulty attitudes and values – will end in poverty. This is in line with the functionalist view concerning the incidence and inequality.

We now move on to discuss the structuralist explanation of the distribution of inequality and poverty that stems from the structuralist view. What we shall be specifically discussing are the structural dimensions of society that influence people's job and career opportunities so that they escape or end in poverty. Our approach does not consider such social security administrative categories as old age, disability, unemployment and one-parenthood as the causes of poverty. A person can be in any one of those categories without being in poverty. Not all the elderly, for example, are in poverty – indeed income differences in old age are substantial. Conversely, many of the poor in any of these categories were poor before. Many one-parent families in poverty, for example, were also poor when they were two-parent families or when they were single.

The three structural dimensions that we shall use are class, gender and race. These three influence people's lives separately as well as jointly though we do not intend to enter the debates in any great detail on whether any one of them is more fundamental that the others. In order to present a brief but coherent picture of the influence of these three dimensions, we propose to discuss the influence of each one of them on the educational system and the labour market. These two societal institutions are pivotal to people's earnings and hence to their likelihood of being in poverty or in affluence.

Beginning with class, the argument presented here is that it has a very significant influence on a person's level of education and professional qualification and it also influences, partly as a result but independently too, a person's earnings from work. There is a great deal of evidence on the relationship between class and educational achievement and we need only summarize it briefly here. In Britain, the work of Halsey and his associates showed not only the strong relationship between class and university education but also it demonstrated that this class relationship did not change from the 1920s to the late 1960s. Later research shows that the picture remains the same. This is how Halsey describes this trend: 'A service-class boy [upper-class boy] in our sample was four times as likely as the working-class peer to be found at school at the age of 16, eight times as likely at the age of 17, ten times as likely at the age of 18, and eleven times as likely to enter university' (Halsey *et al.* 1980, p. 204). The political conclusion of the study was that those reformers who put their faith in education as the means of equalizing access 'to the top 5 or 10 per cent of jobs' would be disappointed (Halsey *et al.* 1980, pp. 218–9). In the US, a very similar picture emerges: a close connection between family background and college entrance for both whites and blacks and for both boys and girls. Moreover, this holds true even when intelligence in terms of IQ scores is taken into account. At all levels of ability, children from high socioeconomic backgrounds have much higher chances of entering and graduating from colleges than children from middle and low socioeconomic backgrounds (Gilbert and Kahl 1987, chapter 7). Schiller provides abundant statistical evidence from government data which show that in 1977 'the likelihood of attending college increases markedly with family income' for white, black and Spanish-speaking youth (Schiller 1980, p. 140). In a later edition of his book, he shows that the situation was very much the same for 1985 (Schiller 1980, table 9.4, p. 146). Similarly, Hearn's study of a random sample of 5211 students

(2617 men and 2594 women) in the mid-1970s came up with a very similar conclusion. This is one of the main conclusions of the study. 'The present results reinforce the findings of earlier college destination studies that, in the high-school-to-college transition, the academically and socioeconomically "rich" become richer (i.e. attend schools having superior intellectual and material resources) while the academically and socioeconomically "poor" become poorer' (Hearn 1984, p. 28). These and many other studies confirm Jencks's earlier conclusion that 'the most important determinant of educational attainment is family background' (Jencks 1972, p. 158) and that this 'correlation appears to have been stable throughout the first half of the twentieth century' (Jencks 1972, p. 138).

Thus for both Britain and the US, the educational system reproduces existing educational inequalities even though it does provide opportunities for many very able working-class children to gain a higher education which their parents did not have. In both countries, the wastage of ability is substantial but perhaps more so in Britain where the proportion of young people going on to higher education is about half that of the US.

That education is associated with earnings from work is generally agreed. The disagreements are around the degree of this association relative to the importance of other factors. Moreover, Jencks's recent work shows that this relationship is not linear in the sense that a year in university is more important to earnings than a year in high school (Jencks *et al.* 1979, chapter 6). We shall be discussing the relevance of race and gender below but here we need to discuss the importance of the job on earnings, reminding our reader of our earlier discussion of dual labour theories. Duncan's work is the most relevant for our purposes. Looking at the careers of white male workers for the period 1968–78, he estimated that education accounted for 15 per cent of the difference in their earnings, and when the influence of work experience, IQ, achievement motivation and father's education were taken into account, a total of 23 per cent of earnings differences were explained, leaving the remaining 77 per cent unaccounted for. He concludes his findings as follows:

> Workers in the highest-status white collar occupations – professionals and managers – generally earn more than the average for individuals with similar measured characteristics, while workers in the lowest status occupations – labourers for example – earn less. Thus for white male workers both individual characteristics resulting from mainly structural factors and

institutional labour market factors affect people's earnings. (Duncan 1984, p. 115)

What this amounts to is that workers with the same occupational and educational abilities and experience can earn very different wages because of the type of job they do. The other implication is that efforts to reduce income inequalities through the educational system will not come to much. The chances of achieving this goal are greater through direct reduction of differences in earnings between jobs. Education cannot rectify the inequalities of the market, as many educational commentators have pointed out over the years.

The importance of class becomes even stronger when we take wealth into account. Wealth does not merely increase income but it also provides economic security and economic power. As we saw in the previous chapters, wealth is highly concentrated in both Britain and the US with the result that only a small minority at the top enjoy its benefits. The group below it enjoys good salaries and good fringe benefits so that its economic security is fairly good even though it possesses far less economic power. The lower down the income scale we travel, the less economic security we encounter so that the lower income groups are totally deprived of it. They have to rely on the state for whatever protection they can get.

Another important aspect of class relevant to our discussion is the differential risks that it involves for different socioeconomic groups. On the whole, the degree of risk varies inversely with class – the lower the class the higher the risk. Thus accidents, illness, unemployment and one-parenthood are more prevalent both in incidence and duration among the lower than the higher socioeconomic groups. The end result is the creation of what we could call *the inverse protection law*. In other words, the lower a person's socioeconomic background, the greater the risk of economic insecurity and the lower the degree of protection the individual possesses or is offered by the state. As we shall see in the next section, the social security system tends to offer little or no protection for several eventualities that tend to be primarily lower-class risks.

Finally, family formation is influenced by class. Men and women tend to marry within their social circles – what has come to be known as 'assertive mating' or 'class endogamy'. In this way, family wealth and family income can be reinforced and economic security either enhanced, or the opposite can happen. Class endogamy is the norm in both Britain and the US, particularly among the top professional and business group. Laumann's study in Massachusetts brings out well the main points in this issue. Having divided the respondents into five occupational groups, the study found that 44 per cent of the respondents had married women from the same occupational group; the proportion was 60 per cent in the case of professionals and managers. Moreover, 71 per cent had married women from within the same or the next socioeconomic group (Laumann 1966, pp. 74–81). A great many factors account for this high degree of class endogamy – schools, colleges, clubs, associations, workplace or mere residential proximity since most neighbourhoods are class segregated to a greater or lesser extent. Class endogamy is obviously reinforced by race endogamy with the result that the risk of poverty among lower socioeconomic groups for many ethnic groups is reinforced.

To conclude, class has a permeating and all-embracing effect on the economic prospects of individuals. Its association with wealth, high income and poverty is very strong though not total. Its influence on education, career and marriage is again substantial though not total. The net effect of all this is that poverty is largely a working-class problem and it is largely the result of structural factors. There are the few in poverty with middle-class or upper-class family backgrounds in the same way that there are a few in poverty as a result of their own individual faults and personal inadequacies. But the exceptions do not negate the general conclusion. The majority of the poor today walk along economic paths that are familiar to their parents and which, most probably, will be trodden by most of their children as adults and parents in the future.

The effects of class, however, are mediated through gender and race, i.e. they are compounded as far as women and various ethnic groups, mostly black, are concerned. Beginning with gender, there is abundant evidence that the earnings of women are lower than those of men in both the UK and the US and that very little change has taken place during the period covered by this study. True enough, the proportion of women in paid employment, full-time and part-time, has increased substantially over the years so that it has approached but not reached the corresponding proportion for men. Thus in the US in 1986 55 per cent of all women were in employment compared with 35 per cent in 1960; in Britain, 60 per cent of women were employed in 1985 – 34 per cent full-time and 26 per cent part-time – compared with 53 per cent in 1973 (Dale and Glover 1989, p. 302).

Very little progress, however, has been made in bridging the gender earnings gap. In the US the earnings of white women in full-time employment working full-year, amounted to 56 per cent of those of men in corresponding employment status in both 1960 and 1980. The proportions were understandably lower for all women workers because of the greater proportion of women than men working part-time but the trend was the same – no change over the years. The same picture emerges if one looks at earnings of men and women taking age into account. Interestingly enough, the only significant improvement has been in the case of black women working full-time, full-year: their earnings were 36 per cent of those of white men in 1960 but by 1980 the proportion rose to 52 per cent, a figure that was almost the same as that for white women (Finnie 1988, table A1, p. 189). In Britain, according to Beechy, women's full-time earnings amounted to 63 per cent of men's earnings in 1970 and 74 per cent in 1983 (Beechy and Whitelegg 1986, table 10, p. 97), figures which appear to be slightly higher than those for the US.

The explanation for the gender gap in earnings cannot possibly be due to differences in educational achievement because in both countries, but particularly in the US, there is no difference in the educational achievements of men and women. In the US the proportion of women and men in colleges and universities is the same while in Britain it is almost the same when the entire higher educational sector, rather than universities only, is taken into account to make the comparison with the US appropriate. It is thus no surprise that several studies which have attempted to explain the differences in earnings between men and women have found the role of education insignificant. Thus in an analysis of PSID of employed white men, black men, white women and black women in 1975, Corcoran and Duncan found that education explained only 2 per cent of the differences between the earnings of white men and white women; 11 per cent of the differences in earnings were attributable to years of training on the job, 28 per cent by other work history, 3 per cent by reasons of labour force attachment, leaving 56 per cent unexplained. A similar picture emerged in relation to the earnings differences between white men on one hand and black women and black men on the other. These findings led to the authors' conclusion that

> those who claim that the labor market treats workers 'fairly' in the sense that equally productive workers are paid equally, are likely to be wrong.

Furthermore, skill-augmenting education and training programs alone probably will not eliminate the earnings advantage enjoyed by white men. (Corcoran and Duncan 1979, p. 19)

A more recent analysis of earnings and education in the US by Finnie also shows that education does not narrow the earnings gap. Taking the two extremes of educational level, white women with no high school education and those with a graduate degree, the picture was as follows: the first group had earnings which amounted to 58 per cent of those of white men in 1960 and 51 per cent in 1980. The corresponding figures for the second group were 54 per cent and 50 per cent respectively. In Britain, education seems to make slightly more difference than in the US. Thus the median annual earnings of women with higher education amounted to 75 per cent of those of men in 1978 while the earnings of women with secondary school education only was only 65 per cent (Arnot 1986, table 2, p. 143).

In advanced industrial societies such as Britain and the US women do not form a monolithic occupational group. Their position in the stratification system cannot therefore be attributed to gender only. It is determined by both class and by gender which interact in a variety of ways but particularly in various covert forms of discrimination in the labour market. Thus in both countries, women are concentrated in a far smaller number of occupations than men and these tend to be low-paying jobs; and they tend to gain promotion and advancement far less than men. Reviewing the evidence for the US, Gatlin concluded that 'from one-half to two-thirds of the earnings gap can be attributed to various forms of discrimination. These range from excluding or discouraging women from entering or advancing in the more lucrative employment areas to systematically underpaying certain jobs because they are held mainly by women' (Gatlin 1987, p. 234).

Another aspect of women's inferior employment position, which stems from their dual role as mothers and workers, is their tendency to work part-time. This is particularly the case in Britain which tends to make women's position worse than that of women in the US. Thus Dex and Shaw in their comparative study of Britain and the US found three main differences: first, 'British women spend more years out of the labour market' than American women; second, 'they are much more likely to take part-time jobs; and third, they suffer more from downward mobility when they return to work after childbirth (Dex and Shaw 1986, p. 124).

Women's employment and earnings patterns have at least three direct implications for poverty. First, for many two-parent families, women's earnings make the difference between the whole family being in or out of poverty. Second, for about two-thirds of mother-only families, full-time employment would not bring in sufficient earnings to lift them out of poverty – their wages are too low. Third, the spread of part-time employment disqualifies an increasing number of women from social security benefits and thus raises the possibilities of poverty.

The debate around the relative importance of class and gender to women's earnings and family poverty is similar to the debate on racism and class and some repetition in these discussions is inevitable. Clearly discrimination in earnings against women is sexist in outcome but is it also sexist in origin or in intent? In both the US and Britain recent anti-discrimination legislation has removed most rules and regulations that were openly sexist in social security and it has made open discrimination in employment against women illegal. In this respect discrimination against women is increasingly a matter of class than gender in origin. There are of course many situations where discrimination by employers is sexist, though not openly committed to make it illegal. There are also many situations where the informal network is so weighted against women that sexist practices are almost inevitable. This is the case in promotion of women to senior positions in predominantly male institutions. But there are also situations where class and gender coalesce so that it is difficult to say how much of the discrimination is due to class or to gender. This is the case in the concentration of women in low-paying jobs. Whether class or gender or both are the causes of discrimination is an important issue for it has direct implications for policy programmes and also because, for many women, gender discrimination is more stigmatizing than class discrimination even though the financial effects are similar.

Race is an important determining factor for employment and income in both the US and Britain but perhaps more so in the former because of its history and the greater ethnic heterogeneity of its population. Most of the theoretical and empirical work on race relates to the US and the discussion here inevitably reflects this. There is no doubt that in the prewar years race was the main factor determining the earnings of blacks. But the expansion of the economy, the changes in the employment structure of the country, the rise in educational opportunities, the anti-discrimination and affirmative action legislation and the rising black consciousness have led to a substantial differentiation in the employment patterns of the black community. Thus in terms of both the type of jobs and the earnings of black people it is now not possible to refer to them as a monolithic ethnic group. In other words, class has increasingly become a main determinant of life chances. It follows that, conversely, race has lost some of its previous strength with the result that today both class and race, and the various ways in which they interact, are important in determining black men's job positions, earnings and risk of poverty. For black women, the dimension of gender has also to be added to the formula, thus making their position not only the most complex but also, potentially, the most vulnerable to the ill-effects of low class and black colour. In brief the position taken here is in line with an interactionist position on class and race which holds that 'racial phenomena generally operate differently across class lines just as class phenomena generally operate differently across racial lines" (Pettigrew 1985, p. 337). It is not a position that, as Wilson pointed out, either ignores 'the legacy of previous discrimination' or one that argues that racial discrimination has disappeared. Rather it is a position that reassesses the role of race in advanced industrial societies (Wilson 1980, p. 167). Having said this, a warning is necessary against the complacent view that given time race and gender will disappear as discriminating factors. There are no inevitabilities in this field. It all depends on the balance of political forces within specific economic situations prevailing in different countries at any one time. Thus whilst it is most unlikely that the clock can be put back, it is quite possible that a severe and prolonged economic recession can slow down, impede and even reverse some of the gains that women and black people have made recently.

All the evidence points to several main trends in the economic position of black people in the US. First, their present economic position is considerably inferior to that of whites despite the improvement that has taken place in recent years. Thus the earnings of all black men in full-time, full-year employment amounted to only 71 per cent of those of white men in the same employment status in 1980 but this figure was substantially higher than 1960 when it stood at 56 per cent. The position is exactly the same when one compares the position of 'prime-aged' earners, those aged 35–44 years – the corresponding figures are 57 and 70 per cent respectively, suggesting that any further improvements towards earnings equality are going to be slow, difficult and perhaps not possible in the foreseeable future (Finnie 1988, table

A.1, p. 189). Second, this improvement has not been so spectacular when one looks at the careers of a sample of workers over a period of time. Duncan's work with PSID indicated, as Table 4.2 shows, that the proportion of blacks always in the top fifth of the income distribution was very small indeed during the 12-year period despite some improvement; conversely, their proportion among the lowest fifth, though declining over the years, remained substantial.

Third, the changes in employment opportunities in inner city areas have resulted in a substantial rise in unemployment among young blacks which has had severe adverse effects not only on their own incomes but also on family life and poverty in these areas. There has been an enormous growth in black mother-only families most of which, as Chapter 3 showed, are in poverty. As Wilson argues, this rise in female-headed families is a symptom of the economic hardships experienced by all lower-class and particularly lower-class black families and not a cause of them (Wilson 1980, p. 161). The implication, of course, is that any realistic policies to deal with this problem must involve a substantial regeneration of employment opportunities with decent wages for all, i.e. wages that enable people to maintain themselves and their children at a standard that is at least of the social coping level discussed in Chapter 1.

Fourth, though there has been a substantial growth in the number and proportion of young black people graduating from colleges and though this has improved their occupational status and earnings, it has not bridged the earnings gap with white college graduates. The earnings of black men in full-time, full-year employment with college degrees amounted to 76 per cent of those for white men in the same employment and education groups in 1980 – a figure that was exactly the same as that of black men versus white men with not even high school education (Finnie 1988, table A.3, p. 198). It suggests that race still plays an important part in the determination of earnings irrespective of the level of education. In a study of the effects of race, education and gender on earnings, Sandefur and Pahari conclude that 'in 1959 black male weekly earnings would have increased by 31.8 per cent if their characteristics had had the same effects as those of white men. This figure declined to 28.1 per cent in 1969 and 21.4 per cent in 1979'. For black women the corresponding figures are 107.9 per cent, 84.6 per cent and 58.4 per cent respectively (Sandefur and Pahari 1988, p. 24). Thus despite the declining significance of race and gender, they still exert a great deal of influence on people's earnings and the risk of poverty. Put in a different way, in both countries the real debate should not be whether the influence of gender and race is declining but why it is so stubbornly persisting.

Fifth, the improvement in the economic position of the black community must be seen in the overall context of what happened to the earnings of other minority groups. As Tienda points out, since the mid-1970s, 'Puerto Ricans have begun to rival Blacks as the most economically disadvantaged group' in US society (Tienda 1989, p. 24). The reasons for this are not clear but one of the main points made in the first section of this chapter is relevant here, i.e. so long as these are low-paid jobs, individuals will be found to fill them even though the characteristics of the individuals change over time.

It may be useful to summarize the structuralist perspective on the incidence and distribution of poverty before examining the ways in which the social security systems of the two countries deal with poverty. The structure of the economy of the two countries with its dual labour markets, the unequal distribution of power and the dominant ideology of individualism combine to produce inequality and poverty. The weak groups in society are inevitably those that will be the low-paid and in poverty. These groups are determined by class, gender and race in both countries. It is the operation of these three factors through the institutions of education and the labour market that individually and jointly determine people's earnings from work and which affect their life chances. Thus when people find themselves in certain contingencies – unemployment, old age, disability, one-parenthood and so on – their risk of being in poverty depends on their primary characteristics in terms of class, gender and race and their labour and educational features. But it also depends on the protection that they enjoy under their country's social security system.

POVERTY AND THE SOCIAL SECURITY/INCOME MAINTENANCE SYSTEM

The social security systems of the two countries are similar in one important respect but they are different in one significant way, too. They are similar in that they are both dominated by the insurance principle; they are different in that the British system contains a national anti-poverty safety net whilst the US system contains a patchwork of anti-poverty mini-systems which do not add up to a national system.

Thus in Britain the great majority of those who do not qualify for an insurance benefit or whose qualification has expired will receive a means-tested benefit which should bring them up to the official poverty line. In the US there is no such anti-poverty safety net provided through a national assistance scheme.

Let us begin, however, by looking at the effects of the insurance principle on the social security systems of the two countries. It has three main effects which have direct implications for the distribution of poverty. The first of these is that insurance benefits are provided for those risks in life which are, on the whole, considered involuntary. The loss of earnings through old age is the best example of an involuntary risk since there is nothing that the individual can do to avoid old age. The net result of the notion of involuntary risk is that certain other risks are considered voluntary and hence are not covered by insurance benefit. The main risk not covered as a result of this is family break-up other than through widowhood. This means that a large number of one-parent families have to rely on means-tested benefits which are inferior to insurance benefits in several ways. Second, the insurance principle has meant that even where an insurance benefit exists, those who do not pay enough insurance contributions will not qualify for a benefit. Thus many people not at work on account of unemployment, sickness and even old age find themselves without an insurance benefit. These people tend to come from the groups that have a weak position in the labour market – the unskilled and semi-skilled on the whole. Women have particularly suffered because of the assumption that their role as mothers and wives should override their role as workers. Third, the insurance principle has been very sensitive to the fear of undermining work incentives. Thus in both countries, insurance benefits for the unemployed are paid for short periods – the maximum period being 12 months in Britain and 26 weeks in the US with the possibility of a further 13 weeks in states with high rates of unemployment. Moreover, unemployment benefit is not paid if it is considered that the individual was voluntarily unemployed or was made unemployed through misconduct. In all these three broad ways the range of insurance benefits, despite their mounting costs, allow and require that a large number of individuals, mostly from the low socioeconomic groups, do not quality for a benefit and hence run the risk of being in poverty. Despite this overall similarity, however, the US insurance scheme is less foolproof than the British in terms of coverage and qualifications even though it provides far higher benefit amounts for the higher-income groups because of the earnings-related nature of all its benefits.

The main difference between the two systems, however, lies in their provisions for a poverty safety net. In Britain persons who do not qualify for an insurance benefit because there is no insurance scheme for them, or because they did not pay enough contributions or whose period of qualification expired or who were disqualified because of their behaviour can apply for a means-tested benefit the amount of which is the same as or very similar to the insurance benefit and which does not vary from one part of the country to another. Thus any elderly person who does not qualify for a retirement pension can apply for this means-tested benefit; any unemployed person whose unemployment insurance period of 12 months has expired can also apply; similarly any unemployed person who was disqualified from the insurance benefit on the grounds of misconduct or voluntary unemployment can apply but will qualify for a reduced amount; all one-parent families can apply because there is no insurance benefit for them other than that for widows; and so on. In the US there is no one national assistance benefit. Instead there are several schemes each of which applies to a specific group and most of which vary from state to state. There is an assistance scheme for the elderly described as 'the most fundamental new departure in US public welfare policy since the 1930s' (Bickle and Wilcock 1974, p. viii quoted in Warlick 1984, p. 2) in the sense that it is federally financed and it provides a uniform amount based on national eligibility criteria. Assistance benefits for all the other groups, however, are based on state eligibility criteria and on state-determined amounts. Thus the largest of these, the scheme for one-parent families, provides benefits which vary from a maximum monthly benefit of $118 plus food stamps in Alabama for a family of three persons in January 1987 to $779 plus food stamps in Alaska. In that year the income threshold used to calculate the extent of poverty in the US was $9056 per annum for a family of three which meant that, apart from Alaska, the maximum cash benefit in all states was below the national poverty line. Even when the value of food stamps is taken into account most states provided less than the national poverty line (US House of Representatives, Committee on Ways and Means 1988, table 12, p. 546 and table 1, p. 941).

Inevitably the US assistance benefit is less satisfactory than the British in ensuring that those who fall through the insurance net do not end up in poverty. State sovereignty in assistance benefits and variations among beneficiary groups have resulted not in generous amounts of benefits and in liberal qualifying conditions but, on the whole, the opposite. In both countries, however, the existence of a means test has always deterred many people from applying for their benefits and as commentators in both countries have noted neither country has found a way out of this problem.

Finally, there is the question of poverty among families with children where one or both parents are in full-time employment. Britain has adopted two policy measures which, despite their weaknesses, have reduced poverty among this group. There is first a weekly allowance in respect of each child paid to the mother irrespective of any conditions and, second, there is a scheme of wage supplementation for family heads in full-time employment and on low wages. The main weakness of both these schemes is the low level of benefits that they provide. The US has persistently refused to introduce any benefits for families where the parents are at work partly on the grounds that it is the parents' responsibility to maintain their children and partly because of fears that any such schemes would undermine work incentives. The net result, however, has been that a far higher proportion of children in the US are in poverty than in Britain. The existence of a national minimum wage in the US has not provided much help to families with children partly because of its low level and partly because of its lax enforcement.

The aim of this section was not to discuss the social security systems of the two countries in any detail but rather to outline the main reasons why they have failed to abolish poverty, officially defined. It has been pointed out that though both systems have had noticeable success in the reduction of poverty, neither has fully succeeded in this and that the US system is less effective in reducing poverty than the British scheme. We have given the administrative reasons for the differences between the two schemes but behind these lurk the broader, more fundamental reasons. Three such reasons stand out for the differences between the two schemes. There is first the political reason. The history of the two countries makes it abundantly clear that the forces of the Left – political parties and trade unions – which have pressed for social security benefit provision, as well as for the type of provision, have been stronger in Britain than in the US. The British Labour Party and trade unions have always pursued a more pro-welfare state and more egalitarian policies than US political parties and trade unions. Second, the central–local government relationship has been more *laissez-faire* in the US than in Britain. US states have managed to retain a greater degree of independence from the federal government than British local authorities have. Theoretically, local authority independence does not necessarily lead to lower-quality benefits but in practice it has done so. Third, the value of individualism has recently been far more entrenched in the US than in Britain. This was not necessarily the case in the past, for individualism in its most extreme forms was the dominant value in Britain during the nineteenth and early twentieth century and it permeated government policies under the poor law system. The situation today, however, is that public support for individualism is stronger in the US than in Britain. All US studies have shown that the majority of the public support the view that a person's socioeconomic position is the result of such individualistic characteristics as drive, skill, motivation, work effort, initiative and enterprise. Poverty is thus seen as the result largely of laziness, lack of effort or thrift, loose morals and suchlike personal inadequacies. On the other hand, wealth is seen largely as the result of hard work, initiative, skills and enterprise (Feagin 1972 and 1975; Huber and Form 1973; Nilson 1981; Kluegel and Smith 1986; Smith and Stone 1989). The few British studies have found strong support for structural explanations of poverty. Furnham's study arrived at two main conclusions: the majority of respondents favoured societal rather than individualistic factors as the causes of poverty; and equally important, Labour Party supporters were more likely to support structural explanations than Conservative Party supporters (Furnham 1982) Moreover, public attitudes towards government measures to reduce poverty, towards the provision of universal social services at the risk of higher taxation and a national minimum for all are more acceptable in Britain than in the US (Smith 1987, pp. 416–9).

In brief, the social security systems of the two countries reflect in varying degrees the historical balance of political forces as well as the dominant values of their society. Recent changes in technology, in business practices and in family patterns which have resulted in a sharp rise in part-time employment, increased labour changes and a substantial growth in one-parent families have undermined further the utility of the insurance principle as the main mechanism for the provision of state benefits to alleviate poverty. As a result, increasing numbers of people rely on means-tested benefits in both countries. The need for some fundamental changes in the structure of the social security systems of both countries has become very urgent indeed, if poverty is to be abolished.

CONCLUSION

Table 4.2 provides a snapshot of the main theses within this chapter. Interestingly enough these same divisions of opinion on the causes of poverty within countries exist also in relation to the causes of poverty and affluence at the international level. In the same way that the poor within Britain and the US have been held responsible or even blamed for their poverty, so have third world countries been seen as responsible for their low economic standards which result in mass and abject poverty among their people (George 1988).

We have argued that a structuralist explanation best explains both the existence and the distribution of poverty in Britain and the US. A structuralist explanation, however, does not claim that each and every person in poverty is totally free from any responsibility for his or her condition. Rather, it claims that the *vast majority* of the poor owe their condition to economic, political and social forces that are wholly or largely beyond their control. A structuralist explanation does not seek to ignore or to minimize the individuality of people as parents, workers or children. Rather it argues that this is shaped by outside forces and though some people are able to prevail against all odds the vast majority are inevitably unable to do this.

We have also argued that even if there were maximum upward and downward mobility – in other words, if family background became irrelevant to children's future careers – there would still be poverty so long as low-paid jobs continued to exist at the same high proportions as they do today. It is for this reason that ideally solutions to the problem of poverty should be sought first and foremost within the labour market and secondarily within the social security system. In the past, however, the labour market has proved far more resistant to government regulations than the social security system and, no doubt, this will continue to be so in the future. The social security system becomes, therefore, the main avenue through which governments can ensure that all their citizens have an income that is at least as high as the official poverty line. Both countries have the resources to achieve this modest but important goal. It is not so much economics as politics that will shape the nature as well as the course of future anti-poverty policies in both countries.

Table 4.2   *Implications of the functionalist, structuralist and marxist theories*

Area	Functionalist	Structuralist	Marxist
Structure of society	Consensus among various groups in society	Conflict among classes and groups in society	Class conflict dominates. Group conflict subordinate to class conflict
Ideology of society	Dominant values benefit all in society alike	Many dominant values to the advantage of higher socioeconomic groups	Dominant values benefit most the capitalist class
Distribution of power in society	No one group has more power than other groups at all or most times	The élites have more power than other groups on most issues	Capitalist class is the most powerful
Why inequality of wealth?	Because of private initiative and inheritance. Wealth guarantees economic growth for all	Through inheritance and private initiative. Wealth generates economic growth which benefits groups unequally	Mainly through inheritance. Wealth generates economic growth for the benefit of mainly capitalist class
Why inequality of earnings?	In order to encourage the most able persons to occupy the most important jobs in society	Mainly because of segmented labour markets	Private profit motive as well as segmented labour markets
Who are the most highly paid?	The most able in terms of IQ, knowledge, skills and values	Those with the greatest marketable skills and the most socially favoured	Those with the closest affinity to the capitalist class
Who are the most lowly paid?	The least able in terms of IQ, knowledge, skills and values	Those most discriminated and those with least marketable skills	Those most discriminated and those with least industrial power
Who benefits out of inequality?	The whole society, including the low-paid and poor	The higher income groups	The capitalist class and the higher income groups
Who are the poor?	Same comments as for the low-paid	Same comments as for low-paid	Same comments as for low-paid
Can poverty be abolished?	Either not possible or not desirable because it would be detrimental to economic growth	Very difficult but possible within welfare states	Not possible so long as capitalism exists

5. Policies for the Abolition of Poverty

It is clear from the discussion in Chapters 2 and 3 that poverty levels have remained high in both the UK and US even when poverty is defined in official subsistence terms. What is more, these high poverty levels have persisted despite the rise in public expenditure on social security programmes, as they are known in the UK, and income maintenance programmes, as they are known in the US. The discussion in Chapters 2 and 3, however, also showed that poverty levels would have been far higher had it not been for these government expenditures. This indicates that the abolition of poverty can only be achieved through government intervention policies and it is a fallacy to believe that the private market can by itself abolish poverty even when the economy is performing satisfactorily. Clearly, however, some policies are more effective in reducing poverty than others and it was no surprise that the Reaganite policies in the US and the Thatcherite policies in the UK during the 1980s were less effective than previous anti-poverty programmes.

Chapter 4 examined the causes for both the existence and the distribution of poverty and showed their predominantly structural nature. It also reviewed briefly the theoretical reasons why the social security/income maintenance programmes of the two countries have failed to abolish poverty altogether, although they reduced it. The structural nature of the roots of poverty inevitably means that its eradication is a very difficult policy task for even willing let alone unwilling governments. Indeed, there are those who maintain that the power structures and the dominant value systems of capitalist societies are such that the eradication of poverty is not possible. Our position has been rather different: a great deal has been achieved in the reduction of poverty during the past 50 years and there is no reason to believe that more cannot be achieved in the future provided the right blend of political and economic conditions prevail.

What is absolutely clear, however, from the history of both countries is that a continuation of existing policies will not abolish poverty even if it leads to higher levels of public expenditure. New policy initiatives are needed and it is these that this chapter discusses and evaluates. For the sake of clarity these various proposals are divided into incremental and comprehensive policies. The first category includes policy proposals that can be made within the existing edifice of the social security/income maintenance system whilst the second category of proposals involves the substantial or total replacement of existing programmes. Incremental policy proposals obviously vary between the two countries and hence they are discussed separately whilst comprehensive policy proposals are applicable to both countries and they are discussed as such though the literature from both countries is included in the discussion. Though the abolition of poverty is the central criterion by which these proposals are evaluated, four other criteria are also used as they have often been cited in the relevant debates: cost implications, administrative complexity, work incentives and income redistribution. These five criteria can often be in conflict with one another and choices between them are inevitable as the discussion in the chapter will show.

INCREMENTAL POLICY PROPOSALS IN BRITAIN

It is not the purpose of this section to discuss in detail all the various incremental proposals for the reform of the British social security system. Rather, the intention is to examine the thrust of the main proposals, their chief aims and the general direction in which they envisage the social security system should develop. Despite the plethora of such proposals in recent years, they are essentially of two main types: expansionist and contractionist. Expansionist policies advocate a growth of the scope of the insurance benefit component of the social security system leading to higher levels of social security expenditure. Contractionist policies head in the opposite direction – a reduction in public expenditure through greater concentration of benefits on those in need and a greater role for private provision. Basically, however, both approaches agree that the principles and assumptions underlying the existing social security system are essentially satisfactory and what is needed is some fine tuning to the system to make it more relevant to the conditions of the 1990s rather than those of the 1940s when the system was set up. It is, therefore, necessary to outline these underly-ing principles if we are to understand fully the significance of the expansionist and contractionist approach, both of which aim at the reduction of poverty.

The social security system of Britain has been based on the princi-ples enunciated in the Beveridge Report of 1942 and it is these princi-ples that need explaining here. The Report outlined six such principles in the hope that poverty in the country would then be largely abolished (Beveridge 1942, p. 121). The first of these was the idea that the amount of benefit should be flat-rate and adequate for subsistence. In other words, benefits should not be earnings-related but should be of the same amount irrespective of the level of earnings that a person had while in employment. This principle remained intact up to the mid-1960s, when earnings-related additions to flat-rate benefits were intro-duced for unemployment, sickness, disability, widowhood and mater-nity by the Labour government, only to be abolished by the Conserva-tive government in the early 1980s. After prolonged conflict between the Labour and Conservative Parties, earnings-related additions for retirement pensions were introduced by the Labour government in the late 1970s for those employees who were not adequately covered by pensions provided by their employers. Again, this has recently been changed by the Conservative government so that the number of em-ployees covered and the level of earnings-related addition to the flat-rate retirement pension have been reduced. It is part of the government's drive to reduce public expenditure and to encourage private and occu-pational pension provision.

The second principle of the Beveridge Report that was incorporated into the social security system of the country was that of flat-rate insurance contributions. The rationale behind this was that since people would be receiving the same amount in benefits it was right and proper that they should also be paying the same amount in contribu-tions. As the costs of social security rose, however, governments found it impossible to adhere to this principle since it would have meant that low-paid workers would be expected to pay contributions that were well beyond their means. The result has been the abandonment of this principle so that today people pay earnings-related contributions even though they receive flat-rate benefits. These earnings-related contribu-tions, however, are paid up to a certain income which is about one-and-a-half times the national average earnings with the result that the most highly paid employees benefit most. Fundamentally, however, the British social security system has been based on the insurance principle, i.e. that people quality for benefits only if they have paid the required amount in contributions. Others have to apply for means-tested benefits.

The third Beveridge principle was unification of administrative responsibility for the social security system. Instead of the multitude of agencies responsible for different parts of the system with different rules and benefit levels, the Report recommended that the entire system should become the responsibility of a government ministry with regional and local offices, with uniform rules and benefit levels. This has been part and parcel of the social security system over the years despite the endless changes in administrative regulations, benefit levels and so on.

It was, however, the fourth and fifth principles that captured the imagination of the British public at the time: adequacy of benefit and comprehensiveness. The Report recommended that the amount of the flat-rate benefit should in itself 'be sufficient without further resources to provide the minimum income for subsistence in all normal cases' (Beveridge 1942, p. 122). We saw in Chapter 2 that the amount of the benefit was based on the subsistence definition of poverty and this has continued to be the case over the years. From the implementation of the Report in the late 1940s to the early 1970s, benefits were increased from time to time and often lagged behind rises in prices and wages. From the early 1970s to the early 1980s benefits were increased automatically every year according to the rise in wages or prices, depending on which of the two was the higher. One of the first changes of the Conservative government in the early 1980s, however, was to change the formula so that benefits are increased every year according to the rise in prices. The net effect of this has been that in the last ten years benefit levels in relation to wages have declined, since wages tend to rise faster than prices. Thus, during most of the 1970s, when benefits were increased according to the rise in earnings, real benefit levels rose by 9 per cent or by 1.1 per cent a year whilst during the 1980s, when benefits were increased according to prices, real benefit levels fell by 3.7 per cent or by 0.4 per cent per year. As Field comments, this evidence shows that the living standards of the poor 'rose most in real terms during the 1970s, when the overall economic performance of the economy was less impressive than since 1981'. This is yet another reminder that economic growth by itself does not necessarily reduce poverty levels (Field 1990).

Poverty Amidst Affluence

The principle of comprehensiveness meant that any risk that was general, uniform and involuntary should be covered by an insurance benefit for everyone in employment. Thus unemployment, sickness, disability, maternity, widowhood and old age were provided with insurance benefits while lone parenthood, other than widowhood, was left out and had to rely on means-tested assistance benefit on the grounds that it was largely a voluntary act. Thus the principle of comprehensiveness was limited from the start, particularly in view of the implications of the sixth principle, that of classification. This principle stated that only those in full-time employment as employees would be covered for all insurance benefits. The self-employed would be covered for only some of the benefits while those in part-time employment would be excluded altogether. Bearing these exclusions in mind and the fact that many people in full-time employment could also be disqualified because they might not have paid sufficient insurance contributions, the principle of comprehensiveness was rather weak. Feminists also criticized it from the start because domestic labour was seen as different and not worthy of insurance coverage. The report, however, required that those not covered by insurance benefits could apply for means-tested assistance though it envisaged that the number of assistance recipients would be a small and declining minority. These principles have been part of the social security system though several minor changes have taken place over time. As we shall see below, the numbers of people on assistance benefits have risen very substantially over the years, signifying that all is not well with the insurance benefit network.

Government expenditure on social security has grown substantially: it amounted to 4.7 per cent of GDP in 1949/50, 5.3 per cent in 1959/60, 7.0 per cent in 1969/70, 9.0 per cent in 1979/80 and 11.1 per cent in 1984/5 (DHSS 1985, p. 27). The composition of this expenditure has also changed significantly: a rise in income-tested benefits and a decline in insurance benefits and non-contributory benefits. Thus in 1949/50, insurance benefits accounted for 63.3 per cent of all social security expenditure, non-contributory benefits 24.0 per cent and the remaining 12.7 per cent were income-tested benefits. In 1984/5, however, the corresponding proportions were 57.4 per cent, 17.0 and 25.6 respectively. Most of this growth in expenditure is due to the rise in the number of people receiving benefits – the elderly, the unemployed and the lone parents; a small proportion is the result of the creation of some new benefits and only a small proportion in the result of improvements in the relative levels of benefits.

The growth in the number of people relying on means-tested benefits and the growth in social security expenditure have given rise to the two opposed reform movements. Neither wants to replace the existing social security system with something totally different; rather each wants to make certain changes to the existing system which, in its view, will make it more effective. The reaction against means testing has come from writers and politicians of the Centre and Left whilst the reaction against rising levels of expenditure has come from the Right. So let us examine these two contrasting approaches, beginning with the expansionist approach.

It has been argued that the growth of means testing is a negation of the Beveridge principles and what is needed is a return to these principles where the insurance benefits dominated and means testing was for a small minority of people. It is for this reason that this reform movement is sometimes referred to as the 'Back to Beveridge' approach. More specifically it has been argued that the growth of means testing has resulted in increased stigmatization; it has made the system even more complex; it has reduced the take-up rates of benefits; and it has created even more poverty traps for benefit recipients. At least three reforms are needed, according to this group: to reinstate the dominance of insurance; to curb means testing; and to reduce poverty to the very minimum as the Beveridge Report envisaged.

First, insurance benefit levels should be raised so that fewer claimants have to supplement their insurance benefit with income-tested benefit. Such a change would be particularly useful to retirement pensioners where so many resort to means-tested benefits to supplement the rather low flat-rate pension. Second, the period of entitlement to unemployment benefit should be increased from its present 12 months to as long as unemployment for the individual lasts, as Beveridge recommended. Again this would lift a large number of the unemployed out of means-tested benefits as Chapter 2 showed. Third, it is necessary to create some kind of insurance benefit for lone parents since such a high proportion of them now rely on means-tested benefits. This recommendation is not strictly in line with the Beveridge principles because though the Report was not necessarily against such an insurance benefit it felt that there were far too many problems involved to recommend it as a priority measure.

Applying our five criteria of evaluation, the expansionist, 'Back to Beveridge' approach will certainly reduce but it will not abolish poverty since it will not benefit the ever-increasing number of part-time employees who pay no contributions and qualify for no insurance benefits. Moreover, it will not alter the benefit position of those in irregular full-time employment who have no adequate insurance contribution record for benefit entitlement. Many of the men and women who are lone parents will fall into this category, thus making an insurance benefit for lone parents very inadequate in terms of coverage. No doubt the cost of the social security system will increase since more people will be receiving benefits than under the present system, but this rise in costs will not be as high as it first appears since many of those who will qualify for insurance benefit protection receive today means-tested benefits of very similar amounts. The proposals in essence involve a great deal of redirection of expenditure from means-tested to insurance benefits. As for the effects of these proposals on work or savings incentives, they are likely to be marginal but, even so, they are likely to be positive particularly in relation to savings. The administrative complexity of the system will be slightly reduced and the benefit take-up will improve since all the available evidence shows that means-tested benefits have a much lower take-up rate than insurance benefits. Those who view the social security system as a vehicle for redistributing income from the better-paid to the lower-paid will be disappointed by these proposals since insurance contributions are at best a neutral and at worst a regressive form of taxation. Means-tested benefits are funded wholly through general taxation revenues whilst insurance benefits are funded partly through insurance contributions and partly through general taxation revenues. In general, the expansionist approach will reduce but it will not abolish poverty simply because it is based on the insurance principle that inevitably discriminates against those in part-time or irregular employment, apart from the fact that it disregards domestic employment.

The contractionist approach is primarily a reaction against the growth of social security expenditure and it, therefore, envisages measures designed to reduce it. Two such measures are envisaged – more targeting of benefits through means testing and privatization of various aspects of the social security benefit network. It has been argued that insurance benefits and universal benefits are wastefully paid to all and sundry irrespective of need. Thus both the general manager of a large company and a low-paid worker will eventually receive the same flat-rate state retirement pension; similarly their wives receive every week the same flat-rate child benefit in respect of any children that they have. It is argued that this is a waste of public money and that benefits should be paid only to those in need. Similarly, the frontiers of the state should be 'rolled back' by privatizing as many aspects of the social security system as possible to encourage private initiative. Despite the ideological commitment of the Thatcher government to the contractionist approach, it moved rather cautiously in this direction. It privatized maternity and sickness benefits by making them the responsibility of employers; it declined to increase the value of child benefit annually; it reduced the generosity of the means-tested benefits; it made the entitlement regulations to unemployment benefit more stringent; and it changed the formula for the annual upgrading of benefits using the rise in prices rather than the rise in earnings.

The government claimed that the rationale for these reforms was to produce a social security system 'which is more relevant to the needs of today; and which is capable of meeting the demands into the next century' (DHSS 1985, p. 1). Whatever this rhetoric may have meant, the reality is that these changes had the effect of increasing poverty during the 1980s and, if they remain in force, they will have the same effect in the 1990s and beyond.

In terms of our other four criteria, it is clear that a continuation of contractionist policies will lead to reduced public expenditure even though private expenditure on social security will increase for those who can afford it. Equally clear, contractionist policies will worsen the problems of administrative complexity since means-tested benefits are by their very nature more complex than insurance or universal benefits. Work incentives will suffer particularly if means testing becomes the rule rather than the exception. We shall be discussing in detail the issue of work incentives in the section on the negative income tax later in this chapter. As far as inequalities are concerned, there is no doubt that privatization of benefits will lead to greater inequalities. People's ability to make provisions for themselves will inevitably be determined largely by their incomes. Means-tested benefits, however, do not increase inequalities in themselves since they are paid only to those in need. The real danger of such benefits is that they degenerate in value over time. Benefits for poor people only tend to become poor benefits.

Incremental Policy Proposals and Changes in the US

Incrementalism has dominated reform efforts in the US. The gradual approach to reform has been taken in recognition of 'what the American public will and will not accept with regard to policies affecting poor people' (Heclo 1986, p. 303). The approach then is one which has been sensitive to what is politically feasible, i.e. 'realistic'. This cautionary approach was particularly prominent in the 1980s because of concern about programme costs, a general backlash against government involvement, and concern about economies slowed by continued unemployment, decline in the rate of increase in the Gross National Product (GNP), and concern that a stagnated economy will be unable to provide funds to support proposals for increasing benefits to the needy.

Incremental changes have been particularly prominent in alterations made to both social insurance and means-tested public assistance programmes. The retirement system now offers benefits to wives and survivors of retirees even though they have not contributed to the support of those benefits. The benefits of retirees are increased by one-half to provide support for their wives. And the formula for determining benefits has been increased over time to provide benefits which far exceed contributions made by retirees when working. Unemployment benefits have been expanded to cover long periods of unemployment and requirements that unemployed must look for a job have been liberally interpreted. Disability benefits have been given to those who are able to work despite original programme objectives that benefits should be provided only in the event of an incapacitating disability. Gradualism has also been the predominant technique for expanding public assistance programmes as is evident from the changes made to AFDC and other means-tested programmes.

But the most dramatic example of piecemeal changes relates to the provision of health insurance. Efforts to include some form of national health insurance in the Social Security Act in 1935 failed because of intense opposition. And later efforts also were unsuccessful. In 1948 President Harry Truman's call for a universal and comprehensive system was soundly rejected by Congress. And similar postwar proposals were also rejected. What was adopted instead was Medicaid and Medicare which provide national and state subsidization so that the poor and the elderly can get medical care. Private insurers are expected to provide medical insurance for those not covered by these programmes. The approach to health care has been described as a 'stunning symbol of the art of political compromise' and recognition of the 'American way' of depending on the private marketplace except in unusual cases (Anderson, 1968, p. 191).

Examples of the piecemeal approach to change are also suggested by the emphasis on 'hands-up' rather than 'hands-down' policies.

Hands-down policies refer to traditional government income maintenance policies. The hands-up (or helping hand) approach focuses on rehabilitating the needy to enable them to compete in the labour market rather than depend on welfare benefits. Workfare programmes have been part of this approach to poverty alleviation.

So taken have Americans been with this approach that those programme expansionists and reductionists have joined forces. Thus it was the liberal Kennedy administration which led the drive to find a 'new approach' to help people overcome individual inadequacies which prevented them from using their own initiative to escape poverty (Steiner 1966, p. 36). The idea was enthusiastically supported by conservatives in the US who had long maintained that it was individual defects which caused poverty and that therefore only limited government income maintenance programmes were necessary. The 'War on Poverty' programmes initiated in the late 1960s built on the Kennedy approach since it was predicated on the belief that improving human resources and opportunities for the needy was preferable to merely expanding income maintenance programmes. A massive series of legislative enactments designed to improve job skills, job opportunities and living conditions were reflections of this policy approach.

The decade of the 1980s provides even more evidence of US dependence upon incremental changes for reducing poverty. An implicit consensus developed that reform should recognize:

1. that different populations had different needs;
2. that benefits increases should be provided only for those clearly unable to work e.g. the elderly and the disabled;
3. that welfare recipients (those receiving means-tested benefits) should work after being 'rehabilitated', and that this should take preference over the provision of benefits;
4. that absent fathers should be required to provide financial support for families; and
5. that all programmes should be cost-effective (Focus, Vol. 11, No. 1 Spring, 1988).

The consensus represented a significant change in the position by those who had usually argued for a universal approach to government transfers which included elements of a guaranteed income. The support for differentiated aid suggested a commitment to principles of selectivity rather than universalism. And the willingness to force absent fathers to support their families under the Family Support Act of 1988 is further evidence of an abandonment of a previous view that systemic rather than personal defects were the primary cause for the prevalence of needy families in the US. The latter position, as we know, had resulted in much support for converting AFDC into a programme which provides guaranteed benefits for all needy families.

The new consensus had an impact. During the Reagan administration Medicaid and Medicare expenditures were reduced, as were services provided under these programmes. Efforts to adopt national health insurance, a promising reality a few years earlier, were abandoned. Instead Medicare catastrophic legislation was approved in 1988 which expanded subsidization for hospital and physician care, and provided for additional nursing and home health care funding. However, in order to control costs, elders were taxed to help pay for the additional benefits. The outcry against the requirement was so great that the legislation was repealed in 1989 – a highly unusual occurrence. In addition federal and state funding for AFDC was reduced, restrictions were placed on eligibility by both the federal and state governments, and workfare provisions were incorporated in the new Family Support Act of 1988.

COMPREHENSIVE POLICY PROPOSALS

Our brief review of the changes in social security/income maintenance programmes during the postwar period showed the dominance of 'disjointed incrementalism' in policy making in both countries. It is not simply that changes were piecemeal and incremental but rather that they did not form part of a coherent strategy that was designed to achieve one of the main goals of social security, i.e. the elimination of poverty. It is, therefore, no surprise that disjointed incrementalism has resulted in both higher levels of public expenditure and in a confusing array of programmes which are sometimes contradictory and which are often so baffling to potential recipients that they discourage take-up. Disjointed incrementalism, by its very nature, cannot be expected to eliminate poverty in the future because of its fundamental premise that 'muddling and compromises are the only rational approaches' (Rein 1976, p. 162) in dealing with problems and issues. Some form of rational, comprehensive planning is urgently needed even though its implementation may of necessity have to be made in stages.

The urgency for a comprehensive plan to abolish poverty becomes even stronger when it is recognized that many, if not all, of the basic assumptions which underlay the social security/income maintenance programmes of the two countries when they were set up are today invalid. Purdy's summary of these basic assumptions is a useful guide to the discussion here. These assumptions were:

1. there is a sexual division of labour whereby men perform paid work whilst women perform unpaid domestic work;
2. paid employment provides sufficient earnings or, when interrupted, sufficient benefits to prevent poverty;
3. paid employment is full-time in nature;
4. full employment is both feasible and desirable;
5. similarly high rates of economic growth are feasible and desirable;
6. only a small minority of individuals will not be able to support themselves and their dependents through earnings and insurance benefits and will have to rely on means-tested benefits (Purdy 1988, p. 202).

It is now generally recognized that assumption 1 is invalid not only because such a high proportion of married women are in paid employment but also because the unpaid nature of domestic work is not so generally accepted today as it was in the 1940s. The discussion in Chapters 2 and 3 showed how invalid assumption 2 has become. Many people are in poverty because of low wages and the inadequacies of insurance benefits. Assumption 3 has become increasingly less valid with the growth of part-time employment, particularly among married women and young people. As for the claim that full employment is sustainable, the postwar history of both countries shows that this is not always the case and that there are also parts of the country with high levels of unemployment even when the national statistics suggest otherwise. The same applies just as much to the fifth assumption and it will become even more questionable in the future with the gradual depletion of natural resources. As for assumption 6, all the evidence shows that those who rely on means-tested benefits or who are even refused such benefits are not a small and declining minority but a sizeable proportion of the population.

Because of these changed conditions and the dawning awareness that the social security systems of both countries have lost sight of one of their main objectives – the elimination of poverty – there has re-

cently been increased interest in new more comprehensive approaches
to the problem of poverty. As Baumol put it, 'the methods we are
currently using may simply not be up to the task' (Baumol 1986) and
new approaches are urgently needed. It is clearly not possible to review all the various comprehensive or semi-comprehensive policy
proposals put forward in the two countries. Instead we shall concentrate
on what we consider to be the four main such approaches: benefits as
of right, negative income tax, basic income guarantee and the starting
even scheme.

The Benefits as of Right Scheme

The insurance principle is now part and parcel of the social security
systems of all advanced industrial societies. People in employment pay
contributions which entitle them to benefits when their employment is
interrupted or when it ceases. It was widely welcomed when first introduced because it reduced the scope of means testing which people found
humiliating and stigmatizing. In many advanced industrial societies,
including Britain and the US, the weekly contributions by the insured
persons account for only a minority of the total income of the social
security scheme. Thus in 1982–83, according to comparative data provided by the International Labour Office (ILO), the income of the social
security/income maintenance programme of the US was made up as
follows: 22.6 per cent from contributions by the insured persons; 34.3
per cent from employers; 28.6 per cent from the central government; 6.3
per cent from other public authorities; and 8.2 per cent from interest on
capital. For Britain during the same year the corresponding figures were
17.9, 23.9, 49.8, 5.8 and 2.1 per cent respectively (ILO 1988, table 6, p.
103–15). Second, a person's insurance contributions are only very loosely
connected to the benefits which he or she receives. Some persons, for
example, experience sickness or unemployment more often than others
and hence receive benefits more often. In other words, no one pays for
his or her benefits in a strict actuarial manner as is the case with private
insurance. Finally, and as a result of the above, social security schemes
are not strictly funded schemes but rather pay-as-you-go schemes so
that there is a great deal of subsidization of benefits among the generations. Thus the working population of today pays contributions which
pay, among other benefits, for the pensions of the retired. In all these
ways, the insurance principle is a myth (Prowse 1988) but a very popular
one because it protects people in need from means testing.

More importantly for the purposes of this discussion, however, the insurance principle inevitably means that many people cannot qualify for insurance benefits and have to rely on means-tested benefits or receive no benefits at all. These can be irregularly employed workers who do not always satisfy the contribution conditions; the increasing number of part-time employees who are not required to pay contributions; those who are unemployed for periods longer than those covered in the insurance scheme; the severely disabled from birth or early life who do not enter the labour market; the lone parents who are not covered by an insurance scheme; and other such groups. It is possible to rectify some of these problems, but by no means all, by a 'Back to Beveridge' scheme discussed earlier simply because that approach retains the insurance principle.

It is for these reasons that many have called for the abandonment of the insurance contribution record as the qualifying criterion for the receipt of benefits (George 1973, p. 132; Field 1981, p. 186; Esam *et al.* 1985, p. 37; Alcock 1985, p. 46; Lister 1989, p. 221). People will qualify for benefits if they are in certain positions which society has recognized as meriting state support – the low-paid, unemployed, sick, disabled, lone parent and retired. It is for this reason that this approach is sometimes referred to as 'positional benefits' scheme. The same methods of verification as today will be used to establish whether a person is low-paid, sick, unemployed, lone parent, retired and so on. Some of the advocates of this approach propose that insurance contributions should continue to be paid while others advocate their complete abolition, leaving the scheme to be financed entirely out of general taxation like defence, education, roads and so on. Those who advocate the continuation of insurance contributions for funding the system do so on pragmatic considerations and grounds of social solidarity, reminiscent of Beveridge's view that the notion of social insurance implied 'that men stand together with their fellows' (Beveridge 1942, p. 13). However the scheme is funded, though, it will have no relationship to the determination of benefit entitlement. People's entitlement to benefits will be justified on the grounds that as citizens they would have contributed to the general taxation of their country in direct or in indirect taxes or both. In other words people have certain political, legal and social rights but they also have certain duties and the fulfilment of one presupposes the fulfilment of the other.

How then does the benefits as of right or positional benefits approach measure up to the five criteria set out at the beginning of the chapter?

There is clearly no doubt that such a scheme will virtually abolish poverty as officially defined. The only group of individuals that will remain in poverty is likely to be those who persistently refuse to take up employment. They thus refuse to contribute to society, which is a fundamental duty (Esam *et al*. 1985, p. 37). In terms of costs, there is no doubt either that the scheme will be more expensive than at present but not as much more as first appears, since part of the extra cost will be met through reductions in means-tested benefits. This is particularly the case in Britain where a large proportion of those who at present do not qualify for an insurance benefit eventually receive a means-tested benefit of about the same amount. These comments on costs are based on the assumption that benefit levels will be the same as under the present scheme. Many of the advocates of this approach, however, envisage higher benefit levels, in which case the overall costs will also be higher. Another complicating consideration is the type of benefit that will be paid to people in part-time employment who become unemployed or sick, or retire. Would they be paid the full benefit or part of the benefit? Administratively the scheme will be far less complex than at present since it will do away with most means-tested benefits and, as a result, take-up rates will also be higher. There is no reason why the scheme should be any more or less detrimental to work incentives. In most ways the scheme will be administered in the same way as today with the same rules and regulations which are designed to protect the system against abuse. One area of reputed potential difficulties is the case of lone parents, expressed as the fear that a benefit as of right might discourage work incentives and may even lead to the growth in the number of one-parent families. Logically, however, it is difficult to see why the situation would be any different from today since lone parents can qualify for means-tested benefits. Field's suggestion for a generous child benefit for all children would help to encourage lone parents to take up employment and would make a benefit as of right to lone parents 'much more politically acceptable' (Field 1981, p. 191). Another area of potential difficulties is the treatment of the part-time employed. If they were to be awarded the same benefit amounts as those in full-time employment when their employment is interrupted or ceases, work incentives may well suffer. In terms of vertical redistribution of income, the scheme would not depart substantially from the present situation unless it were financed completely out of general taxation in which case it would be more redistributive, particularly in countries where most of the government revenues come from direct rather than indirect taxation.

So far, the benefits as of right scheme has received no support from any political party in either of the two countries apart from some rather guarded and lukewarm approval by the Labour Party in Britain in its recent rethinking of future policies. A discussion document by the Labour Party begins by endorsing the insurance principle but it concedes the point that

> social insurance must allow for those denied the opportunity to earn an income high enough or long enough to build up an adequate contribution record... Where necessary, payment of basic benefit should not turn on contributions but on qualification for the conditions it covers – old age, unemployment, maternity or disability. (Labour Party 1988, p. 19)

Negative Income Tax

The central idea of negative income tax schemes (NIT) is that in the same way the government collects income taxes from people when their incomes are above a certain line, it should also pay them an income subsidy when their incomes fall below that line. Put in a different way, under the present tax system, people can either pay tax if their incomes are above a certain line or not pay tax if they are below that line. Under the NIT there will be a third alternative – the government pays people a tax subsidy when their incomes are low. Over the years, a multitude of NIT proposals have been made in both countries, some aiming to replace the entire social security/income maintenance system whilst others were designed to replace only parts of it.

In essence there have been two dominant motivations behind NIT proposals, each reflecting a different ideological position. The first 'dominant' motivation, reflecting a Right-wing political position, was to reduce public expenditure while the second, reflecting a Centrist or Left-wing position, was to provide a simpler and more effective way of dealing with subsistence poverty irrespective of costs. It is for this reason that NIT proposals have come from people from across the political spectrum. A close examination of these proposals shows that they vary a great deal in generosity to the poor. Their differences centre around four main areas: the dividing line between the payment of taxes and the receipt of benefit; whether the whole difference or a certain proportion of the difference between a person's income and the entitlement income should be paid; the marginal tax rate for incomes above the dividing line; and whether the amount of benefit paid should be the same for all or whether it should vary somewhat to take account of very specific needs, as in the case of the disabled.

Debates on NIT began first in the US and the proposals attracted more academic and political attention there than in Britain. The initial NIT proposal came in 1962 from Friedman, whose opposition to government provision and whose support of the unregulated free market are well known. His general position was that private insurance should be the main line of defence against poverty but since this would prove inadequate for some people, a second line of defence was necessary to avoid poverty. Private charity would be 'in many ways the most desirable' recourse but again this would not work in the large impersonal communities of the US and therefore, reluctantly, some form of government intervention was necessary (Friedman 1962, p. 190). Such government intervention, however, should satisfy two basic criteria: it should be 'directed at helping the poor' only rather than all and sundry; and 'so far as possible the program should, while operating through the market, not distort the market or impede its functioning' (Friedman 1962, p. 191). He called his proposal a negative income tax scheme designed to replace the existing 'rag-bag of measures' and to abolish poverty at a much lower cost and with more efficiency than the existing programmes. He summarized the advantages of his proposal as follows:

> It is directed specifically at the problem of poverty. It gives help in the form most useful to the individual, namely, cash. It is general and could be substituted for the host of special measures now in effect. It makes explicit the cost borne by society. It operates outside the market. (Friedman 1962, p 192)

Under the Friedman plan, people whose incomes were so low that they need not pay taxes would receive a state subsidy of 50 per cent of the difference between their incomes and the tax-paying line. The plan encouraged recipients of NIT to work by permitting them to keep 50 per cent of their work earnings. Thus after a certain level of income from work, a break-even point was reached when recipients lost all the NIT subsidy. In brief, the Friedman plan used a very austere poverty line and equally austere conditions for NIT qualification. A non-tax-paying family of four was guaranteed an income of $1500 a year which was only one-half of the poverty line then in existence. If the family earned $1000 through work, it would lose half of it and would thus end with a combined NIT and wages of $2000. It is under these conditions that one should view Friedman's claim that his NIT proposal provided 'a floor below which no man's net income could fall' (Friedman 1962, p. 192).

Although there was considerable support for the idea of an NIT there was concern that the income guarantee under the Friedman plan was too low, especially since other income maintenance programmes would have been abolished. A series of counter-proposals were offered, all of which adopted the idea of the NIT but provided a higher guaranteed income or a reduced marginal tax rate. For example, Theobald recommended a $3200 guarantee which would be in addition to payments from income-tested programmes. He also supported government subsidization of medical care for the elderly in recognition of how medical care costs can affect the finances of those on limited income. In 1969 the Heineman Commission recommended a $2400 guarantee to qualified families of four (Patterson 1981, pp. 188–90).

Despite the support for NIT proposals Congress failed to act on any of the proposals brought before it for consideration. The inaction reflected conflicting views about the various provisions of different proposals. There was dispute about whether the guarantee was too low or too high. There was concern that a guarantee would act as a work disincentive, and considerable uneasiness still existed about the radical nature of the NIT, i.e. the provision of an income guarantee to all the poor. Finally, there was much concern about the cost attendant on offering an income guarantee to all the poor. Much of the uncertainty centred around the effort by the NIT to accomplish three objectives: the provision of an 'adequate' income guarantee; the reduction of overall programme costs; and the maintenance of work incentives. Since the same problem exists regarding proposals in Britain we shall now examine why these objectives seem so mutually exclusive.

As we can see, the NIT is a tax-related proposal because it provides an income guarantee to those who are too poor to pay taxes. Those with lowest income can receive the full guarantee; those with higher income receive less of the guarantee. Those interested in generous benefits support a high guarantee; those interested in controlling costs while providing an income guarantee support a lower guarantee. But the NIT is also tax-related because it provides for a 'marginal tax rate' (mtr). For instance under the Friedman proposal NIT recipients would keep 50 per cent of their wages, i.e. they would have been taxed at a 50 per cent rate on their earnings.

As one might anticipate, programme cost, the amount of the income guarantee and the mtr are intimately related ingredients of the NIT–and they are ingredients which are incompatible unless significant concessions are made by those who hold to all three objectives. The Friedman

NIT proposal provided an income guarantee and a work incentive because it allowed recipients to keep 50 per cent of what they earned. However, critics argued that the plan was designed to keep overall costs down by providing a low income guarantee. To correct the problem Theobald and others recommended higher income guarantees and lower marginal tax rates. Compared to the Friedman plan their recommendations would have increased the total income available to recipients. For example, increasing the guarantee to $2000 and reducing the mtr to 25 per cent would mean that working recipients earning $1000 per year would have a total income of $2750 instead of $2000 as would have been the case under Friedman's scheme. Maintaining the $1500 guarantee provided under Friedman's NIT scheme and lowering the mtr to 25 per cent would also increase the total income, albeit by a smaller amount, i.e. $2250. An NIT with these ingredients would also have increased work incentives because of the lower mtr. However, such a proposal would also have increased programme costs because of the higher income guarantee. Thus a big problem with the NIT is how to resolve the 'three distinct goals commonly associated with welfare systems: income provision, work incentives, and cost minimization' (Schiller 1980, p. 173). As Schiller notes 'these goals are worthwhile [but] mutually exclusive. We cannot move in all three directions at once' (Schiller 1980, pp. 176–77). The difficulties associated with attempting to amalgamate these choices into an acceptable political compromise stymied NIT efforts in the US and created similar problems in Britain.

Attempts were made in the US to meet the problems associated with achieving these three goals by adopting programmes which had elements of an NIT guarantee but which contained provisions designed to overcome the problems of a pure NIT proposal. However, they too floundered over the obstacles associated with achieving cost controls, adequate income guarantees, and work incentives. In 1979 President Nixon introduced a family assistance plan (FAP) as a substitute for the much hated AFDC programme. The FAP proposal was similar in many respects to the Friedman plan. Under FAP there would be a $1600 guarantee for each two-parent family of four and an mtr of 50 per cent to encourage recipients to work. A workfare programme would force recipients into a training programme. Those who refused to participate would lose their FAP benefits. But the proposal failed because of suspicion between supporters and detractors about how to accomplish programme goals. Liberals felt that the benefit was too low, objected to the workfare provisions and pointed to the futility of workfare without assuring those on the programme that employment would be available. Others, however, concerned about the costs associated with providing an income guarantee, felt that the guarantee was too high, and argued that even with workfare recipients would prefer the income guarantee to working. The opposition resulted in defeat for what had been described as the 'most ambitious effort for welfare reform [since the] creation of the welfare state in 1935' (Patterson 1981, p. 197; Aaron 1978, p. 3 et seq.).

But the drive for an NIT guarantee under the FAP proposals did create support for the passage of the Supplemental Security Income (SSI) programme in 1972. SSI provides a basic federally funded income guarantee for the poor elderly, disabled and blind. A 50 per cent mtr was included to encourage work in the unlikely event that the elderly and the incapacitated were so inclined. Before SSI federal and state programmes provided benefits to these people. Typically eligibility varied between and within states, as did amounts of benefits and their duration. The programme was hailed as a 'revolutionary right to cash income' for the elderly blind and disabled (Patterson 1981, p. 197). However, it was clear that it was easier to provide an income guarantee to the aged and the incapacitated than for needy families who were not yet considered deserving of an income guarantee.

Despite the defeat of the FAP efforts continued to provide an NIT-oriented guarantee for needy families. The Commission for National Agenda in the 1980s advocated what was in effect an NIT when it proposed a guarantee which would be three-quarters of the poverty line plus a 50 per cent mtr (Patterson 1981, pp. 203–4). The concept was adopted by President Carter, who proposed the Programme for Better Jobs and Income (PBJI). PBJI would have abolished most means-tested programmes, established an income guarantee of $4200 for a family of four, an mtr of 50 per cent, and a workfare programme for able-bodied recipients. Benefits would have been reduced if recipients refused to participate in the programme. And most importantly PBJI also recommended funding 1.4 million jobs for those unable to find work in the private labour market place. However the proposal, attacked on all sides because of usual concerns about cost, size of the guarantee and work incentives, was also defeated (Patterson 1981, pp. 206–7).

By the early 1980s support for proposals which incorporated the elements of the NIT had disappeared. Martin Anderson, an advisor to Presidents Nixon and Reagan, wrote that proposals for 'radical reform [i.e. the NIT] come essentially from a small group of committed ideologues who want to institute a guaranteed income under the guise of welfare reform' (Anderson 1978, p. 67). NIT proposals, he charged, underestimated the negative impact on work incentives which he suggested would be as much as 50 per cent. The estimate was at odds with studies of NIT experiments in a number of US states which found little impact on work incentives. Focusing specifically on the difficulty of achieving cost reductions and work incentives under such programmes Anderson noted that NIT proposals:

> have three basic parts that are politically sensitive to a high degree. The first is the basic benefit level... The second is the degree to which the program affects the incentive of a person on welfare to find work or earn more; the third is the additional cost to the taxpayers......
>
> To become a political reality the plan must provide a decent level of support for those on welfare, it must contain strong incentives to work, and it must have a reasonable cost. *And it must do all three at the same time.* If any one of these is missing or deficient the reform plan is nakedly vulnerable to anyone who wishes to attack and condemn it. (Anderson 1978, p. 135)

The political tide had turned completely against NIT and by 1980 even Friedman had to concede that 'our proposals are not currently feasible politically'. He rightly insisted, however, that 'what is not politically feasible today may become politically feasible tomorrow' (Friedman and Friedman 1980, p. 157).

Despite some early flirtations with partial NIT schemes, the Left in Britain has always been, on the whole, hostile to means-tested schemes even when administered in non-stigmatizing ways. Thus the Labour Party in its election manifesto for 1964 proposed a variant of NIT in an attempt to reduce the extent of personal, individual means testing for the elderly and widows. When the Labour Party was elected to government in the same year, however, the proposal was abandoned in favour of liberalizing reform of means-tested assistance benefits. Interestingly enough, the Labour Party's NIT variant proposal envisaged a 100 per cent supplementation rate, rather than 50 per cent as on the Friedman plan. A year later in 1965 the Child Poverty Action Group, a poverty pressure group, examined an NIT proposal for working families with children but again abandoned it in favour of higher universal child benefits (Barker 1971, p. 46). The Left in Britain has always favoured universal benefits as the main method of provision using means-tested benefits where necessary within this universalist framework. The Labour Minister of Social Security in 1967 expressed the dominant Left opposition to NIT schemes and other means-tested benefits when she claimed that: 'NIT would be a direct, explicit subsidy to wages; it would involve a tacit acceptance of the evils and inequalities which produce "haves" and "have-nots"; it would have harmful effects on incentives; and it would provide no help for those just above the line' (Barker 1971, p. 49). These are objections of principle and they are in addition to several other objections of administrative nature.

The first detailed proposal for an NIT in Britain was put forward by Lees in 1967. Apart from the fact that it was only a partial scheme confined to working families with children, the Lees proposal had all the hallmarks of the Friedman scheme: its subsidy rate and its marginal tax rate were both set at 50 per cent. Lees, however, was very conscious of the possible administrative difficulties and unintended consequences of his scheme: 'Such a scheme', he wrote, 'is without doubt fiscally feasible. Whether it is administratively feasible and would have the effect intended is quite another matter' (Lees 1967, p. 14). Lees's proposal was warmly received by various prominent figures within the Conservative Party and for almost a decade the NIT or different variants of it were seriously considered within the Conservative Party. Barker concludes his survey of NIT and the Conservative Party in the early 1970s by saying 'I have been unable to find any Conservative who has argued against the scheme, and the party's 1970 election manifesto, without making a firm commitment, expressed support for the idea' (Barker 1971, p. 48). Indeed in 1972 the Conservative government published a Green Paper for the introduction of a tax credit scheme – a variant of NIT – but went no further since it lost the election two years later. By the late 1970s, the Conservative Party lost interest in the NIT and the Thatcher government of the 1980s never raised the issue again.

In Britain today only the two Centre parties are committed to the NIT scheme as well as several academics of the Right and Centre. Like the US, Britain has toyed with the concept of an NIT but has gradually turned its back on it. The reasons for this loss of interest in the NIT are similar to those in the US discussed earlier and need not be repeated at length. As Deacon and Bradshaw comment: 'The twin problems of administrative feasibility and incentives raise serious doubts about the viability of the NIT proposal' (Deacon and Bradshaw 1983, p. 185). They could have also added such other reasons as fears of gradually escalating costs from the Right and ideological objections to wholesale means testing from the Left.

How, then, does NIT measure up to our five criteria of evaluation? To begin with, can it abolish poverty as officially defined? The simple answer is that it all depends on the detailed provisions included in the NIT scheme. To abolish poverty, an NIT scheme must have the following features: it must see that the dividing line between paying taxes and receiving subsidies equals the official poverty line; it must provide for a 100 per cent subsidy between a person's income, if any, and the dividing line; and it must include a payment for actual or reasonable housing costs that can vary from one individual recipient to another. In other words, only the most generous of NIT proposals can hope to abolish poverty. What about the overall cost of an NIT scheme? Obviously the more generous the provisions of a scheme, the higher its costs. But how would the costs of an NIT scheme that abolishes poverty on the lines suggested above compare with current social security/income maintenance expenditure? In Britain the costs will be lower even if one assumes a 100 per cent take-up rate of NIT simply because under the existing insurance and assistance benefit network only a small proportion of the population – around 5 per cent – have incomes below the official poverty line while benefits are paid to a much higher proportion of the population whose incomes would still be well above the poverty line without the receipt of benefits. In the US, Table 3.1 showed that while the proportion of the population in official poverty before the receipt of benefits was 24 per cent – the pre-transfer figure – the corresponding proportion after the receipt of benefits was 15 per cent in 1983, a decline of only 9 per cent. Bearing in mind the overall total costs of the US income maintenance/social security budget it must mean that a large part of it is taken up by persons who would not be in official poverty without it. The conclusion, therefore, must be the same as for the British situation, i.e. an NIT scheme that abolished poverty in the US would not be more costly than the current system. What of the effects of NIT on work incentives, i.e. on whether people opt out of the labour force or on whether they reduce their hours of work? As mentioned earlier, the higher the marginal tax rates, the greater the risk of work incentives suffering and *vice versa*. If the cost of the NIT scheme is to be kept lower than that of current social security schemes, marginal tax rates will need to be high. Yet research evidence from the NIT experiments in the US suggest that work incentives did not prove a significant problem (Haveman and Watts 1977; Hall 1975). A similar conclusion was reached by a government study in Britain of the effects of state subsidy of wages under the government's family credit scheme (DHSS 1975). People's involvement in the labour market is affected not only be economic considerations but by social and psychological reasons as well. As for the issue of vertical redistribution of income, an NIT scheme will be more redistributive than the present system partly because benefits will only be paid to those with no or low incomes and partly because the scheme will be financed out of general taxation rather than through a combination of insurance contributions and general taxation as at present. Since, however, NIT subsidies will be made only to those with low incomes, some of the vertical redistribution will be from those just above the poverty line, i.e. from the almost poor, to the poor. It is because of this, together with its institutionalized poverty traps, that the NIT is seen by the Left as shoring up the existing unequal social structure. Finally, what of the administrative complexities of the scheme? An NIT which replaces all existing benefits and contributions will obviously be simpler than the existing system. Yet it will not be as simple as many of its protagonists maintain for three main reasons, the first of which is that if it is to meet the needs of recipients, it must respond speedily to their changing circumstances. Thus annual assessments of income and benefit are not sufficient – they have to be readjusted as often as necessary to take account of the changing circumstances of individual beneficiaries. Second, if the scheme is to meet some or all of a person's housing costs – as the current system in Britain does – then it will need to be concerned not only about a person's income but also about 'appropriate' housing costs, which adds another complexity. Finally, some of the NIT proposals envisage benefits which vary slightly from one client group to another, reflecting different needs. Thus benefits for the disabled, under some schemes, are higher than those for the unemployed. Moreover, some NIT proposals, like those of the Social Democratic Party in Britain, provide for reduced benefits to those just above the dividing line in an effort to make the system 'fairer'. To summarize, a generous NIT scheme can abolish poverty as officially defined; it will be less complex and its costs will not be higher than existing schemes; it runs some risk of undermining work incentives; it institutionalizes poverty traps and it leaves the existing income and wealth distribution unaltered.

Basic Income Scheme

The idea of providing a basic income scheme was first put forward in Britain in 1942 by Lady Rhys Williams as a response to the Beveridge Report. It subsequently disappeared from public debate for over two decades, resurfaced briefly in the late 1960s and has made a strong comeback in the 1980s. The scheme enjoys an elegant simplicity that no other proposal approaches. Every man, woman and child, irrespective of income, employment status, family position or any other criterion, would receive a weekly grant from the state adequate for basic subsistence. Additional benefits would be paid for such special needs as disability or very advanced age but children would receive lower benefits than adults. The basic income will replace all other benefits as well as all tax allowances. The only exception to this is housing benefit which will still need to be paid on a means-tested basis. The scheme will also mean the abolition of insurance contributions since it will be funded from general taxation. The basic income benefit itself will not be taxable but, obviously, all income above it will be liable to taxation.

Its advocates see numerous advantages in it. One of the early advocates of the 1980s claimed 12 such advantages (Ashby 1984, pp. 8–9), many of which have been advanced by subsequent supporters in Britain and in Europe in books, articles and in the journal of the Basic Income Research Group.

1. The scheme would achieve greater 'social equality' than the existing system of benefits simply because it will be a benefit payable to all without means tests, insurance contribution conditions or any other criterion. It is part of the wider social policy debate which has always claimed that universal services improve social cohesion and individual self-respect while conditional services, and means-tests in particular, exacerbate social divisions in society and stigmatize service users. It is one of those claims which is difficult to put to the empirical test though the limited research evidence does suggest that means-tested services and benefits tend to stigmatize recipients particularly when they are administered without sufficient thoughtfulness and tact.

2. It would put an end to the poverty trap simply because the receipt of benefit does not result in any deduction from earnings or incomes from other sources. In this respect, it differs from an NIT scheme which inevitably involves marginal tax rates. While the NIT provides a ceiling above which many families find it difficult to go, the basic income provides a floor on which people can build through their work, savings and so on.

3. It would promote equality and independence of women *vis-à-vis* men within the household. Under the current system and under

the NIT , the family or the household is treated as a unit and any benefit paid is for all its members whilst under a basic income scheme each member will receive his or her own benefit. Children's benefits will be paid to their parents, most probably the mother, up to the age of 16, after which they will be paid to them. Bearing in mind the evidence about the dominance of the father in the distribution of income within the family, the basic income will certainly give women greater independence.

4. It 'should remove the disincentives to unemployed people taking up employment' (Ashby 1984, p. 16). The reason for this is that under the present scheme any unemployed person receiving benefit can only earn a small amount through part-time employment before his benefit is reduced. This will no longer apply under the basic income scheme though it is possible that an unemployed person may take up part-time employment without declaring it not because of fear of losing some or part of his basic income benefit but because he will be taxed on his work earnings.

5. It would encourage more flexibility in the labour market, particularly for disadvantaged groups. In a sense this is similar to the fourth argument but extended to groups other than the unemployed. It is also slightly different in the sense that a basic income scheme will encourage people to supplement their benefit through part-time work to the extent that they consider it necessary. This is particularly useful for lone mothers, retired persons and so on.

6. It would create more jobs and thus ease the problem of unemployment. The logic behind this is that employers 'would no longer be required to pay the subsistence component of income' (Ashby 1984, p. 17), i.e. they would feel free to pay lower wages. This is a rather dubious argument since it assumes that the scheme would not involve higher taxation than today. If it did, then workers would be demanding higher wages to enable them to maintain their standard of living.

7. It would encourage employers to retain their labour force intact rather than introduce new technology without undermining their competitiveness. In this respect unemployment will be checked without loss of productivity or profits. Again this is a dubious argument for it is based on the assumptions of the previous claim.

8. It would make it possible for governments to increase the standard of living of everyone as the economy grows. In other words,

instead of the benefits accruing to employers and to workers in the most dynamic sectors of the economy, the government would raise the level of the basic income benefit for all, presumably by keeping down wage rises in the dynamic sectors of the economy. This would require a great deal of government intervention in wage negotiations and it has the added disadvantage that it may discourage work effort in the profitable sectors of the economy.

9. It would encourage more flexible patterns of training and higher education since individuals can use their benefit to finance themselves through training schemes and college education when they consider best suitable to themselves either on a part-time or full-time basis. In theory this appears a reasonable claim though it is difficult to know how people will actually behave in a real situation.

10. It should find support not only among employers but among trade unions as well, thus securing a broad base of support in society. We have already referred to the possible attitude of employers. As far as the unions are concerned, Ashby admits that it is not all that certain that they will all support a basic income scheme since many of them prefer a minimum wage and some of them see it as a threat to their bargaining power.

11. It would not be more costly than the existing system of benefits and tax allowances. This is certainly an erroneous claim because all other advocates of the scheme accept that it will be more costly. This is not necessarily the same as saying that Britain or the US cannot afford it but in terms of present-day expenditure the scheme will make greater demands on resources. It is for this reason that many supporters of the scheme, including the Basic Income Research Group, accept that at present only a partial basic income can be acceptable in terms of costs (Walter 1989; Parker 1989). A full basic income in Britain, i.e. one whose level of benefit is equivalent to the official poverty line, would require a tax rate on all other income, apart from the benefit, 'of at least 70% (Basic Income Research Group 1989, p. 6). Such a rate of taxation will not only be unacceptable but it will affect work incentives for many people.

12. It will abolish poverty and it will reduce inequalities in society. This will certainly be the case particularly if it is accompanied, as it must be, by a housing benefit as discussed earlier under the NIT.

As expected, the two main political parties in Britain have shown no interest in the basic income scheme. The current leader of the Liberal Democratic Party, however, endorsed the idea of a basic income but pointed out that at present only a partial scheme could be introduced partly because of costs but also because of fears that a full basic income might be seen as a threat to the security of some of the existing benefit recipients (Ashdown 1990, pp. 5–6). The discussion has concentrated on the British situation because no interest has so far been shown in a basic income scheme in the US of the type discussed here.

How then does the basic income scheme stand up to our five criteria? First, it will certainly abolish poverty; second, it will reduce inequalities considerably; third, the scheme will be easier and cheaper to administer than the other schemes discussed so far; fourth, it will be more costly than all the other schemes – in fact so costly that political support for it at present is non-existent. As far as its effects on incentives are concerned, it is difficult to be certain but a great deal will depend on how it is administered. Purdy, for example, argues that the benefit should be paid unconditionally without any legal obligation on able-bodied adults to take up employment on grounds of practicality and on matters of principle (Purdy 1988, p. 196). Such an approach is likely to increase problems of work incentives. It is based on a very liberal interpretation of the notion of citizenship. Interpreted more precisely, however, the notion of citizenship implies that people have both rights and duties in a society and the fulfilment of one presupposes the fulfilment of the other.

In conclusion, a basic income scheme would reduce inequalities and abolish poverty far more effectively than the other schemes discussed so far. It will also form the foundations for a more socially cohesive and caring society 'with a universal basis of inclusive citizenship' (Jordan 1988, p. 121). It is this ethical and egalitarian streak that makes the basic income scheme the favourite among radicals of the Centre and Left in Britain. Its Achilles heel is its high costs and hence high taxation rates. This makes it even less politically feasible than the other two comprehensive proposals discussed so far.

Starting Even Scheme

This proposal has recently been put forward by Haveman in the US and it reflects the country's search for an anti-poverty policy that combines labour market programmes and income maintenance benefits (Haveman 1988). This approach is in clear contrast with the other three schemes we have discussed which seek to abolish poverty almost exclusively through income transfers. The explanation for this approach lies in the widespread belief in the US that the income maintenance/social security system has, at best, reduced poverty and, at worst, made the problem worse. We saw in the previous chapter how writers such as Gilder, Murray and others blame the income maintenance/social security system for the country's poverty and other problems and how they see the solution to these problems as lying in the virtual disbanding of the whole income transfer network.

Many US writers do not see government programmes in these bleak terms. Haveman points out that government programmes, despite their weaknesses, have had an overall positive effect on US society – they 'reduced individual insecurity and uncertainty, reduced poverty and inequality, and [resulted in] an improved social and political environment' (Haveman 1988, p. 144). Nevertheless, he maintains that there is nothing to be gained by expanding further these programmes because 'we have about exhausted the poverty–inequality–insecurity reduction potential of the taxation–income transfer strategy', (Haveman 1988, p. 145). Hence a new approach is needed, one which combines the pursuit of equality with efficiency, one which attempts to give all citizens an even start in life.

Haveman's scheme consists of five interrelated strands combining government programmes in the labour market, in education and training as well as income transfers. The first strand of his scheme, reminiscent of the NIT, proposes what is in effect an income guarantee through a tax credit for low-income families, both one- and two-parent. The amount of the subsidy would vary according to the size and composition of the family and the degree of its financial need. Those with minimum income would receive a subsidy which would be 'one-half to two-thirds of the poverty level' set by the government (Haveman 1988, p. 157). Families with incomes above the minimum would receive smaller subsidies while 'better-off families would receive no net payment at all' (Haveman 1988, p. 157). Arguments for this proposal are similar to those used by advocates of the basic income, i.e. that it would increase work incentives, 'strip away the complexity of the melange of current programs', remove the stigma attached to existing means-tested programmes, and 'increase equity' (Haveman 1988, p. 158). The guarantee is obviously designed to reduce poverty among the poorest families in the US and reflects an effort to abandon the selectivity of the US AFDC programme which has traditionally provided money only to single-parent families but at varying rates because of state and local government control over the programme.

Haveman offers a second level of income guarantee, i.e. 'an above-poverty minimum for working citizens who have retired' (Haveman 1988, p. 163). One objective of the guarantee is to help the new category of elders who are in poverty because they receive low benefits or are not covered by the retirement system. Among those who fall into this category of poor elderly are widows of husbands with poor work histories as well as minority groups, e.g. black elderly who also have been unable to make significant contributions to the social security fund and therefore receive low or no benefits. However, the plan would result in pension reductions for well-off recipients to induce people to save for their retirement, to encourage the development of private pension schemes, government-regulated to assure their adequacy, and encourage retirees to work by reducing the marginal tax rate. The proposal is highly controversial because it would substitute a minimum income guarantee for earnings-related benefits.

A third aspect of income guarantee is recommended to relieve the problem of children's poverty. Thus a 'universal child-support system' for children in mother-only families is offered to reduce the high incidence of poverty in these families. The new policy would require 'absent parents' to provide for their children by subjecting them to a 'child-support tax' which would be based on their earnings and the number of children who need support. Revenues from the tax, withheld by the employer, would go directly to the needy children or their custodian. Public funds would be available if support from the absent parent was less than 'a social minimum level'. The object of the proposal is to correct 'the last decade's neglect of children' (Haveman 1988, p. 165).

A fourth part of income guarantee would be made available to relieve poverty among youths in the US, especially minority youths. Thus Haveman proposes a 'universal capital grant' of $20 000 which would be given to 18-year-olds. The money would be used as a reserve from which individuals could draw to help acquire adequate education, medical care and work experience. Haveman offers the grant as an alternative to existing 'paternalistic subsidy schemes', and suggests that the new approach will 'go far toward reducing a major set of inequalities in the U.S. society' (Haveman 1988, p. 169).

A final piece in this ambitious plan to revamp the US system of government transfers is designed to help minorities, youths, disabled workers and single mothers whose skills and education are too poor to enable them to compete successfully in the job market and whose wages are too low to provide them with an adequate standard of living. Haveman offers a programme of subsidized employment as the means for improving wages of people in these groups. Under the plan public funds would be available to subsidize the earnings of low-wage workers and tax credits would be given to encourage employers to hire unskilled workers. The employment subsidy for 'disadvantaged workers' would make 'marginal workers' available at low cost to the employer; increase the wages of low-skilled workers; be more cost-effective than alternative policies which attempt to meet the problem by creating jobs or through public works employment. And of especial importance, the plan would 'reduce inequality in employment and earnings in a way that encourages independent work, and initiative' (Haveman 1988, p. 168).

The Haveman proposals are the most radical reform ideas current but there are other proposals which also offer sweeping recommendations for an even start for all Americans (Ellwood 1988; Lerman, 1988; Ford Foundation 1989). They all share the belief that the new approach needed to deal with poverty should not rely exclusively on income transfers but it should on the one hand make it possible for individuals, through the labour market, to become independent and on the other to use income transfers both as a means towards this end and as a way of helping those who do not make it. How do the Haveman proposals measure up to our five criteria? First, will they abolish poverty as officially defined? They will certainly go a long way towards that goal but some poverty will remain. Since the tax credit will at best amount to only 75 per cent of the poverty line, there will be many who may not be able to make the remaining 25 per cent through their own effort. The restriction of child benefits to mother-only families is another weakness of the scheme for it assumes that wages are always sufficient for family needs. The proposals for education and training are important but they assume that somehow low-paid jobs will disappear when people are better educated and trained. Our discussion in Chapter 4 showed that this is not always the case. So long as there are low-paid jobs there will be low-paid people, however high education or training standards may be. As far as work and saving incentives are concerned, the scheme goes a long way towards ensuring that they do not suffer. The greater role of general taxes in funding the scheme and the replacement of earnings-related with flat-rate benefits combine to make the scheme vertically redistributive. The extra cost of the proposals, according to Haveman's calculations, will be very modest indeed – about '1 per cent increase in federal government expenditures' (Haveman 1988, p. 177). Finally, the scheme will be administratively less complex than the present largely because it lays down national scales of benefit for families instead of the wide state variations that exist today under the AFDC programme. All in all, the Haveman proposals add up to a well thought-out strategy for reducing poverty in the US even though they might not be of much relevance to other countries.

CONCLUSION

Our examination of current policies and of reform proposals leads to several general conclusions. First, the current complex system of benefits has contributed to the reduction of poverty over the years in both countries. Second, a continuation or even expansion of the current systems will not lead to any further reductions in poverty simply because they are not directly and mainly concerned with poverty reduction. There is, therefore, a very urgent need to rethink the underlying principles in order to create a system that has poverty reduction as its main concern. Third, all four schemes discussed in the previous section will be more effective than the current system in reducing poverty. Indeed, all four schemes will virtually abolish poverty, as it is officially defined. Fourth, the abstract choice between these four schemes depends on how well they perform on the other criteria, apart from poverty reduction, that we discussed. Those who make the control of costs the second primary consideration after poverty reduction will opt for the NIT scheme. Those who make the reduction of inequality the second primary consideration will support the basic income scheme. Those who make the reduction of inequality and the control of costs equal second consideration will lend their support to either the benefits as of right or the starting even scheme. Though the NIT does reduce inequality, it tends to do so at the expense of those whose incomes are just above the poverty line and who, in a real sense, are not that much better off than the poor. Moreover, the NIT scheme is likely to affect incentives more than the other schemes. Fifth, the real choice, as distinct from the abstract choice, must also take into account the political realities and the historical circumstances of the two countries. Britain has had a more fully developed national insurance/assistance system than the US and can, therefore, proceed more easily along the benefits as of right scheme. The US has always stressed not only income transfers but education, training and the labour market as avenues for poverty reduction and hence the starting even scheme reflects these traditional practices. Both countries have flirted with and rejected the NIT scheme and neither country is anywhere near ready to take up the challenge and the possibilities of a basic income scheme. Finally, we recognize that the recommendation for a benefit as of right scheme for Britain and the starting even scheme for the US is not likely to meet with strong political support at present. Yet incremental changes, which are more acceptable politically, are not likely to do much to reduce poverty. Trying to reconcile political feasibility with the poverty reduction potential of a scheme poses endless dilemmas. Our analysis of the causes of poverty and of the policy proposals leads us to the firm conclusion that nothing less than a radical reform of existing programmes along the lines discussed in this section will reduce poverty. Excessive fascination with political feasibility and with disjointed incrementalism only serves to perpetuate the current high rates of poverty that exist in both Britain and the US.

6. Conclusion

In this final chapter, we bring together the main conclusions that emerge from the previous chapters, we compare and contrast the situation in the two countries and we look briefly at the possible developments in the two countries during the final decade of the twentieth century.

POVERTY IN BRITAIN AND THE US

Research and debate on poverty have a long tradition in both Britain and the US perhaps more so than in most other advanced industrial societies. From the very early research studies of poverty at the turn of the century to present-day studies, opinions have differed on the definition of poverty. In general, however, the trend has been to move away from subsistence to relative definitions in both countries. Chapter 1 attempted to go beyond this dichotomy of definitions, subsistence versus relative, by placing the various perceptions of poverty along a continuum of want ranging from starvation, to subsistence, to social coping and finally to social participation. Each definition signifies a particular degree of severity of want ranging from the harshest to the mildest. This approach to poverty can be used to study and compare the extent of poverty over time in the same country and comparatively between countries today. Without this continuum of definitions, historical studies can lead to such misleading conclusions that the extent of poverty – differently defined – has not declined over the years, or even worse, that the extent of poverty in Britain or the US is similar to that of India or Kenya. Thus the classification of definitions adopted in Chapter 1 fills a gap in the literature of poverty.

Irrespective of how poverty is defined, it is necessary to operationalize (translate into monetary terms) the definition as precisely as possible if it is going to be useful to research, informed debate and policy making. In other words, one has to express as precisely as one can what starvation, or subsistence poverty and so on add up to. A poverty line has to be established above which people are not in poverty and below which they are, irrespective of whether one refers to poverty as starvation, subsistence, social coping or social participation. Dividing lines are easy targets of attack because the conditions of those just above the line are not that much different from the conditions of those just below it. Yet without dividing lines there can be little meaningful discussion. Over time, three different methodological approaches have been used in the construction of poverty lines: the professional, the consumption and the public opinion approach. Each has its strengths and weaknesses and, as Chapter 1 argued, cannot by itself provide an adequate methodology for the construction of a soundly based poverty line. A combination of all three methodologies is needed even though one may be the dominant. Thus the professional may play the dominant role in the operationalization of what constitutes starvation but it needs to take into account the consumption patterns of the society to which it refers.

Lengthy debates on definitional and methodological issues can divert attention from more important poverty issues: its extent, depth, distribution, persistence, causation and abolition. Clearly, the extent of poverty in Britain or the US varies according to the severity of the definition used. Defined as hunger or starvation, poverty has declined very substantially in both countries over time but the sad fact is that it still persists in both countries to a small extent. It rubs shoulders with immense and glaring opulence, particularly in the inner city areas. No one who walks through the streets of London or New York can fail to notice the manifold centres of opulence and luxury cheek by jowl with a multitude of desperate forms of existence – begging, homelessness, soup kitchens at Christmas, sleeping rough under the railway arches and so on. These are two worlds apart, reminiscent of Disraeli's two nations in Victorian Britain. The tragedy of this situation is compounded by the fact that it has come to be accepted and often to be blamed on the victims. The very poor have been marginalized and their plight evokes the ritual response of charitable provision during Christmas and suchlike public holidays.

Defined as subsistence, poverty is quite widespread in both countries and it is, of course, even more widespread when defined as social coping or social participation. Most of the data on poverty in Chapters 2 and 3 are based on the official definitions of poverty and these reflect subsistence definitions which the public considers to be too low. Thus, in a recent study of poverty in London, Townsend and Gordon found that when respondents were asked to estimate how much income a family or a person needed 'to keep out of poverty' the vast majority gave figures that were higher than the official poverty line. The figures given varied according to various household types but the average amount given for all household types was 61 per cent higher than the official poverty line (Townsend and Gordon 1990, table 3, p. 9).

Though the official poverty lines of the two countries refer to subsistence, they are not strictly comparable. It is not only that what are considered basic needs and basic levels of satisfaction vary between the two countries, but also because such other services as housing and health differ so much between the two countries that they affect the poor differently. Thus health care in Britain is provided free of charge to the poor within the National Health Service which covers the entire population. In the US, however, there is no National Health Service covering the whole population and including the poor. Instead the twin systems of Medicare and Medicaid provide free medical care to most people but not to all. The Medicaid programme provides medical assistance for certain groups of people with low incomes but it varies considerably from one state to another. As an official publication puts it: 'Within broad Federal guidelines, each State determines its own eligibility requirements; the amount, duration, and scope of services; the rate of reimbursement for services; and administers its own program. The Medicaid programs vary considerably from State to State' (Social Security Administration 1989, p. 48). The net result is not only patchy coverage and uneven standards but, worse still, not all the poor receive medical assistance under this programme.

The differences in housing subsidies between the two countries are equally striking. In Britain, people whose incomes are on or below the official poverty line will have, by and large, their housing costs met largely by the central government irrespective of whether they live in privately rented accommodation, in council housing or even if they are buying their own house. Without going into details, the situation is very different in the US. There is no national scheme for meeting the housing costs of people with low incomes. Instead there is a variety of publicly or privately owned housing projects supported by government subsidies for housing the poor. Such schemes, however, vary tremendously from one state to another and the coverage, even in the most generous states, is inadequate compared with the national housing subsidy scheme of Britain.

In brief, the official poverty figures for the two countries do not reflect accurately the differences in either the extent or the severity of poverty in the two countries. Nevertheless, the figures presented in Chapters 2 and 3 showed that the extent of official poverty in the US has been higher than in Britain for the entire period covered by this study. In 1985, at least one in twenty persons in Britain and at least one in seven persons in the US were in poverty, using the official definitions of the two countries. Interestingly enough, however, postwar trends in the prevalence of poverty followed very similar patterns in the two countries. Poverty went largely unnoticed during the 1950s, it became a very lively issue during the 1960s and early 1970s when it also declined, and it was pushed to the background of the political agenda during the 1980s when it rose again to the levels of the early 1960s. All this lends support to the thesis that economic growth by itself does not abolish poverty. Economic growth is not like a tide that raises all boats. It obviously increases the wealth of the country as a whole but it can leave some groups unaffected and even worse-off. The millions of workers made redundant in the 1980s in order to bolster the rate of economic growth couldn't have benefited very much from the experience. Government policies are indispensable for the reduction let alone the abolition of poverty.

The higher incidence of poverty in the US is also shown by the Luxembourg Income Study which defined persons as being in poverty if their net incomes were less than one-half of the national equivalent income. In this way, the poverty line is standardized as the same proportion of the prevailing net average income per person in the country. Table 6.1 shows that the US has the highest overall poverty, the highest poverty among single-parent families and among other families. It also has the second highest poverty rate, after Israel, in relation to elderly families and two-parent families.

COMPOSITION AND RISK OF POVERTY

Poverty risks are higher in the US than in Britain not because problems are more intractable but because its income maintenance/social security system is less well developed as an anti-poverty system. While Britain's social security system involves two national safety nets – the insurance and the assistance systems – plus a system of child benefits, the US system is made up of several insurance systems, an even larger number of state assistance systems and makes no provisions for child benefits. We have already shown in Chapters 2 and 3 that the British

Table 6.1 Percentage of persons in poverty, 1979

Country	Total population	Elderly families	Single-parent families	Two-parent families	Other families
	%	%	%	%	%
Sweden	5.0	0.1	9.2	5.0	7.0
UK	8.8	18.1	29.1	6.5	4.1
Israel	14.5	23.8	11.8	14.9	5.5
US	16.9	20.5	51.7	12.9	9.8
Norway	4.8	4.6	12.6	3.4	5.7
Canada	12.1	11.5	37.5	11.0	8.5
W. Germany	6.0	9.3	18.1	3.9	5.4
Average	9.7	12.7	24.3	8.2	6.6

Source: Smeeding, O'Higgins and Rainwater 1990, table 3.4, p. 65.

Table 6.2 Role of taxation and social security benefits in reducing poverty among families with children, 1979–81

Country	Poverty rates			Overall reduction
	Pre-tax/ pre-transfer	Post-tax/ pre-transfer	Post tax/ post-transfer	
	%	%	%	%
Australia	17.6	19.9	15.0	14.8
Canada	13.6	14.4	8.6	36.8
W. Germany	7.9	15.0	6.9	12.7
Norway	12.1	15.9	6.4	47.1
Sweden	10.4	22.5	4.4	57.7
Switzerland	4.4	6.2	4.1	6.8
UK	14.1	20.6	8.5	39.7
US	16.6	18.0	13.8	16.9

Source: US House of Representatives, Committee on Ways and Means 1989, table 15, p. 957.

system is more successful in reducing pre-transfer poverty than its US counterpart using the official definitions of poverty. The picture remains much the same if poverty is defined in standardization terms, i.e. net personal income below one-half of net median income per person, as Table 6.2 shows.

Beginning with those in full-time employment, poverty risks are higher in the US because, unlike the British system, that system does not provide a benefit that supplements the low wages of men or women with children. It is true that the US provides a national minimum wage whilst Britain has a partial one but a minimum wage without adequate child benefits is not a very good protection against poverty. Similarly, children run a higher poverty risk in the US than in Britain because of the absence of child benefits except through the very limited provisions of the AFDC programme. Indeed the US is almost alone in this among advanced industrial societies and a universal child benefit system is long overdue for every child in the US. In a comparison of the treatment of the retired/disabled, the unemployed and the low-paid full-time workers by the US social security system, Ellwood concludes that the low-paid receive by far the worst deal. Indeed, they get very little from the social security system apart from food stamps. As he summarizes the position:

> Worst of all is the treatment of the full-time working poor. Even though these families start out less poor than those in other categories, they get so little aid that they are actually the poorest group after transfers. Over a third have no medical protection, and those who have some protection often have to purchase it with their already limited income. (Ellwood 1988, p. 100)

It is a reflection of the belief that opportunities do exist for those at work to increase their earnings if only they tried harder.

The unemployed are treated more severely than other groups of beneficiaries in both countries but particularly so in the US with its stronger tradition of individualism. In both countries there is an unemployment insurance benefit for those with an adequate insurance contribution record but this is as far as the similarity goes. In Britain the scheme is national while in the US the individual states have a great deal of freedom in devising their own regulations governing eligibility, duration and amount of benefit. As a result, only about one-third of the unemployed were receiving unemployment benefit in 1988; the maximum length of period was 39 weeks but with many states falling well below that usually to 26 weeks; and with an average weekly amount of benefit ranging from $77 in Puerto Rico, $100 in Mississippi to $186 in Columbia and $182 in Michigan. In 1988, the poverty line for a family of three persons was $9428 dollars and for a family of four persons, $12 088 per annum (US House of Representatives, Committee on Ways and Means 1989, table 7, p. 451 and table 1, p. 941). The implication of this is that the weekly unemployment benefit was well below the poverty line for a family of four in all states and below that of a family of three in all but three of the states. Thus when the level of the benefit and the fact that only one-third of the unemployed receive that benefit are considered together, the gross inadequacy of the insurance scheme becomes apparent. This applies to a lesser extent to the British insurance scheme but with the big difference that those who do not qualify for it will, if they have no other substantial income, receive an assistance benefit which is about the same in amount. In the US most of those who fall through the insurance net will fall on hard times and live in poverty. The point has to be made that this harsher treatment of the unemployed is not due to the greater incidence of unemployment. Using the OECD definition, unemployment in the US for the 1980s averaged 7.5 per cent of the labour force compared to 10.1 per cent in the UK. As with the low-paid, it is traditional national attitudes towards work and self-support that account for the US way of treating the unemployed.

In both countries the incidence of one-parenthood has increased considerably so that today one-parent families, headed mostly by women, make up about 15 per cent of all families in Britain and about 25 per cent in the US. Again, both countries provide an insurance benefit for widowed families but all other one-parent families have to rely on the means-tested assistance benefit scheme. In Britain, mothers are under no pressure from the government to go out to work and those who have no other substantial sources of income will qualify for an assistance benefit that will bring them up to the official poverty line. In the US there is greater pressure on mothers to go out to work and the AFDC assistance programme varies in generosity from one state to another. Thus in 1989 a one-parent family of three persons received AFDC benefits that were below the poverty threshold in all states ranging from 11 per cent of the poverty threshold in Puerto Rico and 15 per cent in Alabama to 84 per cent in California (US House of Representatives, Committee on Ways and Means 1989, table 9, p. 539). Even when the value of food stamps is added to the AFDC benefit, only three states reach the poverty threshold.

It is, therefore, no surprise that the risk of poverty among one-parent families is higher in the US than in Britain. Moreover, the prospects of improvement are rather dim at present in view of the increasing criticism from the new Right that benefits are the main cause for the rise in one-parenthood. Yet, as Table 6.1 showed, the US has the highest proportion of one-parent families in poverty among advanced industrial societies. The role of subsistence benefits in the creation of one-parenthood is negligible compared to such other factors as better employment opportunities for women, changed sexual mores and easier divorce laws. The harsher policies of the US reflect again traditional values as well as vague fears stemming from the very high incidence of one-parenthood among black families – half of all black families with children were headed by the mother only in 1984. The net effect of US policies is that a very high proportion of children in one-parent families live in poverty. When this is combined with the poverty rates of children in two-parent families, the US exhibits the highest poverty rate of children among advanced industrial societies, as Table 6.3 shows. Thus, whether poverty is defined in standardized terms as in Table 6.3, or in terms of national definitions, as in Tables 2.3 and 3.5, one-parent families run a higher risk of being in poverty in the US than in Britain.

In both countries, expenditures on the elderly are by far the single main item in the social security budget. This, together with projections

Table 6.3   Poverty rates among children by family type, 1979–81

Country	One-parent	Two-parent	Other	All types
	%	%	%	%
Australia	65.0	12.4	10.6	16.9
Canada	38.7	6.8	5.5	9.6
Germany, F.R.	35.1	4.9	12.1	8.2
Norway	21.6	4.4	12.7	7.6
Sweden	8.6	4.5	.5	5.1
Switzerland	12.9	4.1	3.8	5.1
UK	38.6	9.5	2.5	10.7
US	51.0	9.4	16.2	17.1

Source: US House of Representatives, Committee on Ways and Means 1989, table 14, p. 957.

Table 6.4   Population aged 65 and over as % of total population

Country	1980	2000	2010	2020	2050
Australia	9.6	11.7	12.6	15.4	19.4
France	14.0	15.3	16.3	19.5	22.3
Germany	15.5	17.1	20.4	21.7	24.5
Italy	13.5	15.3	17.3	19.4	22.6
Japan	9.1	15.2	18.6	20.9	22.3
Sweden	16.3	16.6	17.5	20.8	21.4
UK	14.9	14.5	14.6	16.3	18.7
US	11.3	12.2	12.8	16.2	19.3

Source: Adapted from Maguire 1987, p. 5

of the growth in the numbers of the elderly in the near future, has raised doubts among some commentators concerning the ability of governments to continue financing retirement pensions and providing other services particularly for the very elderly. We have argued that such fears are exaggerated and, as Table 6.4 shows, the demographic picture for the next 20 years does not raise any issues for concern in the funding of benefits. After that the proportion of the elderly rises in both countries but, as we argued previously, this has to be seen in conjunction with increased productivity and the increased female participation in the labour market. Table 6.4 also shows that the proportion of the elderly is higher in Britain than in the US and it will remain so for the next 30 years when the figures for the two countries converge.

Benefit arrangements for the elderly in the two countries are very similar: an insurance-based retirement pension and a means-tested assistance benefit for those who do not qualify for the insurance pension. In both countries, but particularly in Britain, social security benefits are the main source of income for the elderly with occupational pensions and private pensions forming the second main source. Income from employment has become increasingly less important in both countries, particularly for those aged 70 and over. The risk of poverty is slightly higher for the US elderly than the British elderly irrespective of whether poverty is defined in country-specific terms or in a standardized way, as Tables 2.3, 3.5 and 6.1 show. Class, gender, race and very old age exacerbate the risk of poverty in both countries. Those of the elderly with a semi-skilled or unskilled employment background are more likely to be in poverty than other elderly people because their savings, their retirement pension as well as their occupational pensions will be lower. Women, as a group, suffer from all these class disadvantages but also because they live longer than men. Race also has the effect overall of exacerbating class disadvantages with the result that black working-class women are the group most vulnerable to the risk of poverty.

Despite their many differences, the social security systems of the two countries share many basic assumptions, as Chapter 5 showed: the importance of full-time employment to benefit qualification, the insurance principle, the irrelevance of domestic labour as far as social security is concerned and so on. An additional assumption not discussed in Chapter 5 is the belief that continuing economic growth is both possible and desirable at all costs. Recent debates on environmental pollution and destruction stemming from the relentless pursuit of economic growth point out that at the very least economic growth needs to take account of environmental considerations and perhaps even slow down in the future. If the latter proves to be the case, then poverty will only be abolished if social security systems adopt an explicit anti-poverty strategy.

CAUSES AND SOLUTIONS

The causes of poverty have long been the centre of intense debate and disagreement because they have clear policy implications. From the very early days of this debate, opinion was divided between those who stressed the immediate 'causes' of poverty – widowhood, old age, unemployment, etc. – and those who went a step further to examine the more structural 'causes'. One of the members of the Royal Commission on the Poor Law of 1905–9 in Britain commented as follows on this issue:

> Of course there have not been wanting witnesses who have regarded the question from a political point of view, and have assigned the existence of pauperism to such causes as Capitalism, Free Trade, and the system of Land Tenure. The Commission felt it to be beyond their reference either to endorse or to controvert such suggestions. (Bosanquet 1909, p. 42)

A second bone of contention in this area concerns the distinction between the causes of the incidence of poverty and the causes of its distribution. As Chapter 4 argued, the incidence of poverty refers to the root question of why there is poverty whilst the distribution of poverty raises the related but different question of why some individuals and not others are in poverty at any one time. In other words, the characteristics of the individuals in poverty may change over time without affecting the existence of poverty.

So why does poverty exist amidst such affluence? The review of these debates in Chapter 4 showed that they can be roughly divided into two groups: those which stress individual failings and those which emphasize structural factors. The structuralist explanation adopted in Chapter 4 accepted the limited importance of individual factors but stressed the structural roots of poverty both for the existence and the distribution of poverty. The roots for the existence of poverty are to be found in two interrelated processes: first, the unequal rewards and risk which are attached to different jobs in the labour market and second, the related ideology of individualism that permeates the social security system. Certain jobs provide good wages, regular employment, generous fringe benefits, low health risks and high opportunities for promotion and advancement while other jobs provide the exact opposite in most or all of these dimensions. The reasons for this unequal pattern of job rewards and dangers are to be found in the nature, profitability and centrality of various jobs in a labour market dominated by individualism and private profit. The characteristics of the individual occupants of these jobs exercise only a minor influence on the reward structure of the jobs. Moreover, they are not only likely to be low-paid while in employment but they are also likely to be in poverty while not in employment because of the ways in which social security systems operate.

What then influences the allocation of the poverty-prone jobs? Class, gender and ethnicity are the three structural influences in Britain and the US as they are in other advanced industrial societies. Class influences a person's wealth, income, education, choice of marriage partner and type of residential area. The prevalence of direct and indirect, open or concealed forms of discrimination against women and certain ethnic groups has the obvious effect that they are more likely to occupy the poverty-prone jobs than other individuals. Clearly the three factors of class, gender and race reinforce one another in a variety of ways so that compound advantage is the good fortune of some and compound disadvantage is the bad luck of others. Recent anti-discrimination legislation, the growing power of women and of ethnic groups have tended on the one hand to reduce the significance of gender and race and on the other to increase the importance of class, defined in Weberian terms, in the distribution of jobs. To make this point is not to deny the fact that race and gender are still very significant in both Britain and the US.

The social security systems of both countries operate on the inverse protection law. In other words they provide less protection to those in greatest need because of the dominance of the insurance principle and of work incentives. This is not in any way to deny the significance of the social security system to the weak members of the labour market. As already stressed, without social security benefits their position would be infinitely worse. The point is rather different: a regularly employed and well-paid person will get better protection when in need from the social security system than a low-paid and irregularly employed worker.

The structuralist explanation advocated here does not deny the importance of the individual in surmounting adverse family, ethnic or gender conditions and getting on in life. Clearly many individuals do just that as shown by data on upward social mobility from both countries. The point is rather different: the intergenerational correlation between the earnings of parents and adult children is high particularly when the incomes of the two groups are compared over a long period of time rather than over a single year (Behrman and Taubman 1990). Thus, most people in poverty at any one time come from family backgrounds whose standards of living have hovered around the poverty line. There are, of course, those in poverty from middle and perhaps upper family backgrounds but these have always been the minority. The risk of falling into persistent poverty is clearly much higher among children of the low-paid than among children of the highly paid.

The abolition of poverty in such affluent societies as the US and Britain should be one of the primary moral duties of all governments, equal in standing to the protection of individual freedom. In the same way that governments of all political complexions accept their responsibility to protect individual freedom, so they should equally accept that all their citizens have a right to enjoy a basic standard of living. Indeed, individual freedom is rather hollow for those persistently below the breadline in such affluent countries. As a recent church report in the US put it: 'Dealing with poverty is not a luxury to which our nation can attend when it finds time and resources. Rather it is a moral imperative of the highest priority (National Conference of Catholic Bishops 1986, p. 83).

If poverty is to be abolished, a radical reform of the social security system of both countries is urgently needed. Simply adjusting it here and there or even spending more on it will not abolish poverty. A radical, comprehensive reform is needed and Chapter 5 discussed four such schemes: the benefits as of right, negative income tax, basic income and the starting even scheme. In addition to the abolition of poverty, four other criteria were used to evaluate these four schemes - costs, work incentives, administrative complexity and vertical redistribution of income. It was clearly shown that there can be conflicts between these five criteria and that the choice between them depended on the individual's sense of priorities. What all these four schemes had in common was that they could all abolish poverty though they scored differently on the other four criteria. Our choice, based also on grounds of political feasibility, was for the benefits as of right scheme for Britain and the starting even scheme for the US. Both of these schemes will cost slightly more than the existing network of benefits and tax allowances but both countries possess the resources to meet the extra cost. The US is also in desperate need of some form of comprehensive national health insurance scheme. It cannot be right that the most powerful nation in the world provides no adequate health coverage for many of its citizens.

The abolition of income poverty in both countries depends not only on a radical reform of the social security system but on the adoption of specific policies in other areas – education, child care, health, housing and employment. To take just one example, the abolition of poverty among one-parent families can only be achieved if the right combination of benefit provision, child care facilities and employment programmes is pursued. To cite another example, the abolition of poverty among the unemployed depends not only on a reformed social security system but on better employment and retraining policies that will minimize the extent of unemployment.

POVERTY IN THE 1990S

What, then are the prospects for poverty for the next ten years or so? It is, of course, impossible to predict future trends in poverty in any detailed way. What is possible, however, is to outline those forces and trends in society which have a bearing on poverty levels in the immediate future. To begin with, there are the demographic trends which are easier to chart than others. All the evidence shows that the proportion of the very elderly – those aged 75 and over – is going to rise in the future and this is the group of the elderly that runs the highest risk of poverty. Similarly, the incidence of lone parenthood in society is going to rise, particularly among the younger age group which again is the most vulnerable to poverty. Thus demographic trends will increase the risk of poverty. What about economic trends? These are far more difficult to predict. Beginning with part-time employment, it is safe to say that it is not going to decline in the near future. Indeed, all the industrial changes strongly suggest that the proportion of people in part-time employment will rise as more married women enter the labour force and as more employers in the services industries come to prefer part-time employees. All the indications suggest that unemployment in the 1990s will fluctuate at average levels and that we are not likely to return to either the consistently very low levels of the 1960s or the high levels of the early 1980s. In brief, economic trends are not likely to reduce poverty in the 1990s by themselves.

In other words, in the absence of radical reform initiatives along the lines suggested above, poverty levels are likely to remain the same or even rise in the 1990s. One of the mildly positive factors is the decline in defence expenditure resulting from recent changes in eastern Europe – and so-called 'peace dividend'. But there will be so many other government activities that will compete for a slice of the 'peace dividend' – international diplomatic services, reduction of national debt, improvement of the environment, health care services and so on (Steuerle and Wiener 1990) – that too much reliance on this for poverty reduction would be mistaken. Another possible positive factor in poverty reduction is the increasing awareness that continued economic growth along the environmentally destructive lines of the past must cease. New forms of production and changed attitudes to consumption are necessary to protect the environment and the future of the world. In this new climate, there is a strong possibility that the general public and governments may recognize that poverty cannot be abolished through economic growth but through new social security/income maintenance programmes.

Is there anything that we can learn from the historical development of social policy in the two countries to assist our judgement of poverty trends during the 1990s? Despite their many differences, the historical development of social policy in the two countries shows four important tendencies that are relevant for this discussion. First, the large-scale policy changes in both countries occurred during brief periods of time rather than evenly over the whole period. For Britain, the crucial periods were the first decade of this century, the five years immediately after the end of the second World War and the 1980s. For the US, it was part of the 1930s, of the 1960s and of the 1980s that were the crucial times. Apart from the 1980s which were years of policy contractions, the other periods produced expansions of social policy and anti-poverty programmes. Though there is no strong evidence at present to suggest that the 1990s will be one of these gestating periods of social policy, there are some signs – disarmament, protection of the environment, public reaction against the rise in abject poverty, homelessness and general destitution during the 1980s – which suggest that the 1990s may not be such a bleak period for the poor as the 1980s were. Second, these policy changes appear as radical breaks from the past at the time of enactment but with hindsight they are more accurately described as important extensions of previous trends and practices in, perhaps, the non-government sectors. This is important for this discussion for if any radical reforms are to take place in the future they will be bound by the country's experience from the past. Hence our recommendation for a benefits as of right for Britain and starting even for the US can be seen as making more political sense than the other two radical schemes we discussed. Third, social policies with broad political constituencies survive difficult times better than programmes with narrow, and particularly stigmatized, clientèle. Thus cut-backs in benefits during the 1980s were in those areas that were for the poor rather than in such 'universal' programmes as retirement pensions. It is thus important to support radical reforms which are of a 'universalistic' kind rather than targeted, means-tested schemes for the poor. Fourth, the poor are not a homogeneous group and government policies have tended to favour the 'deserving' groups. As Chapter 4 pointed out, the 'undeserving' groups have always been dealt with rather harshly in both countries but particularly so in the US. The lesson for future reform movements is for the various groups of the poor to unite and to campaign jointly for reforms. This will not be easy but the logic for unity among the poor is inescapable.

The abolition of poverty in such affluent countries as Britain and the US is imperative for moral, economic and ecological reasons. It cannot be right that some people cannot afford even the basic necessities of life while so many of their fellow citizens enjoy unprecedented affluence. It cannot be right for governments to use such double standards in their policies as tax cuts for incentives to the highly paid and benefit cuts to the poor for the same purpose. The economic ill-effects of poverty are many and varied and often difficult to quantify. Poverty is related to ill-health both directly and indirectly in a variety of ways. Poverty affects the educational achievement of children and results in large-scale wastage of ability that in turn affects their well-being as well as the economy of the country. Ecologically friendly economic growth has now been generally accepted if the destruction of the environment is to be prevented. Some have even called for reduced consumption to save the environment. Whether one accepts the light green or the dark green view of sustainable development, the fact remains that government responsibility for the abolition of poverty is heightened. Both views imply reduced rates of economic growth and hence greater government responsibility for poverty reduction. Both views, but particularly that of the dark greens, argue for a less acquisitive society, and a greater concern for fellow citizens, for the third world and for future generations. From all three perspectives, poverty is not so much a paradox in affluent societies as a destructive anachronism. Poverty can be abolished in affluent societies and its abolition will strengthen rather than weaken them in moral, economic, ecological and political terms.

In both Britain and the US the 1980s were a decade for the highly paid and the rich. Tax rates were reduced and public expenditure squeezed in the belief that they would trigger higher rates of economic growth as a result of which everyone in society would benefit more or less alike. The results have been nothing of the kind. The highly paid and the rich benefited enormously whilst the low-paid and the poor lost out in a very big way. In addition rates of economic growth did not improve. This ought to be a lesson for the 1990s. The public as voters, we hope, will reject the politics of the 1980s and elect governments that will deal with the deteriorating situation of poverty in both countries. Despite all the uncertainties the 1990s may well turn out to be the decade of the low-paid and the poor.

Bibliography

Aaron, Henry J. (1978) *Politics and the Professors: The Great Society in Perspective*, Brookings Institution.

Abel-Smith, B. and Townsend, P. (1965) *The Poor and the Poorest*, Bell.

Alcock, P. (1985) 'Socialist Security', *Critical Social Policy*, no. 13.

Alcock, P. (1987) *Poverty and State Support*, Longman.

Anderson, M. (1978) *Welfare*, Stanford University Press.

Anderson, O.W. (1968) *The Uneasy Equilibrium: Private and Public Financing of Health Services in the U.S. 1875–1965*, College and University Press.

Arnot, M. (1986) 'State Education Policy and Girls' Educational Experiences' in Beechy and Whitelegg.

Ashby, P. (1984) *Social Security After Beveridge – What Next?*, Bedford Square Press.

Ashdown, P. (1990) 'Breaking the Poverty Trap: A Basic Income'. *Basic Income Research Group*, Bulletin no. 10, pp. 5–7.

Ashford, S. (1987) 'Family Matters' in Jowell, R. and Witherspoon, S., *British Social Attitudes: The 1987 Report*, Gower.

Atkinson, A.B. (1969) *Poverty in Britain and the Reform of Social Security*, Cambridge University Press.

Atkinson, A.B. Maynard, A.K. and Trinder, C.G. (1983) *Parents and Children: Incomes in Two Generations*, Heinemann.

Atkinson, A.B. (1989) *Poverty & Social Security*, Harvester Wheatsheaf.

Auletta, K. (1982) *The Underclass*, Random House.

Bane, M. and Ellwood, D. (1986) 'Slipping Into and Out of Poverty: The Dynamics of Spells', *The Journal of Human Resources*, vol. 21, no. 1, pp. 1–23.

Banfield, E. (1968) *The Unheavenly City*, Little Brown.

Barker, D. (1971) 'The Negative Income Tax' in Bull, D.

Basic Income Research Group (1989) *Basic Income*, London.

Baumol, W. (1986) *Superfairness*, MIT Press.

Bazen, S. (1988) *On the Overlap between Low Pay and Poverty*, Discussion Paper no. TIOI/120, London School of Economics.

Becker, C. (1964) *Human Capital*, Columbia University Press.

Beckerman, W. (1979) *Poverty and the Impact of Income Maintenance Programmes*, ILO.

Beckerman, W. and Clark, S. (1982) *Poverty and Social Security in Britain since 1961*, Oxford University Press.

Beechy, V. and Whitelegg, E. (eds) (1986) *Women in Britain Today*, Open University Press.

Behrman, J. and Taubman, P. (1990) 'The Intergenerational Correlation Between Children's Adult Earnings and their Parent's Income', *Review of Income and Wealth*, vol. 36, no. 2, pp. 115–27.

Bell, D. (1960) *The End of Ideology*, Free Press.

Berthoud, R. (1976) *The Disadvantages of Inequality*, Macdonald and Jane's.

Berthoud, R. (1989) *Credit, Debt and Poverty*, HMSO.

Beveridge, W. (1942) *Social Insurance and Allied Services*, Cmd 6404, HMSO (The Beveridge Report).

Bickle, G. and Wilcock, D. (1974) The *Supplemental Security Income Program*, Bureau of Social Science Research, Washington, D.C.

Black Report (1980) *Inequalities in Health*, DHSS.

Blackman, T. *et al.* (1989) 'Housing and Health', *Journal of Social Policy*, vol. 18, no. 1, pp. 1–16.

Blaug, M. (1972) *An Introduction to the Economics of Education*, Penguin.

Bluestone, B. (1970) 'The Tripartite Economy: Labor Markets and the Working Poor', *Poverty and Human Resources*, vol. 5, July–August, pp. 15–35.

Bonilla, F. (1970) 'Rio's Favelas' in W. Mangin (ed.) *Peasants and Cities*, Houghton Mifflin.

Bosanquet, H. (1909) *The Poor Law Report of 1909*, Macmillan.

Bowles, S. (1972) 'Schooling and Inequality from Generation to Generation', *Journal of Political Economy*, vol. 80, pp. 5219–51.

Bradshaw, J. *et al.* (1983) 'The Impact of Unemployment on the Living Standards of Families', *Journal of Social Policy*, vol. 12, no. 4, pp. 433–52.

Bradshaw, J. Mitchel, D. and Morgan, J. (1987) 'Evaluating Adequacy: The Potential of Budget Standards', *Journal of Social Policy*, vol. 16, no. 2, pp. 165–81.

Bradshaw, J. (1989) Lone Parents: Policy in the Doldrums', Family Policy Studies Centre, London.

Brenner, M. (1973) *Mental Illness and the Economy*, Harvard University Press.

Briggs, E. and Rees, A. (1980) *Supplementary Benefits and the Consumer*, Bedford Square Press.

Brown, J. (1989) *Why Don't They Go to Work? Mothers on Benefit*, HMSO.

Brown, J.C. (1988) *In Search of a Policy, The Rationale for Social Security Provision for One Parent Families*, National Council of One Parent Families.

Brown, J.L. (1989) 'When Violence has a Benevolent Face: The Paradox of Hunger in the World's Wealthiest Democracy', *International Journal of Health Services*, vol. 19, no. 2, pp. 257–77.

Brown, M. and Madge, N. (1982) *Despite the Welfare State*, Heinemann.

Bryson, A. (1989) 1880s–1980s. The '80s: decade of poverty, *The New Review of the Low Pay Unit*, no. 1, pp. 11–15.

Bull, D. (1971) *Family Poverty*, Duckworth.

Burtless, G. (1986) 'Public Spending for the Poor' in Danziger S. and Weinberg D. (eds) *Fighting Poverty*, Harvard University Press.

Byrne, D. *et al.* (1986) *Housing and Health*, Gower.

Callan, T. *et al.* (1988) *Poverty and the Social Welfare System in Ireland*, Combat Poverty Agency, Dublin.

Callan, T. and Nollan, B. (1987) 'Concepts of Poverty and the Poverty Line' Working Paper no. 2, *ESRI Project on Income Distribution, Poverty and Usage of State Services*, Dublin.

Central Statistical Office, *Social Trends*, no. 5 (1974), no. 6 (1975), no. 8 (1977), no. 10 (1980), no. 16 (1986), no. 17 (1987), no. 19 (1989), no. 20 (1990), HMSO.

Coates, K. and Silburn, R. (1970) *Poverty: The Forgotten Englishman*, Penguin.

Cole, D. and Utting, J. (1962) *The Economic Circumstances of Old People*, Codicote Press.

Cole-Hamilton I. and Lang, T. (1986) *Tightening Belts: A Report on the Impact of Poverty on Food*, London Food Commission.

Cohen, B. (1989) *Eliminating Hunger: A Food Security Policy for the 1990s*, The Urban Institute.

Commission of the European Communities (1977) *The Perception of Poverty in Europe*, Brussels.

Corcoran, M. and Duncan, G. (1979) 'Work History, Labor Force Attachment, and Earnings Differences Between Races and Sexes, *Journal of Human Resources*, vol. 14, no. 1, pp. 3–21.

Corcoran, M. *et al.* (1985) 'Myth and Reality: The Causes and Persistence of Poverty', *Journal of Policy Analysis and Management*, vol. 4, no. 4, pp. 516–39.

Council of Economic Advisers (1964) *Economic Report to the President, Washington.*

Craig, F.W. (ed.) (1970) *British General Election Manifestos 1918–1966*, Political Reference Publication.

Dale, A. and Glover, J. (1989) 'Women at Work in Europe', *Employment Gazette*, June, pp. 299–308.

Danziger, S. and Gottschalk, P. (1985) 'The impact of budget cuts and economic conditions on poverty', *Journal of Policy Analysis and Management*, vol. 5, pp. 587–593.

Danziger, S. and Weinberg D. (eds) (1986) *Fighting Poverty: What Works and What Doesn't*, Harvard University Press.

Danziger, S. *et al.* (1984) 'The Direct Measurement of Welfare Levels: How Much Does it Cost to Make Ends Meet?' *Review of Economics and Statistics*, vol. 66, pp. 500–505.

Davis, K. and Moore, W. (1945) 'Some Principles of Stratification', *The American Sociological Review*, vol. 10, no. 2, pp. 242–9.

Dawson, A. and Evans, G. (1987) 'Pensioners' Income and Expenditure, 1970–85', *Employment Gazette*, May, pp. 243–53.

Deacon, A. and Bradshaw, J. (1983) *Reserved for the Poor*, Blackwell, 1983.

Department of Employment (1988) 'Measures of Unemployment and Characteristics of the Unemployed', *Employment Gazette*, January, pp. 28–38.

Department of Employment (1988) 'Ethnic Origins and the Labour Market', *Employment Gazette*, December, pp. 633–46.

Department of Health and Social Security (1975) *Two-Parent Families Receiving Family Income Supplement,* HMSO.

DHSS (1985) *Reform of Social Security*, Cmnd 9517, HMSO.

DHSS (1976) *Two-Parent Families receiving Family Income Supplement* in 1972, HMSO.

DHSS (1979) *Nutrition and Health in Old Age*, HMSO.

DHSS (1980) *Inequalities in Health*, HMSO.

DHSS (1986) *Low Income Families 1983*, HMSO.

DHSS (1988) *Social Security Statistics*, HMSO.

DHSS (1988) *Low Income Families 1985*, HMSO.

DSS (1989) *Children Come First*, vols One and Two, HMSO.

Desai, M. (1986) 'Drawing the Line: On Defining the Poverty Threshold' in Golding, P. *Excluding the Poor*, Child Poverty Action Group.

de Schweinitz, K. (1943) *England's Road to Social Security*, Barnes.

Dex, S. and Shaw, L. (1986) *British and American Women at Work*, Macmillan.

Disraeli, B. (1845) *Sybil*, Longmans.

Doeringer, P. and Piore, M. (1971) *International Labor Markets and Manpower Analysis*, Lexington.

Donnison, D. and Ungerson, C. (1982) *Housing Policy*, Penguin.

Drewnowski, J. (1977) 'Poverty: Its Meaning and Measurement' *Development and Change*, vol. 8, no. 2, pp. 183–206.

Duncan, G. *et al.* (1984) *Years of Poverty, Years of Plenty*, University of Michigan.

Ellwood, D. (1988) *Poor Support: Poverty in the American Family*, Basic Books.

Employment Gazette (1988) 'Measures of Unemployment and Characteristics of the Unemployed', *Employment Gazette*, January, pp. 28–38.

Engels, F. (1892, reprinted 1969) *The Condition of the Working Class in Britain*, Panther Books.

Esam, P. Good, R. and Middleton, R. (1985) *Who's to Benefit?* Verso.

Eysenck, H. (1971) *Race, Intelligence and Education*, Temple Smith.

Fagin, L. and Little, M. (1984) *The Forsaken Families*, Penguin.

Feagin, J. (1972) 'When it Comes to Poverty, it is still "God Helps Those Who Help Themselves"', *Psychology Today*, vol. 6, pp. 101–29.

Feagin, J. (1975) *Subordinating the Poor*, Prentice-Hall.

Feather, N. (1974) 'Explanations of Poverty in Australian and American Samples', *Australian Journal of Psychology*, vol. 26, pp. 199–216.

Fiegehen, G. (1986) 'Income after Retirement', *Social Trends*, no. 16 HMSO, pp. 13–19.

Field, F. (1981) *Inequality in Britain*, Fontana.

Field, F. (1990) 'The Trickle of Wealth that Dried Up', *Guardian*, 24 April.

Finnie, R. (1988) 'Changes in Well-Being and Inequality, 1960–1985' in Haveman, R. *Starting Even*, Simon and Schuster.

FAO/WHO (1973) 'Energy and Protein Requirements: Report of a Joint FAO/WHO Expert Committee; *WHO Technical Services Report No. 522*, Geneva.

Ford Foundation (1989) *The Common Good,* Ford Foundation, New York.

Friedman, M. (1962) *Capitalism and Freedom*, University of Chicago Press.

Friedman M. and Friedman R. (1980) *Free to Choose*, Pelican.

Fuchs, V. (1967) 'Redefining Poverty and Redistributing Income', *Public Interest*, no. 8, pp. 88–96.

Furnham, A. (1982) 'Why are the Poor Always with Us? Explanations for Poverty in Britain', *British Journal of Social Psychology*, Part 4, pp. 311–22.

Galbraith, J.K. (1958) *The Affluent Society*, Houghton Mifflin.

Gans, H. (1962) *The Urban Villagers*, Free Press.

Gans, H. (1973) *More Equality*, Patheon Books.

Gatlin, R. (1987) *American Women since 1945*, University of Mississippi.

George, V. and Wilding, P. (1972) *Motherless Families*, Routledge and Kegan Paul.

George, V. (1973) *Social Security and Society*, Routledge and Kegan Paul.

George, V. and Lawson, R. (1980) *Poverty and Inequality in Common Market Countries*, Routledge and Kegan Paul.

George, V. and Wilding, P. (1984) *The Impact of Social Policy*, Routledge and Kegan Paul.

George, V. (1988) *Wealth, Poverty and Starvation*, Wheatsheaf.

Gilbert, D. and Kahl, J. (1987) *The American Class Structure*, Dorsey Press.

Gilder, G. (1982) *Wealth and Poverty*, Buchan & Enright.

Goodwin, L. (1972) *Do the Poor Want to Work*? Brookings Institute.

Gordon, D.M. (1972) *Theories of Poverty and Underdevelopment*, Lexington.

Gouldner, A. (ed) (1962) *Durkheim E: Socialism and Saint-Simon*, Collier Books.

Government Actuary (1983) 'Pension Scheme Membership in 1983', *Employment Gazette*, December, pp. 494–7.

Government Actuary (1990) *National Insurance Fund – Long Term Financial Estimates*, HMSO.

Government Statistical Service (1990) *Households Below Average Income. A Statistical Analysis 1981–87*, Department of Social Security.

Hagenaars, A. and Van Praag, B. (1985) 'A Synthesis of Poverty Line Definitions', *Review of Income and Wealth*, Series 31, no. 2, 139–55.

Hall, R. (1975) 'Effects of the Experimental NIT on Labor Supply' in Pechman, J. and Timpane, P. (eds) *Work Incentives and Income Guarantee*, Brookings Institute.

Halsey, A. Heath, A. and Ridge, J. (1980) *Origins and Destinations*, Clarendon Press.

Harrington, M. (1962) *The Other America – Poverty in the United States*, Macmillan.

Harrington, M. (1985) *The New American Poverty*, Penguin.

Haskey, J. (1989) 'One parent Families and their Children in Great Britain', *Population Trends*, no. 55, pp. 27–33.

Haveman, R. (1988) *Starting Even*, Simon and Schuster.

Haveman, R. and Watts, H. (1977) 'Social Experimentation as Policy Research: a Review of NIT Experiments' in Halberstadt, V. and Culyer, A. (eds) *Public Economics and Human Resources*, Cujas.

Hearn, J. (1984) 'The Relative Roles of Academic, Ascribed and Socio-economic Characteristics in College Destinations', *The Sociology of Education*, vol. 53, pp. 22–30.

Heclo, H. (1984) 'The Political Foundations of Anti-Poverty Policy' in Danziger, S. and Weinberg, D. (eds) *Fighting Poverty*, Harvard University Press.

Hernstein, R. (1971) 'I.Q.' *The Atlantic Monthly*, September.

Hernstein, R., (1973) *I.Q. and the Meritocracy*, Allen Lane.

Hill, M.S. (1985) 'The Changing Nature of Poverty', *Annals of AAPSS*, pp. 31–47.

HMSO (1985) 'Reform of Social Security', *Background Papers*, vol. 3, Cmnd 9519, HMSO.

Holman, R. (1978) *Poverty*, Martin Robertson.

House of Commons, Social Services Committee (1990) 'Low Income Statistics', *Fourth Report*, HMSO.

Huber, J. and Form, W. (1973) *Income and Ideology: An Analysis of the American Political Formula*, Free Press.

Hughes, M. (1989) 'Concentrated Deviance and the "Underclass" Hypothesis', *Journal of Policy Analysis and Management*, vol. 8, no. 2, pp. 274–82.

Hunter, R. (1904) *Poverty*, Macmillan.

International Labour Office (1988) *The Cost of Social Security, 12th Inquiry*, Geneva.

Jahoda, M. *et al*. (1933) *Marienthal: The Sociography of an Unemployed Community*, Tavistock Press.

Jencks, C. *et al*. (1972) *Inequality*, Basic Books.

Jencks, C. *et al*. (1979) *Who Gets Ahead*, Basic Books.

Jencks, C. (1989) 'What is the Underclass – and Is It Growing?' *Focus*, vol. 12, no. 1, pp. 14–27.

Johnson, P. and Webb S. (1990) *Poverty in Official Statistics: Two Reports*, Institute of Fiscal Studies.

Jordan, B. (1988) 'The Prospects for Basic Income', *Social Policy and Administration*, vol. 22, no. 2, pp. 115–23.

Joseph, K. and Sumption, J. (1979) *Equality*, Murray.

Jowell, R. and Witherspoon, S. (1987) *British Social Attitudes: The 1987 Report*, Gower.

Kahn, A. (1986) 'Poverty Research in International Perspective', *Focus*, vol. 9, no. 2.

Kaim-Caudle, P. (1953) *Studies in Poverty*, University of Durham, Manuscript.

Keegan, V. (1990) 'Country and Western Marxism may be Music to the Poor', *Guardian*, 13 August.

Keyserling, L. (1964) *Progress or Poverty: the U.S. at the Crossroads*.

Kluegel, J. and Smith, E. (1986) *Beliefs About Inequality: Americans' View of What is and What Ought to Be*, Aldine de Gruyter.

Labour Party (1988) *Social Justice and Economic Efficiency*, Labour Party, London.

Laumann, E. (1966) *Prestige and Association in an Urban Community*, Bobbs-Merrill.

Layard, R. (1968) *How to Beat Unemployment*, Oxford University Press.

Leacock, E. (1971) *The Culture of Poverty: A critique*, Simon and Schuster.

Lees, D. (1967) 'Poor Families and Fiscal Reform', *Lloyds Bank Review*.

Le Grand, J. (1982) *The Strategy of Equality*, Allen and Unwin.

Lerman, R. (1988) 'Non-welfare Approaches to Helping the Poor', *Focus*, vol. 11, no. 1.

Levy, F. (1977) 'How Big is the American Underclass?' Working Paper, The Urban Institute, Washington.

Lewis, H. (1967) 'Culture, Class and Family Life Among Low-income Urban Negroes' in Ross, A.M. and Hill, H. (eds) *Employment, Race and Poverty*, Harcourt, Brace and World.

Lewis, O. (1961) *The Children of Sanchez*, Random House.

Lewis, O. (1966) 'The Culture of Poverty' *Scientific American*, vol. 215, October.

Lewis, O. (1967) 'The Children of Sanchez, Pedro Martinez and La Vida: A C.A. Book Review', *Current Anthorpology*, vol. 8, pp. 480–500.

Lewis, O. (1968) *La Vida*, Panther Edition (first published by Random House, 1965).

Lewis, O. (1969) 'Review of Charles A. Valentine "Culture of Poverty: Critique and Counter-Proposals"', *Current Anthropology*, vol. 10, no. 2–3.

Liebow, E. (1967) *Tally's Corner*, Little Brown.

Lister, R. (1989) 'Social Benefits' in Alcock, P. *et al. The Social Economy and the Democratic State*, Lawrence and Wishart.

Low Pay Unit (1988) *The Poor Decade: Wage Legislation in the 1980s*, Low Pay Unit.

MacDonald, M. (1985) 'Evaluating Basic Needs to Determine Welfare Benefits', Institute for Research on Poverty, Discussion Paper, University of Madison.

Mack, J. and Lansley, S. (1985) *Poor Britain*, Allen & Unwin.

McLanahan, S. and Garfinkel, I. (1988) 'Single Mothers, the Underclass and Social Policy,' Institute for Research on Poverty, Discussion Paper, University of Madison.

Macnicol, J. (1987) 'In Pursuit of the Underclass", *Journal of Social Policy*, vol. 16, no. 3, pp. 293–318.

MAFF (1985) *Household Food Consumption and Expenditure 1983*, National Food Survey Committee, Annual Report, HMSO.

Maguire, M. (1987) 'Making Provisions for Ageing Populations', *OECD Observer*, no. 148, October–November, p. 5.

Mansfield, M. (1986) 'The Political Arithmetic of Poverty', *Social Policy and Administration*, vol. 20, no. 1, pp. 47–57.

Marcuse, H. (1964) *One-Dimensional Man*, Routledge and Kegan Paul.

Martin, J. *et al.* (1985) *The Prevalence of Disability Among Adults*, HMSO.

Martin, J. and White, A. (1988) *The Financial Circumstances of Disabled Adults Living in Private Households*, HMSO.

Mayer, S. and Jencks, C. (1989) 'Poverty and the Distribution of Material Hardship', *The Journal of Human Resources*, vol. 24, no. 1, pp. 88–113.

Mead, L. (1989) 'The Logic of Workfare: The Underclass and Work Policy', *Annals of American Academy of Political and Social Science*, no. 501, pp. 156–69.

Miller, H. (1951) *Rich Man, Poor Man*, Apollo.

Moon, M. (ed) (1977) *The Measurement of Economic Welfare: Application to the Aged*, Academic Press.

Moylan, S. *et al.* (1984) *For Richer, for Poorer: DHSS Cohort Study of Unemployed Men*, HMSO.

Moynihan, P. (1986) *Family and Nation*, Harcourt, Brace, Janovitch.

Munnell, A.H. (1987) 'The Current Status of our Social Welfare System', *New England Economic Review*, July/August p. 3–12.

Murray, C. (1984) *Losing Ground: American Social Policy 1950–1980*, Basic Books.

Naseem, S.M. (1977) 'Rural Poverty and Landlessness in Pakistan' in ILO *Poverty and Landlessness in Rural Asia*, Geneva.

National Conference of Catholic Bishops (1986) *Economic Justice for All*, Washington.

Nelson, M. and Naismith, D. (1983) 'The Nutritional Status of Poor Children in London', *Journal of Human Nutrition*, vol. 13, no. 1.

Nilson, L. (1981) 'Reconsidering Ideological Lines: Beliefs About Poverty in America', *The Sociological Quarterly*, vol. 22, no. 4. pp. 531–48.

Novak, T. (1988) *Poverty and the State*, Open University Press.

OECD (1976) *Public Expenditure on Income Maintenance Programmes*, Paris.

OECD (1988) *Reforming Public Pensions*, Paris.

Orshansky, M. (1969) 'How Poverty is Measured', *Monthly Labour Review*, vol. 92, no. 2, pp. 37–41.

Oster, S Lake, E. and Oksman, C. (1978) *The Definition and Measurement of Poverty*, vol. 1, Westview Press.

Pacey, A. and Payne, P. (eds) (1985) *Agricultural Development and Nutrition*, Hutchinson.

Palmer, J.L. Smeeding, T. and Torrey, B.B. (eds) (1988) *The Vulnerable*, The Urban Institute Press.

Parker, H. (1989) *Instead of the Dole*, Routledge.

Parkin, F. (1971) *Class Inequality and Political Order*, McGibbon & Key.

Patterson, J. (1981) *America's Struggle Against Poverty*, Harvard University Press.

Pettigrew, T. (1985) 'New Black-White Patterns: How Best to Conceptualise them?' *Annual Review of Sociology*, vol. 11, pp. 329–46.

Physician Task Force on *Hunger in America: The Growing Epidemic*, Wesleyan University Press.

Piachaud, D. (1979) *The Cost of a Child*, Child Poverty Action Group.

Piachaud, D. (1981) 'Peter Townsend and the Holy Grail', *New Society*, 10 September, pp. 419–21.

Piachaud, D. (1987) 'Problems in the Definition and Measurement of Poverty', *Journal of Social Policy*, vol. 16, no. 2, pp. 147–64.

Piachaud, D. (1988) 'Poverty in Britain 1899 to 1983', *Journal of Social Policy*, vol. 17, part 3, pp. 335–51.

Plowden Report (1967) *Children and their Primary Schools*, HMSO.

Prowse, M. (1988) 'The Mirage of Social Insurance', *Financial Times*, 26 February.

Purdy, D. (1988) *Social Power and the Labour Market*, Macmillan.

Rainwater, L. (1974) *What Money Buys: Inequality and the Social Meaning of Income*, Basic Books.

Rein, M. (1976) *Social Science and Public Policy*, Penguin Books.

Ricketts, E. and Sawhill, I.V. (1988) 'Defining and Measuring the Underclass', *Journal of Policy Analysis and Management*, vol. 7, no. 2, pp. 316–26.

Ringen, S. (1988) 'Direct and Indirect Measures of Poverty', *Journal of Social Policy*, vol. 17, part 3, pp. 351–74.

Rodman, H. (1963) 'The Lower Class Value Stretch', *Social Forces*, vol. 42, December, pp. 205–15.

Rokeach, M. and Parker, S. (1970) 'Values as Social Indications of Poverty and Race Relations in America', *The Annals,* vol. 388, March, pp. 87–111.

Root, L. (1986) 'Redundancy Payments in Britain: A View From Abroad', *Policy Studies*, vol. 7, no. 1, pp. 30–51.

Rowntree, B.S. (1901) *Poverty: A Study of Town Life,* Macmillan.

Rowntree, B.S. and Lavers, G. (1951) *Poverty and the Welfare State*, Longmans.

Royal Commission on the Distribution of Income and Wealth (1974) *Lower Incomes*, Cmnd 7175, HMSO.

Ruggles, P. and Williams, R. (1988) *Measuring the Duration of Poverty Spells*, Urban Institute Publication.

Sandefur, G. and Pahari, A. (1988) 'Racial and Ethnic Inequality in Earnings and Educational Attainment', Institute for Research on Poverty, Discussion Paper, pp. 863–88. University of Madison, Wisconsin.

Sawhill, I.V. (1988) 'Poverty in the U.S: Why is it so Persistent?' *Journal of Economic Literature*, pp. 1073–1119.

Schiller, B. (1980) *The Economics of Poverty and Discrimination*. 3rd edition, Prentice-Hall.

Sen, A. (1981) *Poverty and Famines*, Clarendon Press.

Sidel, R. (1986) *Women and Children Last*, Viking.

Slipman, S. and Hadjipateras, A. (1988) *Helping One Parent Families to Work*, National Council for One-Parent Families, London.

Smeeding, T. O'Higgins, M. and Rainwater, L. (eds) (1990) *Poverty, Inequality and Income Distribution in Comparative Perspective*, Harvester/Wheatsheaf.

Smith, K.B. and Stone, L. (1989) 'Rags, Riches and Bootstraps: Beliefs about the Causes of Wealth and Poverty', *The Sociological Quarterly*, vol. 30, no. 1, pp. 93–107.

Smith, T.W. (1987) 'The Welfare State in Cross-National Perspective' *Public Opinion Quarterly*, vol. 51, no. 3, pp. 404–421.

Social Security Administration (1989) 'Social Security Programmes in the United States', *Social Security Bulletin*, vol. 52, no. 7, July, pp. 2–78.

Social Security Advisory Committee (1983) *Benefits for Disabled People: A Strategy for Change*, HMSO.

Steiner, Gilbert Y. (1966) *The State of Welfare*, Brookings Institution.

Steuerle, C and Wiener, G. (1990) *Spending the Peace Dividend: Lessons from History*, The Urban Institute.

Stigler, G.J. (1965) 'The Economist and the State', *American Economic Review*, vol. 55, no. 1, pp. 1–18.

Sukhatme, P. (1982) 'Measurement of Undernutrition', *Economic and Political Weekly*, vol. 17, no. 50, pp. 2000–2016.

Thane, P. (1981) 'The Growing Burden of An Ageing Population?' *Journal of Public Policy*, vol. 17, no. 4, pp. 373–87.

Tienda, M. (1989) 'Race, Ethnicity and the Portrait of Inequality: Approaching the 1990s', *Sociological Spectrum*, vol. 9, pp. 23–52.

Townsend, P. (1952) 'Poverty: ten years after Beveridge', *Planning*, vol. 19, pp. 21–40.

Townsend, P. (1957) *The Family Life of Old People*, Routledge and Kegan Paul.

Townsend, P. (1979) *Poverty in the U.K.* Penguin.

Townsend, P. (1983) 'A Theory of Poverty and the Role of Social Policy' in M. Loney *et al.* (eds) *Social Policy and Social Welfare*, Open University Press.

Townsend, P. (1985) 'Review of Poor Britain', *Poverty*, no. 61, pp. 42–5.

Townsend, P. (1987) 'Deprivation', *Journal of Social Policy*, vol. 16, no. 2, pp. 125–46.

Townsend, P. Phillimore, P. and Beattle, A. (1988) *Health and Deprivation*, Croom Helm.

Townsend, P. and Gordon, D. (1990) 'Let Them Eat Cake! The idea of meeting minimum needs is abandoned', *The New Review of the Low Pay Unit*, no. 4, June/July, pp. 6–10.

Tumin, M. (1953) 'Some Principles of Stratification: A Critical Analysis', *The American Sociological Review*, vol. 18, no. 4, pp. 387–404.

Tussing, A. Dale. (1975) *Poverty in a Dual Economy*, St Martin's Press.

Uhr, E. and Evanson, E. (1984) 'Poverty in the United States: Where do we stand now?' *Focus*, vol. 7, no. 1, pp. 1–13.

US Bureau of Labor Statistics, (1948) *A Worker's Budget in the United States*, Bulletin no. 927, Washington.

US Dept of Health, (1987) 'Human Resources and Social Security Administration', *Social Security Bulletin, Annual Statistical Supplement*, 1986, Washington.,

US House of Representatives, Committee on Ways and Means (1989) *Background Material and Data on Programs within the Jurisdiction of the Committee*, US Government Printing Office.

US House of Representatives, Committee on Ways and Means (1990) *Overview of Entitlement Programs, 1990 Green Book*, Washington, D.C. Government Printing Office.

Veit-Wilson, J. (1987) 'Consensual Approaches to Poverty Lines and Social Security', *Journal of Social Policy*, vol. 16, no. 2, pp. 183–211.

Vincent J. and Burke, V. (1974) *Nixon's Good Deed: Welfare Reform*, Columbia University Press.

Wachtel, H. (1972) 'Capitalism and Poverty in America: Paradox or Contradiction', *American Economic Review* vol. 62, no. 2, pp. 187–94.

Walker, R. Lawson, R. and Townsend, P. (1984) *Responses to Poverty: Lessons from Europe*, Heinemann.

Walter, T. (1989) *Basic Income: Freedom from Poverty, Freedom to Work*, Boyars.

Warlick, J. (1984) 'How Effectively Does SSI Guarantee Minimum Income for the Low-Income Aged', Discussion Paper no. 751–84, Institute for Research in Poverty, Univ. of Madison, Wisconsin.

Weale, A. *et al.* (1984) *Lone Mothers, Paid Work and Social Security*, Bedford Square Press.

Weisbrod, B.A. and Hansen, L.W. (1968) 'An Income-Net Worth Approach to Measuring Economic Welfare', *American Economic Review*, vol. 58, no. 5, pp. 1315–29.

Westergaard, J. and Reisler, H. (1975) *Class in a Capitalist Society*, Heinemann.

Wilson, W.J. (1985) 'Cycles of Deprivation and the Underclass Debate', *Social Service Review*, vol. 59, no. 4, pp. 54–60.

Wilson, W.J. (1980) *The Declining Significance of Race*, University of Chicago Press, 2nd edition.

Wilson, W.J. (1987) *The Truly Disadvantaged: The Inner City, the Underclass and Public Policy*, University of Chicago.

Wintour, P. (1989) 'Number in Poverty up by over 3 Million', *Guardian*, 28 April.

Index